WRITING FROM EXPERIENCE

Marcella Frank

American Language Institute, New York University

PRENTICE-HALL, INC., ENGLEWOOD CLIFFS, NEW JERSEY 07632

Library of Congress Cataloging in Publication Data

FRANK, MARCELLA.
    Writing from experience.

    Includes index.
    1. English language—Study and teaching—Foreign
students. I. Title.
PE1128.A2F68 1983   808'.042   82-9097
ISBN 0-13-970285-7   AACR2

Printed in the United States of America

10 9 8 7 6 5 4 3 2 1

0-13-970285-7

Editorial/production supervision and interior design by Virginia Rubens
Cover design by Ray Lundgren
Manufacturing buyer: Harry P. Baisley

PRENTICE-HALL INTERNATIONAL, INC., *London*
PRENTICE-HALL OF AUSTRALIA PTY. LIMITED, *Sydney*
PRENTICE-HALL CANADA INC., *Toronto*
PRENTICE-HALL OF INDIA PRIVATE LIMITED, *New Delhi*
PRENTICE-HALL OF JAPAN, INC., *Tokyo*
PRENTICE-HALL OF SOUTHEAST ASIA PTE. LTD., *Singapore*
WHITEHALL BOOKS LIMITED, *Wellington, New Zealand*

Contents

Preface

 Writing from Experience is a writing workbook for adults at the high intermediate or low advanced level of English as a second or a foreign language. With some modification, however, it can also be used by low intermediate or more advanced students.

 This workbook is the result of ten years of classroom testing, both in the United States and abroad. During this time I have constantly modified my approach to make the text more useful in the classroom. I have also benefited greatly from the suggestions made by other teachers at New York University and Brigham Young University who have tried out the materials.

 Writing from Experience has great flexibility of use. It may be the only text in a writing class, or it may be a supplementary text in a grammar class or a class for combined language skills. Because of the great amount of controlled practice in the text, it may also be used in a writing workshop or in a tutorial program staffed by teaching assistants.

 The great variety of language practice in *Writing from Experience*—speaking, writing, listening, grammatical structure—represents a careful integration of the language skills and is designed to maintain student interest. Each unit begins with a discussion-writing stage and ends with a listening-writing stage.

 Built into the writing practice is a systematic provision for correction, with materials and procedures that enable the students to make their own corrections. In addition, an accompanying text, *Writer's Companion,* gives students help with many of their writing problems. The two books together provide a total package for composition writing which relieves the teacher of having to spend time explaining particular usages and gives students the maximum opportunities for self-help.

Because *Writing from Experience* is intended for students who are still struggling with problems on the sentence level, the workbook does not require them to explore a composition subject in depth. The topics involve mainly rhetorical patterns that are relatively easy to handle, such as description and explanation. The text contains ten units, each dealing with one particular subject. The topics in these units become progressively more comprehensive, and the level of difficulty increases.

UNIQUE FEATURES OF CONTROL

1. RHETORICAL CONTROL (of the organization and development of compositions)

Rhetorical control comes essentially from an outline given for each composition. This outline guides the two stages that are preliminary to the writing of the composition. The first stage provides for a discussion of each item in the outline. The second stage, introduced in Unit 4 after students have gotten used to working from an outline, requires the completion of an organizational worksheet based on the outline. This worksheet, which offers students the opportunity to make preliminary notes, serves as the basis for the final draft of the composition.

Constant use of such outlines makes students aware of the need for an organic structure to their compositions—a structure which the rhetorical rules of English require, but which may differ from the writing conventions of other languages.

The repeated use of outlines also gives students an awareness of paragraph development within the context of the composition, so they get a better feeling for writing effective paragraphs than if they wrote them in isolation.

2. GRAMMATICAL CONTROL (of the structures needed to write about a particular subject)

The text sets up the preliminary discussion stage in such a way that the teacher can help the students with any of the grammatical structures needed to discuss the subject of the composition. In addition, the text provides many reinforcement exercises for oral and written practice in these structures.

3. SEMANTIC CONTROL (of the vocabulary needed to write about a particular subject)

The discussion stage also offers an opportunity for the teacher to supply needed vocabulary. Furthermore, vocabulary related to the subject is found throughout the exercises.

In addition, many units give students the opportunity to enlarge the vocabulary needed for different functions, such as describing (geography and scenic views, personal characteristics), givng instructions (including recipes), writing letters, writing a newspaper announcement, filling out applications.

4. COMMUNICATIVE CONTROL (of the subject matter)

Each unit consists of a concrete topic that lends itself readily to discussion—such as holidays, superstitions, courtship and marriage customs. Thus students can talk and write about subjects that come from their own knowledge and experience. What they want to say is merely channeled through an outline. Each unit helps the students expand their thinking on the subject and increases the range of vocabulary needed to discuss the subject.

The discussion of the subject matter in each unit provides the opportunity for cross-cultural exchanges between student and student as well as between students and teacher.

ORGANIZATION OF THE UNITS

Each unit is divided into four sections:

1. Discussion and Composition

2. Reinforcement Practice

3. Extra Speaking and Writing Practice

4. Listening-Writing Practice

DISCUSSION AND COMPOSITION

While each unit is about the subject in general, most of the compositions are specifically geared to the student's own country.[1]

This section is set up in two parts.

[1] Obviously, for students of English as a second language who do not remember much about their native country, these compositions can be about the English-speaking country in which they are presently living.

1. DISCUSSION: Preliminary outline for the composition (prewriting stage)

The guidance for this stage is presented in two columns. The left column is the outline. The right column suggests guidance that the teacher can give as the students discuss the items on the outline. This guidance includes ideas, grammar and usage, vocabulary, as well as elements of composition building.

This outline-discussion format facilitates the integration of all the levels of writing—sentence, paragraph, and full composition—in one process.

2. COMPOSITION (to be done before or after the reinforcement practice)

A. ORGANIZING THE COMPOSITION

From Unit 4 on, each unit includes an organizational worksheet, which is based on the discussion outline and which requires students to set up the structural framework of their compositions.

The worksheet requires students to indicate the contents of their introductions and conclusions, to write many of the opening sentences of paragraphs, and to list supporting details in each paragraph. Textual notes for each point on the outline guide the students in the use of their paragraphs. Thus, much of the guidance in rhetorical control that was first given orally during the discussion is noted at the appropriate place on the worksheet.

B. WRITING THE COMPOSITION

In this stage, instructions are given for writing the composition based on the notes made on the organizational worksheet. Also, instructions for the composition's format—title, paper, margins, spacing—are repeated in each unit as a reminder of the form that is to be followed.

C. CORRECTING OR REWRITING THE COMPOSITION

The text sets up a procedure for students to correct their own compositions and to learn from their corrections. A chart of correction symbols for both the teacher and the students is given in the back of the book. This system of symbols is modeled after the one commonly used in freshman composition texts. However, the number of symbols has deliberately been limited so that they will be easy for the teacher to use and for the student to follow.

Each unit also includes a correction page which students should use to write down corrections of mistakes they have made in their compositions. This requirement provides a convenient way for students to actively correct their errors and serves as a constant reminder to avoid repeating the same mistakes.

REINFORCEMENT PRACTICE

This section includes a variety of oral and written drills on structure and vocabulary, many of which are on the sentence level. The choice of grammatical structures has been determined by the need to communicate about a particular subject matter.[2] For this reason, the structures are not graded for degree of difficulty, nor do they cover all problems of grammatical usage. However, an effort has been made to include as many of the basic structures as possible, as a kind of review (and in some cases, an expansion) of structures students have previously learned. An effort has also been made to keep the explanations short and clear, with a minimum of grammatical terminology but with abundant examples.

The contents of the drills are all related to the subject matter of the unit. The vocabulary represents a mixture of formal and conversational styles appropriate for writing. Like the grammatical structures, the vocabulary is not graded.

Among the types of exercises are two of special note that appear in each of the units. One is on word forms. This type has been included because even advanced students continue to have difficulties with the use of the proper part-of-speech suffixes. The other contains strings of lexical items that must be made into full sentences. This exercise serves both as a review of sentence structures already practiced in the unit and as further practice in using the appropriate verb forms and structure words such as articles and prepositions.

EXTRA SPEAKING AND WRITING PRACTICE

The exercises in this section provide a variety of language activities that lead to speaking and writing practice, or both. Many of them can be done in pairs or in larger groups. These exercises may begin with oral work based on visual material such as a map, a chart, a diagram, or an airline ticket. Other oral practice, often leading to writing, may take the form of dialogs, role playing, or interviews.

LISTENING-WRITING PRACTICE

Each unit has two selections for dictation and two for dicto-comps (dictations-compositions), all based on the subject matter of the unit. Dicto-comps are somewhat longer selections than dictations; students write summaries from the dicto-comps that their teachers read to them.

[2] Examples of such structures are: in Biography: prepositions of time; in Instructions: passive for a process, conditions for precautions; in Telling Stories: direct and indirect speech.

In some units the Extra Speaking and Writing Practice section or the Listening-Writing Practice section includes partial or full written models for the composition. These sections may also include contextualized practice with the grammatical structures from the reinforcement exercises.

END MATERIAL

1. Partial answers to all the reinforcement drills in each unit. These answers are particularly useful for students who are doing any of the exercises on their own.

2. Chart of symbols for correction of compositions.

3. Index of exercises in the units.

4. A general index of all usage and writing practices.

TEACHER'S MANUAL

This manual contains specific suggestions for handling the work in each of the units. The manual also includes complete answers for all the exercises in each unit. In addition, there are two forms of a usage test that can be administered before and after the practice work with the text, not only to determine student progress, but also to pinpoint areas of student weakness.

ACCOMPANYING TEXT

Writer's Companion is a small, compact text designed to complement this volume. Its purpose is to take care of individual writing problems, especially on the sentence level, so that the teacher does not need to engage in endless explanations of usages that have not been mastered by particular students.

Writer's Companion consists of two parts:

1. An Index of Usage and Rhetoric. This is the main section of the book, arranged in the same alphabetical order as the correction chart in this book. Thus students can easily find information when they are writing compositions or making corrections. Some entries in the Index are mainly for correction of errors, such as dangling constructions and fragments. Other entries give more detailed information, such as the entries under verbs, spelling, punctuation.

Entries for rhetoric include introductions, conclusions, paragraphing, and transitions.

2. A Grammar Review and Practice section, consisting of a brief overview of basic grammar. This section is intended for those students whose lack of knowledge of English grammar interferes with their understanding of the rules of usage. This part of the text includes some exercises (with answers) which can be done as class work or assigned individually.

ACKNOWLEDGMENTS

The author would like to acknowledge with thanks the invaluable help given by Marianne Russell and Virginia Rubens of Prentice-Hall in the production of this book. Thanks are also due to the many teachers at the American Language Institute of New York University, and at other institutions, who tried out the materials and offered useful suggestions for strengthening parts of the book.

To the Student

The method of writing compositions that you are going to follow in this book may be quite different from the way you have been taught before. In this book you will write compositions that are controlled by an outline. The use of such an outline will enable you to construct well-developed compositions. In order for you to concentrate on these techniques of composition building, you will be asked to write only about subjects that you know from your own experience.

Units 1 through 3 will help you get accustomed to following an outline. Beginning with Unit 4, you will be writing compositions that have three basic parts: an introduction, a body, and a conclusion. Such an organization may not be required in all types of writing, but it is the one most commonly used for formal papers and reports of the kind you might need for academic work. The introduction prepares the reader for what you are going to concentrate on, the body contains the main points that you are going to make, and the conclusion rounds out in some satisfying way what you have just said.

The following sections give a brief explanation of the use of introductions and conclusions, as well as of other elements of composition building. The examples are taken from Unit 7, Superstitious Beliefs.

1. INTRODUCTIONS

An introduction often makes general statements that lead into the specific subject (or the body) of your composition. There are a number of ways of making such general statements. One way that is suggested in this book is to give a definition of the broad term which you will treat in a narrower sense in the composition. For example, in the composition on "Superstitious Beliefs in (*name of your country*)," you will be asked to begin the composition with a general definition of superstition. The text suggests that such a definition might include references to the fact that superstition:

- is an unreasonable belief that supernatural forces can cause good or bad things to happen

- results from ignorance and fear of the unknown

- often involves magic and witchcraft

- may have a religious origin

2. TRANSITIONAL LEAD-INS

A transitional lead-in helps you move from the general comments of the introduction to the body of your composition. This transition indicates how you are going to narrow down the general statements in your introduction to the specific subject of your composition. Also, the transition may actually mention the main points on your outline so that the reader can anticipate the way you are organizing your composition. For example, a transitional lead-in suggested for the composition on "Superstitious Beliefs in (*name of your country*)" is: "Superstitions are often attached to numbers, animals and birds, and things." This transition tells the reader that you are going to organize your composition about superstitions under the headings of:

    I. Superstitions about numbers

   II. Superstitions about animals and birds

  III. Superstitions about things

3. PARAGRAPHING

The outline is very important in guiding you in the construction of your paragraphs. Each item on the outline is generally developed in a separate paragraph. The opening sentence of each paragraph (often called a *topic sentence*) includes a reference to the point on the outline. For example, the open-

xiv   TO THE STUDENT

ing sentence of point I, Superstitions about numbers, might be: "There are several superstitions about numbers in my country."

The sentences that follow this opening sentence should be only about the topic from the outline—in this example, superstitions about numbers. Also, the sentences that follow the opening sentence of a paragraph should be connected properly. Suggested connectives that might link sentences after the opening sentence of the paragraph about numbers are:

For example, we have *one* about number 13.

OR

The most common *one* concerns number 13.

4. CONCLUSIONS

The conclusion gives the composition a sense of completion by opening up from the main part of the composition to more general comments about the subject. Thus, the composition begins and ends with general statements about the subject.

For the conclusion of the composition on superstitions, the book suggests that general statements might refer to:

- the kind of people who still believe in these superstitions

- your own belief

A conclusion need not be long, and it can sometimes be omitted if the main part of the composition ends on an important point or if a story merely comes to an end.

The general statements of introductions and conclusions given in this book are only suggestions. You might want to use your own ideas instead. However, introductions and conclusions should be kept short so that you can concentrate on the main part of your composition, which comes from the other points on the outline.

This kind of tight control through the use of an outline with an introduction and a conclusion may seem artificial to you, and in fact this control is not always so strict as in this book. However, it is useful for you to practice such a control at first so that you may have the rules for composition building firmly in mind. Remember that your reader expects some guidance to the main points on your outline. Your awareness of these principles of writing is important not only for writing but for reading textbooks. In the introduction and conclusion of the entire book, and often in each chapter, the writer of a text will guide the reader to the main ideas. Also, the writer will frequently use headings to draw attention to the main points from the outline.

Procedures
for the Teacher

The teacher's manual that accompanies *Writing from Experience* gives specific suggestions for teaching each of the units in the book. However, since the outline-discussion approach for teaching composition is basically different from other approaches, and since the success of this approach is partly dependent on the procedures for guiding the composition, it is especially important for the teacher to have some general guidelines here.

First, a word about when the compositions should be written. Although each unit begins with the discussion and composition section, the decision of whether students should write the composition before or after the reinforcement exercises is up to the teacher. However, regardless of when the composition is to be written, it is highly desirable to begin the work of the unit with the discussion of the composition. There are several reasons for doing so.

First, this discussion requires students right from the start to face many of the semantic, structural, and rhetorical problems involved in writing about a particular subject. The oral guidance given by the teacher for points on the outline helps students to begin to overcome these problems. This guidance not only forestalls the possible number of mistakes in student compositions, but it helps students retain longer those structural and lexical items that they struggled for in the discussion and that they will also need when they write about the subject.

Furthermore, after students talk about the composition topic, they often realize that their mastery of some of the structures they have already studied is not as secure as they had thought. They are therefore more receptive to doing the reinforcement exercises and can gain more from them.

Another advantage of beginning with the discussion stage is that the cross-cultural exchange that is involved puts students at ease right from the start. Communicating freely and meaningfully with each other creates a friendly and relaxed atmosphere in which the students and the teacher can learn from each other.

PROCEDURES FOR THE DISCUSSION STAGE

Because of the importance of the discussion stage for the work to be done in each unit, specific steps are suggested below for handling this stage. These suggestions are based on the use of the outline page(s) at the beginning of the Discussion and Composition section.

First, write on the blackboard the title and the outline given in the left column. (Some subpoints can be omitted from the outline at first and then added as the discussion proceeds.) Students' books should be closed, in order to allow them to get the most benefit out of the oral work.

For the steps that are to follow, use the information from the right-hand column to help students with the content and expression of the composition. Include elements of the rhetorical development if the composition is to be written immediately after the discussion. Elicit as much of this information as possible from the students.

1. Call on individual students to give a full sentence for each point on the outline.

2. As a student makes a mistake or searches for a word, get the correct information from the class and place it on the board. Have students copy this information in their notebooks.

3. Continue calling on students until they give enough sentences for each point on the outline to enable you to place all the needed structures and vocabulary on the board. Encourage student exchange of information. In some units the discussion column has information on American culture that can be shared with the students.

4. If much student interaction has been generated during the class discussion, you might form student groups to continue discussing the points on the outline with each other.

5. From Unit 4 on, when introductions and conclusions are added to the composition, see how much of the suggested contents for these paragraphs you can get from the students themselves before you give the information from the

discussion column (and of course additional suggestions of your own.)[1] You might also ask the class for alternate transitions and opening sentences of paragraphs.

PROCEDURES FOR THE WRITING STAGE

If some time has elapsed between the preliminary discussion and the writing of the composition, it would be desirable to repeat the discussion based on the outline, especially for the handling of the introduction, conclusion, and transitions. Stress the use of opening sentences of paragraphs in order to start building an awareness of topic sentences.

Have the students fill out the organizational worksheet, which requires them to stay within the structural framework set up by the outline. Suggest that they check against the discussion outline for additional help.

For the first few compositions it is advisable to have students fill out the worksheet in class. Once this is done, the composition can be written, or at least started, in class, or it can be assigned for homework. The compositions in Units 8 through 10, which are rather long, may be broken into two parts, both for the discussion and the composition. The two parts however should hold together as one composition.

It is very important to point out the need for students to revise their compositions several times so that what they hand in is the best they can do. Students can catch many of their mistakes if they take the time to look over their papers carefully.

PROCEDURES FOR THE CORRECTION STAGE

In going over the compositions, mark mistakes with the symbols from the correction chart so that students can correct their papers themselves.

An error may be marked by underlining it and placing the correction symbol directly above it, or better still, in the margin. Students should be asked to insert the correction neatly above the error, preferably in pen for a typewritten composition, or in pencil or a different color ink for a handwritten composition. If there are many errors, it would be best to have students rewrite the composition.

If you feel that this symbol system is too complicated for your students, you might at first select only the starred symbols, which cover the more basic problems in English, and then gradually introduce the other correction sym-

---

[1] The suggested contents of introductions and conclusions are especially important for the weaker or less reflective students. Such students will follow the suggestions rather closely, while the others will be able to express their own ideas more freely.

bols. Also, in some cases you might find it advisable to use some subsymbols—for example, V (tense), P (run-on).

Obviously, you might also add other terms that call for corrections, such as *not clear, unnecessary,* the omission symbol Λ, or the question mark for illegible writing or an incomprehensible point. Such notations have been omitted from the chart because they do not require explanation in the Index of *Writer's Companion.*

Once students have been made sufficiently aware of a particular usage, mistakes in this usage might be merely underlined or circled instead of being labeled.

After the compositions are returned, it is important to have your students list their corrections on the correction page. However, this notation should not be done before you have checked their corrections. For the first set of compositions, you might want to show students how to use the correction chart.

Encourage students to review their lists of corrections as often as possible so that they will avoid making the same mistakes again.

Also encourage your students to make use of *Writer's Companion.* Since the Index to Usage and Rhetoric in the *Companion* contains detailed information about the same items that are in the correction chart, students can get additional help in making their own corrections.

PROCEDURES FOR THE REINFORCEMENT PRACTICE

Although some of the Reinforcement Practice is specifically designated in the text as group work, actually almost all of the exercises can be done in groups. Division of students into pairs provides the most individual practice, but for some activities, larger groups might get the benefit of greater cross-cultural exchange.

Whether students are to do the exercises in class or at home, the explanations should be gone over first, and answers for the first few sentences should be made available to make sure that the students understand what is required in each exercise.

If students are having trouble with the exercises on word forms, it would be helpful for them to study the first two units in the Grammar Review and Practice section of *Writer's Companion.* They may need to do some of the exercises in these chapters in order to get an idea of the signals that indicate the need for a particular part-of-speech form.

Because the general index lists the usage practices, and because answers to the usage exercises are also given in the back of the book, the whole class or individual students can be assigned special exercises to do at home (even if such exercises are not in the particular unit being studied). In a workshop or tutorial the answers allow students to go at their own pace. If these exercises are not sufficient, assignments might be given from my *Modern English: Exer-*

cises for Non-native Speakers (Part One, Parts of Speech; and *Part Two, Sentences and Complex Structures*). The answers to these exercises are available in the teacher's manual that accompanies these texts.

PROCEDURES FOR THE EXTRA SPEAKING AND WRITING PRACTICE

These speaking and writing exercises, which provide a variety of short activities, have varying degrees of control. It would be best to work with these exercises after the composition has been corrected or rewritten.

PROCEDURES FOR THE LISTENING-WRITING PRACTICE

The Listening-Writing Practice consists of dictations and dicto-comps. These can be interspersed with the reinforcement exercises in order to give more variety to the classroom practice. A dictation or a dicto-comp can be assigned for study beforehand or it can be done without previous preparation. In the latter case, it is advisable at the first reading to let students look at the selection in the book and to explain any difficult structures and vocabulary.

DICTATIONS

For the dictations, the standard procedure is recommended:

1. Read the entire selection once at normal speed while students listen.

2. Read the selection again, more slowly but in natural phrases, for students to write.

3. Read the selection a third time at normal speed for students to check what they have written.

After the dictations are collected, have the students refer to the selection in the book immediately, while their interest is still keen on seeing what they got right and what they got wrong.

Other possible procedures are to let students correct their own dictations or to have them exchange papers for correction.

DICTO-COMPS

Dicto-comps are written summaries of selections that are read to the class by the teacher. Students get the most benefit from a dicto-comp if they have not seen it before they listen to it. However, if the selection is difficult for students, it might be assigned beforehand. The danger here, of course, is that students may merely memorize it, which defeats the purpose of the dicto-comp as listening-writing practice (although the memorization is helpful for internalizing certain structural and lexical items).

The dicto-comp, like the dictation, is read three times, but each time at normal speed. It is advisable to have students take notes of what they hear at each reading. After the last reading, to make sure that students have not missed the main points, you might ask a series of questions about the content in chronological order so that they can check their notes, and you might put key words on the board to guide the writing. Also, if there is time, you might form small groups for students to exchange the information with each other before they write their summaries.

After students turn in what they have written, it is useful to have them look at the reading selection to get immediate feedback on problems they had in writing the dicto-comp.

Traveling to Another Country

GRAMMAR AND USAGE

very, too, so with adjectives or adverbs
Irregular verbs (past tense and past participle)
Infinitives versus gerunds
Time: structures with *before, after*
Purpose: structures with *to* or *for*
it versus *there*
Spelling: changing *y* to *i*

RHETORIC

Using an outline to guide the composition

DISCUSSION AND COMPOSITION

1. DISCUSSION: Preliminary outline for the composition (prewriting stage)

Subject: *My Trip to the United States* [or to another foreign country]

Outline (To Be Placed on the Board)	Discussion (Ideas, Grammar and Usage, Vocabulary, Elements of Composition Building)
I. Decision to come to the foreign country	Purpose: With *to:* 　　to continue my studies in this country 　　to specialize in a particular field 　　to visit the country only 　　to get some practical experience 　　to immigrate to this country With *for:* 　　for a visit 　　for business 　　for pleasure 　　for further education Problems: 　　overcoming my parents' objections 　　getting the money to live in the new country
II. Preparations for the trip	
A. Getting the necessary documents	Documents: passport, visa, I-20 for students
B. Taking care of medical requirements	Shots; injections; vaccination; inoculation; 　　immunization—for smallpox, cholera
C. Making the financial arrangements	
D. Buying clothes	
E. Purchasing the ticket for the trip	One-way or round trip, tourist class Plane fare
F. Packing bags	Suitcases, luggage, baggage Shipping trunk ahead
G. Saying goodbye	
III. The trip itself	
A. Saying goodbye to family, friends	Tearful, crying
B. Plane ride	Checking in, boarding pass Long trip, nonstop Delays, plane trouble

Outline (cont.)	Discussion (cont.)
B. Plane ride (cont.)	Comfortable, airsick Service, food Stewardess (or flight attendant) Feelings: sad, homesick, lonesome, worried, anxious, happy, excited Experiences: other passengers Views from the plane
IV. Arrival in the new country	
A. Experiences at the airport	Impression of the airport Difficulty with the language Claiming bags from the baggage (luggage) area Going through customs
B. First impressions of the new country	Ride from the airport to your destination

2. COMPOSITION (to be done before or after the reinforcement practice)

A. WRITING THE COMPOSITION

Place the title of the composition at the top of the page:

My Trip to the United States
[or to another foreign country]

Do not use quotation marks or a period for a title at the top of the page. Use initial capital letters for the first word of the title and for all other words except articles, short prepositions, and short conjunctions.

Write the composition on ''My Trip to the United States'' [or to another foreign country] following the outline that has been discussed. The right column of the outline pages can be of help to you.

Place each of the four main points in a separate paragraph. If any of these paragraphs is quite long, you may break it in two. Be sure to follow chronological order. Use the *past tense*.

Use 8½ - by 11-inch white paper, with lines for handwritten compositions and without lines for typed compositions. Double-space typewritten papers, and skip lines on handwritten compositions. Write on the front of the paper only, and leave wide margins on *both the left and the right sides* of the paper. Indent the beginning of each paragraph.

Look over your composition carefully before you hand it in.

B. CORRECTING OR REWRITING THE COMPOSITION

When your teacher returns your composition, it will be marked with the symbols from the correction chart on page 257. Make the necessary corrections on the composition and hand it back to your teacher. If you have made many mistakes, you may need to rewrite the composition.

Place the corrections on the correction page, and note down the rule that is involved.

(For more help with problems of writing, consult the Index of Usage and Rhetoric in *Writer's Companion*. The items in this index are arranged in the same alphabetical order as in the correction chart.)

CORRECTION PAGE

Use this page to write down the correction of any mistake you have made in your composition on "My Trip to the United States" [or to another country]. Include enough of the words surrounding the corrected part to make the meaning clear. (Do not copy down the mistake itself.) If possible, write down the rule that covers the correction you have made.

Review these corrections from time to time in order to avoid making the same mistakes again.

Corrections	**Rule**
	(See the correction chart if necessary)

REINFORCEMENT PRACTICE

EXERCISE 1: *very, too, so* with Adjectives or Adverbs

Very, too, and *so* are used with adjectives or adverbs to express degree (how much).

Very expresses a large degree.

I was *very* nervous on the plane.

Too expresses an excessive degree, more than is acceptable.

I was *too* nervous on the plane to eat the food.

Sometimes the speaker himself determines how much is excessive.

It was *very* noisy at the airport.
It was *too* noisy at the airport.

So is often an informal equivalent of *very*.

I was *so* nervous on the plane.

This use of *so* for *very* should be avoided in compositions. *So* is appropriately used before adjectives or adverbs that are followed by *that*.

I was *so* nervous on the plane *that* I couldn't eat anything.

Supply *very, too,* or *so*. Do not use *so* for *very*.

1. At the Consulate, I had to wait in a _____*very*_____ long line.

2. There were _____*so*_____ many things I had to do that I thought I would never be ready to leave for my trip.

3. The night before I left, I was _____*too*_____ excited to sleep.

4. My trip was __Very__ nice and comfortable, but I couldn't sleep.

5. During the trip I felt ____So____ depressed.

6. The food on the plane was __Very__ bad that I couldn't eat it.

7. The plane arrived at the airport __Very__ late. It was __too__ late for anyone to meet me.

8. There were ____so____ many people at the airport that I was _____ surprised.

9. I was carrying ____So____ many packages that I was afraid I would lose something.

10. The line at the customs checkout was ___so___ long that I thought I would never get out of the airport.

11. My suitcases were ___too___ heavy for me to carry. A ___very___ nice porter helped me take them to a taxi.

12. There were ___so___ few taxis at this time of the night that I was afraid I might not find one.

13. I was ___very___ happy when I was finally able to get a taxi.

14. The taxi was ___very___ expensive, but I was ___too___ tired to worry about money.

EXERCISE 2: Irregular Verbs (Past Tense and Past Participle)

A. Supply the past tense or the past participle of the irregular verbs in these sentences. (The past participle is the third principal part of an irregular verb [*wear, wore, **worn***] and comes after a form of the auxiliary *be* or *have*.)

1. Last month I (fly) ___*flew*___ to New York in a 747 plane. I had never (fly) ___*flown*___ in such a large airplane before.

2. Before I (leave) ___left___ my country, I (get) ___got___ a passport and a visa. I (put) ___put___ them in my wallet right away.

3. Soon after I had (leave) ___left___ my country, I started to feel homesick. I (begin) ___began___ to wish I had never (go) ___gone___ away.

4. I (feel) ___felt___ depressed in the plane, and I have (feel) ___felt___ depressed many times since.

5. I hardly (eat) ___I ate___ or (drink) ___drunk___ anything on the plane. I should have (eat) ___eaten___ or (drink) ___drunk___ a little more.

6. I have often (think) ___though___ about the easy life I (have) ___had___ in my country.

7. I (know) ___knew___ that I would have to work hard to learn the new language, and I wondered whether I would be (understand) ___understood___.

8. Since I (come) ___came___ here, I have (come) ___come___ to the conclusion that life here is difficult but interesting.

9. I have (write) _written_ many letters home about my experiences here, but I haven't (tell) _told_ my family everything.

10. I haven't (say) _said_ that I was almost (hit) _hit_ by a car and that some of my money was (steal) _stolen_.

11. But I did tell my family about the wonderful plays I've (see) _seen_ and the concerts I've (hear) _heard_.

B. Change the following sentences with irregular verbs to the passive voice. Keep in mind that:

    (1) A passive sentence begins with the original object of the verb.
    (2) The verb consists of a form of *be* plus the past participle.
    (3) The original subject usually is placed in a *by*-phrase.

	Subject	*Verb*	*Object*	
Active	My friends	gave	a party	for me before I left.
Passive	A party	was given		for me *by my friends* before I left.

1. I lost my wallet at the airport a few weeks ago. (omit *I*)

    My wallet was lost at the airport a few weeks ago.

2. My girlfriend had made it for me.

3. I cannot buy such a wallet in this country. (omit *I*)

4. A customs inspector found it.

5. He gave it back to me.

6. He told me to be very careful with money.

7. I have already spent all my money. (omit *I*)

8. My father will send me more money right away.

9. I'll pay some bills with this money. (omit *I*)

10. I'll put the rest in the bank. (omit *I*)

EXERCISE 3: *Infinitives versus Gerunds*

Verbs that come after other verbs may be in infinitive form *(to do)* or in gerund form *(doing)*.

Verbs Followed by Infinitives		**Verbs Followed by Gerunds**	
allow help[1] refuse persuade used	*to do* something	anticipate appreciate avoid enjoy stop	*doing* something

A few verbs are followed by the infinitive without *to*.

have let make	someone *do* something

After some words, *to* is regarded as a preposition and requires the *-ing* form.

be used to object to	*doing* something

After certain expressions, the *-ing* form is required.

be busy spend time	*doing* something

Use the correct form of the verb in parentheses.

1. At first my parents wouldn't let me (leave) _____ *leave* _____ the country.

2. They objected to my (go) _____ *going* _____ away because I wasn't used to (live) _____ *living* _____ alone.

3. I couldn't understand why they refused (give) _____ *to give* _____ me permission to go away.

4. But nothing could make me (change) _____ *change* _____ my mind.

5. Finally I persuaded my parents (allow) _____ *to allow* _____ me (take) _____ *to take* _____ the trip.

6. I spent many days (prepare) _____ *preparing* _____ for the trip.

[1] The infinitive after *help* may be used with or without *to*.

9

7. I was busy (buy) _buying_ the clothes I needed and (get) _getting_ the necessary documents.

8. I had my tailor (make) _make_ some new clothes for me.

9. I made all my friends (gather) _gather_ information about the country I was going to.

10. My whole family helped me (pack) _to pack_ my suitcases.

? 11. I had the clerk at the airport (check) _check_ my baggage.

12. I enjoyed (look) _looking_ at the land from the plane.

13. I used (think) _to think_ I knew English well, but when I arrived at the airport, I didn't understand anything.

14. My heart almost stopped (beat) _beating_ from fear and excitement.

15. Would I ever get used to (be) _being_ in a strange country?

16. I anticipated (have) _having_ lots of problems.

17. I couldn't avoid (think) _thinking_ of the many friends I had left behind.

18. However, I knew I would appreciate (make) _making_ new friends.

EXERCISE 4: Time: Structures with *before, after*

Before or *after* may introduce:

A SUBJECT PLUS A PREDICATE
After *I finished* high school, I decided to come to the United States.

Before *I left* my country, I withdrew money from the bank.

THE *-ING* FORM OF THE VERB
After *finishing* high school, I decided to come to the United States.

Before *leaving* my country, I withdrew money from the bank.

Structures beginning with *before* or *after* may also be used at the end of the sentence, with no commas before them.

I decided to come to the United States *after* I finished high school.

I withdrew money from the bank *before* leaving my country.

A. Change each sentence by using *before* or *after* as indicated. Make the change in two ways: (1) use a subject plus a verb, and (2) use the *-ing* form of the verb. For this exercise, place each *before* or *after* structure at the beginning of the sentence and use a comma after the structure.

1. I got my passport; then I applied for my visa.   *after*

   After I got my passport, I applied for my visa.
   After getting my passport, I applied for my visa.

2. I had to overcome my parents' objections; afterward(s) I was able to come to the United States.   *before*

   Before I was able to come to the United States, I had to overcome my parents' objections.
   Before being able to come to the United States, I had to overcome my parents' objections.

3. I made a reservation for my plane flight; then I picked up my ticket.   *after*

4. I purchased my plane ticket; after that I bought some clothes.   *after*

5. I was inoculated for smallpox; after that I felt ill for a few days.   *after*

6. I was given a big party; afterward(s) I left for the United States.   *before*

7. I checked my luggage; then I boarded the plane for New York.   *before*

8. The stewardesses served the beverages; then they served the food.   *after*

9. I arrived at the airport; then I claimed my luggage.   *after*

10. I had to go through customs; afterward(s) I was able to join my friends who were waiting for me.   *before*

B. Write *true sentences* about a trip you made.
   (1) Use five sentences containing *after* + the *-ing* form of the verb.
   (2) Use five sentences containing *before* + the *-ing* form of the verb.

EXERCISE 5: Purpose: Structures with *to* or *for*

Purpose may be expressed with *to* or *for*.

to + a VERB	I went to the travel agency *to pick up my ticket.* (or *in order to pick up my ticket.*)
for + a NOUN	I went to the travel agency *for my ticket.*

A. Change the information in parentheses to a phrase expressing purpose. Begin the phrase with:

> *to* (or *in order to*) + a verb
>
> OR   *for* + a verb

See if both types of phrases of purpose are possible.

1. I argued for a long time (so that I might overcome my parents' objections to my leaving the country).

   I argued for a long time to (or *in order to*) *overcome my parents' objections to my leaving the country.*

2. I worked hard (in order that I might earn the money to come to this country).

   I worked hard (*in order*) *to earn the money to come to this country.*
   I worked hard for the money to come to this country.

3. I came to this country (so that I might learn about American culture).

4. I went to the bank (so that I might withdraw money to pay for my ticket).

5. I went to the travel agency (so that I might pick up my plane ticket).

6. I went to the doctor (so that I might get a vaccination against smallpox).

7. I went to bed early (so that I wouldn't be tired on the day of the trip). (use *in order not to*)

8. I ate a big meal on the trip (so that I wouldn't be hungry when I arrived). (use *in order not to*)

9. I went to the baggage area (in order that I might claim my suitcases).

10. I had shipped a trunk ahead (so that I might have it when I arrived in the United States).

B. The words in parentheses express purpose. Use *to* or *in order to* with the VERBS, and *for* with the NOUNS.

1. I came to this country (_____*to, in order to*_____ study medicine).

2. I came to this country (_____*for*_____ business reasons).

3. I came to this country (_____*for*_____ a visit).

4. I came to this country (*to, in order to* get some practical experience in my field).

5. I came to this country (*to, in order to* study economics).

6. I wrote to an American university (_____*for*_____ admission to their school).

7. I went to the American consulate (*to, in order to* apply for a visa).

8. I went to the hospital (___*for*___ a smallpox vaccination).

9. I went to the bank (___*for*___ money to pay for my trip).

10. I went to the travel agency (___*to, in order to*___ pick up my airline ticket).

EXERCISE 6: *it* versus *there*

It and *there* are often used as "empty" words that merely fill subject position but have no meaning in themselves.

it — with an ADJECTIVE	*It* was very *noisy* at the airport. (*Noisy* is an adjective)
there — with a NOUN	*There* was a lot of *noise* at the airport. (*Noise* is a noun)

Usually an "empty" *it* or *there* occurs with the verb *be*. In the case of *there*, the verb agrees with the following noun, which is the true subject of the sentence.

There *was* a bad *storm* during my flight. (the singular subject *storm* requires the singular verb *was*)

There *were* several *storms* during my flight. (the plural subject *storms* requires the plural verb *were*)

In the following sentences, use *it was, there was,* or *there were.*

1. ___*There were*___ many people at the travel agency. (*people* is a noun)

2. ___*It was*___ very crowded at the travel agency. (*crowded* is an adjective)

3. ___*There is / was*___ a nonstop flight leaving for New York in the morning.

4. ___*there were*___ many things I had to do before I could leave.

5. ___*It was*___ a little painful to get my shots.

6. ___*there was*___ a bad rainstorm the day before I was to take my flight.

7. ___*there was*___ a lot of excitement at the airport because a plane had been hijacked.

8. ___*It was*___ exciting to feel the plane take off.

9. ___*there was*___ a pretty girl sitting next to me.

10. ___*there were*___ a choice of entrées for dinner on the plane.

11. _It was_ very cold and windy the day I arrived at Kennedy Airport.

12. _There were_ so many buildings at Kennedy Airport that I became confused.

EXERCISE 7: Word Forms (1)

Use the correct form of the word in parentheses. (If you need help with the signals that tell whether a noun, verb, adjective, or adverbial form is needed, refer to *Writer's Companion,* Unit 2, in the Grammar Review and Practice section.)

1. I had made a (decide) _decision_ to come to the United States a long time ago.

2. My parents raised a few (object) _____ to my plan to go away for such a long time, but they finally gave me their (approve) _____.

3. I had to make many (prepare) _____ to go on my long trip.

4. I began to feel some (anxious) _____ as I went to the American (Ambassador) _____ for some documents.

5. I made a (withdraw) _____ from the bank and then I (purchase) _____ my plane ticket.

6. When the day of (depart) _____ arrived, I bid a (tear) _____ goodbye to my family and friends.

7. The (fly) _____ was very (comfort) _____ during the first half of the trip; the stewardesses were (attend) _____ and (help) _____.

8. During the second half of the trip, a severe storm made many of the (passage) _____ airsick.

9. On my (arrive) _____ at Kennedy Airport, I had to pass through the (immigrate) _____ office for the (inspect) _____ of my baggage.

10. Now that I was in my new country, I really felt (nerve) _____ and (fright) _____.

EXERCISE 8: Word Forms (2)

Add the word for either the profession or the person who follows the profession. Also add *a* or *an* for the person.

1. If you want to become __a__ __dentist__, you must study __dentistry__.
2. If you want to become __a__ __doctor__, you must study __medicine__.
3. If you want to become __a lawyer__, you must study __law__.
4. If you want to become __a physicist__, you must study __physics__.
5. If you want to become __an__ __economist__, you must study __economics__.
6. If you want to become __a psychiatrist__, you must study __psychiatry__.
7. If you want to become __an__ __accountant__, you must study __business accounting__.
8. If you want to become __a Chemist__, you must study __chemistry__.
9. If you want to become __a__ __financier__, you must study __finance__.
10. If you want to become __a Stenographer__, you must study __stenography__.
11. If you want to become __a__ __photographer__, you must study __photography__.
12. If you want to become __an engineer__, you must study __engineering__.
13. If you want to become __a psychologist__, you must study __psychology__.
14. If you want to become __a__ __nurse__, you must study __nursing__.

EXERCISE 9: Sentence Review

Make full sentences from the word groups below. Use the past tense for all verbs. Make whatever changes or additions are needed, but do not change the word order. Use commas, semicolons, or periods where necessary.

1. My wallet / lose / airport / few / weeks ago.

   My wallet was lost at the airport a few weeks ago.

2. Last month / I / fly / New York / I never / fly / such / large airplane / before.

3. My parents / object / me / go away / because / I / not / use / live / alone.

4. I / have / my tailor / make / some new clothes.

5. My heart / almost / stop / beat / from / fear / excitement.

6. I / apply / visa / after / get / my passport.

7. I / check / my luggage / then / I / board / plane / New York.

8. I / go / doctor / get / vaccination / smallpox.

9. I / work / hard / money / come / this country.

10. Be / many things / have / do / before / I / can / leave.

11. Be / very cold / windy / when / I / arrive / Kennedy Airport.

12. Be / pretty girl / sit / next / me.

13. I / make / withdraw- / bank / then / I / purchase / my plane ticket.

14. When / day / depart- / arrive / I / bid / tear- / goodbye / my family / friends.

15. The fli- / be / very comfort- / stewardesses / be / atten- / help-.

EXTRA SPEAKING AND WRITING PRACTICE

EXERCISE 10: Spelling: Changing y to i

A. A final *y* is changed to *i* before *-s* or *-ed*.

> study + s becomes *studies* (note that e is added before s)
> study + ed becomes *studied*

There is no change, however, if a vowel appears before the final *y*.

> plays, played.

The ending *-ing* is not changed after final *y*.

> studying, playing

Rewrite the words, adding the required endings.

country + s _____ *countries* _____   difficulty + s _Difficulties_

carry + ed _Carried_   study + ing _Studying_

fly + s _flies_   worry + ed _worried_

delay + ing _delaying_   enjoy + ing _enjoying_

journey + s _journeys_   party + s _parties_

hurry + ed _hurried_   annoy + ing _Annoying - left alone_

accompany + ed _accompanied_   delay + ed _delayed_

travel agency + s _travel Agencies_   employ + ed _Employed_

Bothering

B. A final *y* is also changed to *i* before other endings.

final *y* + a syllable beginning with a *vowel:*

carry + age = carriage

final *y* + a syllable beginning with a *consonant:*

happy + ness = happiness

But there is *no change if a vowel precedes the y.*

employer, enjoyment

Rewrite the words, adding the required endings.

dirty + est _____ *dirtiest* _____   friendly + er _friendlyier_

lonely + ness _lonelynes_   employ + ment _employment._

employ + ee _employee_   vary + ety _Various / Variety_

enjoy + ment _enjoyment_   beauty + ful _beautiful_

lucky + ly _Luckily_   mystery + ous _mysterious_

library + an _Librarian_   pay + ment _payment_

EXERCISE 11: Questions and Answers: An Airline Ticket

Working in pairs, take turns asking and answering the following questions about the information on this airline ticket. Answer in full sentences.

PASSENGER'S NAME FRANK | MARCELLA				DATE OF ISSUE 19 APR 77		PLACE OF ISSUE-AGENCY SUPERIOR TRAVEL SERVICE 100 EFFICIENCY ROAD SALT LAKE CITY, UTAH
FROM	FARE BASIS	CARRIER	FLIGHT NO.	DATE	TIME	
SALT LAKE CITY	Y^1	WA^2	161	APR 26	750^3 A	
TO LOS ANGELES	Y	WA	732	APR 26	845 A	
TO MIAMI	Y	EA^2	28	MAY 1	600 P	
TO NEW YORK JFK	Y	TW^2	900	MAY 15	845 P	PASSENGER TICKET AND BAGGAGE CHECK— ISSUED BY:
TO CASABLANCA						
FARE 554.30						*TRANS WORLD AIRLINES* TWA
TAX 3.00	TOTAL 557.30					

1. Who was the airline passenger?
2. When was the airline ticket issued?
3. What is the name of the travel agent that issued the ticket?
4. Which airline issued the ticket?
5. How much did the ticket cost? How much tax did the passenger pay?
6. Which airline did this passenger take from Salt Lake City to Los Angeles? From New York to Casablanca?
7. What cities did the passenger go to after leaving Salt Lake City?
8. What time did the passenger leave Miami? New York?
9. How many flights did this passenger take in the morning? In the evening?

[1] The symbol Y stands for the economy class (not first class).

[2] WA = Western Airlines; EA = Eastern Airlines; TW = Trans World Airlines.

[3] The time means time of departure. (A = A.M.; P = P.M.) The time of arrival is not shown on the airline ticket.

LISTENING-WRITING PRACTICE

EXERCISE 12: Paragraphs for Dictation

Your teacher will dictate each paragraph three times. The first time is for listening only, the second time is for writing, and the third time is for checking what you have written.

Immediately after you give your teacher the dictation you have written, check the dictation in the book for any problems you had in writing it.

DICTATION 1

To obtain a visa for study in the United States, you must apply to a U.S. embassy or consulate abroad with a passport from your own government and proof that you satisfy certain requirements. You must present evidence that you have been accepted as a full-time student by a recognized U.S. school or special education program, that you are in good health, and that you have adequate financial support to cover your expenses in the United States for the entire period of your proposed study program. Form I-20, "Certificate of Eligibility for Non-Immigrant Student Status," issued by your U.S. institution, is proof that you have been accepted as a student in the United States.

Institute of International Education, *Practical Guide for Foreign Visitors,* p. 12.*

DICTATION 2

If you have traveled to the United States by airplane, it will probably be cheaper for you to use the airport's bus service when you leave the airport. This bus service will take you to the center of town. As airports are usually located some distance from the center of town, a taxi is likely to be extremely expensive. In most parts of the country, taxi fare is registered on a meter. Fares are fixed according to the distance traveled, with an additional charge for suitcases. Taxi drivers should always be tipped, usually 15 percent of the fare.

Institute of International Education, *Practical Guide for Foreign Visitors,* pp. 16–17.*

EXERCISE 13: Dicto-comps

Take notes as your teacher reads each of these dicto-comps to you several times. Then reconstruct the dicto-comp from your notes. The dicto-comp does not need to be written exactly as you heard it, but it should be grammatically correct.

* Reprinted from *Practical Guide for Foreign Visitors,* 1979, by permission of the Institute of International Education, New York, N.Y. 10017, U.S.A. (slightly abridged and adapted).

Before you write the dicto-comp, your teacher may ask the class to get together in groups to check with each other on what you heard.

Immediately after you give your teacher the dicto-comp you have written, check the dicto-comp in the book for any problems you had in writing it.

DICTO-COMP 1

My father had always promised me that when I finished high school, he would let me come to the United States to study business. I studied English privately for a few years so that I would know the language well when I went to the United States.

At last the day of my high school graduation came. It was a great day for me because I knew I would be leaving soon for the United States. But there were many things to do. I wrote to an American university for admission. After I received my I-20 form, I arranged to get a passport. Then I got the shots I needed. Finally, I applied to the American Consulate for an F-1 visa.

When I had all the necessary documents, I picked up my airline ticket at the travel agency, and I made all the financial arrangements for my stay abroad. Then I went shopping for clothes. My mother went with me to be sure I chose suitable clothes. My whole family helped me pack my trunk, which I sent ahead by air freight.

Finally the day of my departure arrived. My family accompanied me to the airport. They bid me a tearful goodbye when I boarded the plane.

DICTO-COMP 2

Now I was alone. The thought that I would not see my family and friends for a long time depressed me. I was already starting to feel homesick. But a very nice lady sitting next to me began to talk to me and soon I became more cheerful.

The plane ride was fairly comfortable, except for a little turbulence now and then. The food on the plane was strange to me, and because of my excitement, I could hardly eat anything.

When my plane landed at Kennedy Airport, I was really nervous. A thousand questions came into my mind. Would my uncle, who was supposed to meet me, be there? Would I have trouble with Immigration? Would I understand what people were saying to me?

I needed to do many things before I could leave the airport. First I had to have my health documents examined by the Public Health officials. Then I had to go to Immigration for the inspection of my passport, visa, and other documents. Finally, I had to go to the customs area to have my bags inspected. Luckily, everything was in order, and I was permitted to leave the airport.

There was such a crowd of people in the terminal that I was afraid I would never find my uncle. So you can imagine how happy I was to see him coming toward me. Now I knew that one part of my life was finished, and another part, more difficult but very exciting, was about to begin.

Geography

GRAMMAR AND USAGE

Points of the compass used with geographic names—capital
   letters, adjective forms, prepositions
the with geographic names
Passive voice
Countable versus noncountable nouns
Passive sentences—natural resources
Reducing coordinate structures containing *and*
Comma faults (run-on sentences)
Nonrestrictive adjectival phrases and clauses—punctuation
Combining sentences with phrases containing *of which*
Combining sentences with adjectivals and appositives
Reversal of subject and verb after initial expressions of place

RHETORIC

Using an outline to guide the composition

DISCUSSION AND COMPOSITION

1. DISCUSSION: Preliminary outline for the composition (prewriting stage)

Subject: *The Geography of* (name of your country)

Outline *(To Be Placed on the Board)*	Discussion *(Ideas, Grammar and Usage, Vocabulary, Elements of Composition Building)*

I. Location on the continent	Names of the continents (seven large land masses): Africa, Asia, Europe, North America, South America, Australia, Antarctica
	
	the with place names:
	    with all bodies of water except lakes
	    with all plural names, especially mountains
	    with all names that end in *of* phrases
	    with all names that include a word for a political union (*the* Dominican Republic)
	
	Choices for position on the continent:
	    in the south of Europe
	    in the southern part of Europe
	
	off the continent: Japan is off the east coast of Asia.
	
	Initial capitals with words for points of the compass:
	    South Africa *versus* in the south of Africa
	    the Middle East *versus* east of Europe
	
	No quotation marks around geographic names
	
	Adjective forms of words for points of the compass: eastern, western, etc. combinations: northeastern, southwestern, north central
	
	Passive voice: My country is located in _____ .
	
	Only *it* (not *she*) is used to refer to a country when discussing its geography.

II. Bordering areas	Prepositions of place and direction:
	    To the north of my country is _____ .
	OR My country is bordered on the north
	    by _____ .
	    in the north is *inside* the country.
	    to the north is *outside* the country.

Outline (cont.)	Discussion (cont.)
II. Bordering areas (cont.)	Passive voice: My country is surrounded by _____ . Additional vocabulary (if needed): peninsula, archipelago

III. Location of principal cities, rivers, mountains	*The* with place names (already given under I.)
	
	Initial capitals for *River, Mountains* when they are part of the name
	
	Passive voice (for a location):
	  The _____ River is located in _____ .
	
	Additional vocabulary (if needed):
	  mountain range
	
	For a river:
	  tributary, mouth, source, drain

IV. Location of principal industries	Passive voice:
	  Coffee is grown in _____ .
	  Cattle are raised in _____ .
	  Gold is mined in _____ .
	
	Vocabulary items (if needed):

Product	Industry	Place
metals (gold, silver, aluminum, etc.), gemstones (diamonds, emeralds, etc.), and coal	mining	mine
crops (rice, cotton, tobacco, coffee, etc.)	agriculture (or farming)	farms (or plantations for very large farms in warm climates)
textiles (cloth: cotton, wool, etc.)	manufacturing	mills
automobiles	manufacturing	plants, or factories
domestic animals, birds	(cattle) raising	farms, ranches for larger animals like cattle, horses

2. COMPOSITION (to be done before or after the reinforcement practice)

A. WRITING THE COMPOSITION

Place the title of the composition at the top of the page:

The Geography of (name of your country)

Do not use quotation marks or a period for a title at the top of the page. Use initial capital letters for the first word of the title and for all other words except articles, short prepositions, and short conjunctions.

Write the composition on "The Geography of *(name of your country)*" following the outline that has been discussed. The right column of the outline pages can be of help to you.

Place items I and II in the same paragraph. Use separate paragraphs for items III and IV. You will thus have three paragraphs in the composition.

Since you are making general statements about your country, use the *present tense* of the verbs.

Use 8½ - by 11-inch white paper, with lines for handwritten compositions and without lines for typed compositions. Double-space typewritten papers, and skip lines on handwritten compositions. Write on the front of the paper only, and leave wide margins on *both the left and the right sides* of the paper. Indent the beginning of each paragraph.

Look over your composition carefully before you hand it in.

B. CORRECTING OR REWRITING THE COMPOSITION

When your teacher returns your composition, it will be marked with the symbols from the correction chart on page 257. Make the necessary corrections on the composition and hand it back to your teacher. If you have made many mistakes, you may need to rewrite the composition.

Place the corrections on the correction page, and note down the rule that is involved.

(For more help with problems of writing, consult the Index of Usage and Rhetoric in *Writer's Companion*. The items in this index are arranged in the same alphabetical order as in the correction chart.)

CORRECTION PAGE

Use this page to write down the correction of any mistakes you have made in your composition on "The Geography of *(name of your country).*" Include enough of the words surrounding the corrected part to make the meaning clear. (Do not copy down the mistake itself.) If possible, write down the rule that covers the correction you have made.

Review these corrections from time to time in order to avoid making the same mistakes again.

Corrections	*Rule* *(See the correction chart if necessary)*

REINFORCEMENT PRACTICE

EXERCISE 1: Points of the Compass Used with Geographic Names—
Capital Letters, Adjective Forms, Prepositions

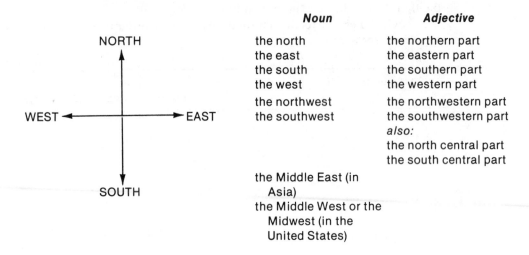

	Noun	*Adjective*
	the north	the northern part
	the east	the eastern part
	the south	the southern part
	the west	the western part
	the northwest	the northwestern part
	the southwest	the southwestern part
		also:
		the north central part
		the south central part
	the Middle East (in Asia)	
	the Middle West or the Midwest (in the United States)	

Note these differences in the use of initial capital letters.

No Initial Capital	*Initial Capital*
He lives in the *south* of France. The *south* is a geographic location, not a name.	He lives in the *South.* The *South* is the name of a definite geographic area in the United States. Compare with *the Middle East, the West.*
He lives in *southern* France. *southern* is the equivalent of *the south of*—a geographic location.	He lives in *South* America. *South* in South America is part of the name of the geographic area.

A word for a point of the compass is not capitalized if it merely gives a direction.

France is to the *south* of England.

Referring to the map on the next page, write full sentences for all the information that is called for in this exercise. Remember to capitalize words for points of the compass when they are part of the name, but not when they indicate direction or simple location.

1. Italy
Write sentences that tell what is (a) to the *north,* (b) to the *east,* (c) to the *south,* (d) to the *west,* (e) to the *northwest* of Italy.

(a)   *To the north of Italy are Switzerland and Austria.*

(b)   to the east of Italy is Adriatic sea.

(c)

(d)

(e)

2. France

Write sentences that tell what borders France (a) on the *north,* (b) on the *east,* (c) on the *south,* (d) on the *west.*

(a)   *France is bordered on the north by the English Channel.*

(b)

(c)

(d)

3. Capital cities

Write sentences that give the location in their country of these capitals: (a) London, (b) Paris, (c) Lisbon, (d) Madrid, (e) Warsaw, (f) Rome, (g) Bucharest, (h) Athens, (i) Berlin.

(a)   *London is located in the southeastern part of England.*

Note that the noun *part* requires the adjective *southeastern.* You may also say:

*London is located in the **southeast of** England.*

(b)

(c)

(d)

(e)

(f)

(g)

(h)

(i)

EXERCISE 2: *the* with Geographic Names

The four most important rules regarding the use of *the* with geographic names are:

1. Use *the* with all bodies of water except lakes: *the Atlantic Ocean, the Mediterranean Sea, the Mississippi River* (but *Lake Erie*).

2. Use *the* with all plural names, especially mountains: *the Rocky Mountains, the Philippines, the Finger Lakes.*

3. Use *the* with all names that end in *of* phrases: *the Gulf of Mexico.*

4. Use *the* with all names that end in a word for a political union: *the British Commonwealth, the Dominican* **Republic.**

(Note the use of capital letters for words like *River, Ocean, Mountains* when these are part of the name.)

Names of continents, countries, and cities are generally used without *the* unless one of these four rules applies.

To the above rules we might add the use of *the* with north, east, south, west when these words are names for geographic areas: *the Middle East, the West.*

Supply *the* where needed.

1. ___*The*___ Pacific Ocean is the largest ocean in the world.

2. ___/___ Lake Geneva is a beautiful lake in ___/___ Switzerland.

3. To the east of India is ___*the*___ Bay of Bengal.

4. ___*the*___ Great Lakes separate ___*the*___ United States from ___/___ Canada.

5. ___*the*___ Soviet Union is in the eastern part of ___/___ Europe.

6. Several of the world's highest mountains, including ___/___ Mount Everest, are in ___/___ southern Nepal.

7. ___/___ Malay Archipelago,[1] the world's largest group of islands, lies off the southeast coast of ___/___ Asia.

8. ___*the*___ Suez Canal separates ___/___ Africa from ___/___ Asia.

9. ___/___ Turkey is bounded on the north by ___*the*___ Black Sea.

10. ___*the*___ Sahara Desert, which is in ___/___ North Africa, extends from ___*the*___ Atlantic Ocean to ___*the*___ Nile River.

11. The Asian part of ___*the*___ U.S.S.R. is separated from the European part by ___*the*___ Ural Mountains.

12. ___*the*___ British Isles consist mainly of ___*the*___ Great Britain and ___/___ Ireland.

13. ___*the*___ Republic of Venezuela exports much of the oil it produces.

14. Many good wines are produced in ___*the*___ Rhine Valley.

[1] *The* is also used with deserts, valleys, peninsulas, archipelagos.

EXERCISE 3: Passive Voice

The passive construction is often used in writing about geography. Use the required passive forms in the following sentences.

1. Yugoslavia (locate) _____*is located*_____ in the southeast of Europe.

2. A peninsula (surround) *is surrounded* by water on three sides; it (attach) *is attached* to land on one side.

3. Czechoslovakia (bound) *is bounding* on the north by Poland.

4. The Pyrenees Mountains (find) *are found* in the northeastern part of Spain.

5. North America and South America (situate) *are situated* in the Western Hemisphere.

6. Various fruits (grow) *are grew* in California.

7. Several kinds of seafood (catch) *are caught* in the waters off the Atlantic Coast.

8. Chickens (raise) *are raised* on New Jersey farms.

9. Cloth (produce) *is produced* in textile mills in the eastern part of the United States.

10. Cars (manufacture) *are manufactured* in Detroit.

11. Tobacco and cotton crops (cultivate) *are cultivated* on large plantations; cattle and other livestock (raise) *are raised* on ranches.

12. In Alaska, seals (trap) *are trapped* for their fur.

13. Dairy products (make) *are made* from milk.

EXERCISE 4: Countable versus Noncountable Nouns

The names for some products are noncountable and therefore do not take the -s plural ending. Also, they require singular verbs when used as subjects.

The *lumber* we need for our bookcase *is* very expensive.

Sometimes words for foods are used in the plural to mean *kinds of, varieties of.*

There are many fishes in the sea.

The wines from France are well-known.

Several citric fruits are grown in Florida.

In the following list, add -*s* to the names of products that are countable.

Products Grown in the Ground
vegetable
tobacco
cotton
beet
potato
grape

Products from Trees
fruit
coconut
cocoa
banana
timber
rubber

Grains
wheat
rye
corn
oat

Products from Mines
coal
iron
silver

Products from the Sea
oyster
fish
shrimp
pearl

Dairy Products
milk
cheese
butter
cream

Products from Animals and Birds
beef
bacon
liver
egg
wool
feather

Animals and Birds Raised for Food
cattle[2]
cow
sheep[3]
poultry
pig
goat
chicken[4]

Products Manufactured or Processed
textile
wine
chemical
paper
leather
handicraft
pottery
fertilizer
machinery
farm equipment

[2] *Cattle* is plural only.

[3] *Sheep* is a countable word. It may be used with a plural verb, but it does not take an ending for the plural: *sheep is, sheep are.*

[4] The plural, *chickens,* refers to the individual birds. As food, the word *chicken* is noncountable.

Natural Resources in the United States

EXERCISE 5: Passive Sentences—Natural Resources

The resource map of the United States shown above indicates where industries such as farming, mining, and fishing are located. Working in pairs, ask and answer questions (in full sentences) about where certain resources are found. Use the *passive voice*.

Keep in mind that:

(1) *A particular crop* is produced (or raised, cultivated, grown).

Fruit is grown in the southwestern part of the United States.

(2) *Certain animals* are raised.

Hogs are raised in the north central part of the United States.

(3) *Certain fish* are caught.

Salmon[5] are caught off the northwestern coast of the United States.

(4) *Certain minerals* are mined (or produced, found).

Oil is found off the southeastern (or south central) coast of the United States.

Note: For variety in your questioning, after an answer is given about the location of an industry, you may also ask questions like:

Where else are cattle[6] raised? (OR *In what other part* of the country are cattle raised?)

---

[5] For names of fish, the plural form is usually the same as the singular, although sometimes the *-s* is added.

[6] Remember that the word *cattle* is plural only.

EXERCISE 6: Reducing Coordinate Structures Containing _and_

Short sentences that are joined by _and_ should be avoided when only small amounts of information are given in each sentence. To improve such sentences, eliminate the _and_ and grammatically reduce one of the sentences. Make whatever change is necessary in the other sentence.

POOR USE OF _AND:_	Brazil is the largest country in South America and it is located in the north.
IMPROVED:	Brazil, which is the largest country in South America, is located in the north.
OR, BETTER:	Brazil, the largest country in South America, is located in the north.

(Note that in the improved sentence, _Brazil_ is the subject of the sentence and _is located in the north_ is its predicate.)

Rewrite the following sentences by eliminating _and_ and reducing the first or second part of each sentence as indicated. Keep the same word order.

1. _Japan is located off the east coast of Asia_ and it is an island country. (reduce the _first_ part)

   Japan, **which is located off the east coast of Asia,** is an island country.

   OR _Japan, **located off the east coast of Asia,** is an island country._
   (Note that the reduced information is put within commas.)

2. Japan consists of four main islands _and they are Hokkaido, Honshu, Shikoku, and Kyushu._ (reduce the _second_ part)

   Japan consists of four main islands, **Hokkaido, Honshu, Shikoku, and Kyushu.**
   (A colon [:] may replace the comma before a list of items.)

3. _Mexico City is the biggest city in my country_ and it is located in the central part of the Republic. (reduce the _first_ part)

4. Two other big rivers in Italy flow into the Adriatic Sea _and they are the Adige and the Piave._ (reduce the _second_ part)

5. _The Amazon is the largest river system in the world,_ and it drains more than one third of South America. (reduce the _first_ part)

6. Czechoslovakia has two large mountain ranges, _and they are the Carpathian in the east and the Sudeten in the west._ (reduce the _second_ part)

7. _Africa is a great plateau._ It is about 5,000 miles long from north to south. (reduce the _first_ part)

EXERCISE 7: Comma Faults (Run-on Sentences)

Short sentences joined by *and,* although often not effective, are grammatically correct because *and* permits two sentences to be joined into one. It is incorrect, however, to join two sentences with only a comma. This error is called a *comma fault.*

The capital city is Madrid, it is located in the central part of the country.

Such a sentence can be made grammatically acceptable by using a period (or a semicolon) instead of the comma. However, when both sentences are short, it is better to reduce one part of the sentence.

The capital city, Madrid, is located in the central part of the country.

Correct the comma faults in these sentences by reducing the part of each sentence that is indicated. Use commas around the reduced structure.

1. *The Nile is the longest river in the world,* it travels 4,000 miles before reaching the Mediterranean. (reduce the *first* part)

   *The Nile, **the longest river in the world,** travels 4,000 miles before reaching the Mediterranean.*

2. Saudi Arabia has two capitals, *they are Riyadh and Mecca.* (reduce the *second* part)

3. *Europe is a huge peninsula,* it is subdivided into a number of lesser peninsulas. (reduce the *first* part)

4. *The islands of Japan rise from great depths of the sea,* they are mostly mountainous. (reduce the *first* part; change *rise* to *rising*)

5. In the northern part of Argentina is the Gran Chaco, *it is a land of forests, lakes, and swamps.* (reduce the *second* part)

6. *Peru was once famous for its precious metals,* today it produces other important minerals. (reduce the *first* part)

7. *Alaska is the largest of the fifty states,* it has a variety of climates ranging from temperate to frigid. (reduce the *first* part)

EXERCISE 8: Nonrestrictive Adjectival Phrases and Clauses — Punctuation

Adjective structures that come after *proper nouns* (names that begin with capital letters) usually require commas.

Manhattan, (which is) surrounded on all sides by water, is a busy seaport.

COMPARE WITH: Manhattan is a busy seaport (which is) surrounded on all sides by water. (no comma after *seaport*)

Such adjective structures with proper nouns may also appear at the beginning of sentences.

Surrounded on all sides by water, Manhattan is a busy seaport.

In this position, the adjective structure must also be set off by a comma.

A. Change the second sentence into an adjective structure and place it after the proper noun in the first sentence. Use commas with each adjective structure. Also, see which structures can be moved to the beginning of the sentence.

1. The Andes Mountains _____
form the longest mountain range in this continent.
They run along almost the entire coast of South America.

> *The Andes Mountains, which run along (or, running along) almost the entire coast of South America, form the longest mountain range in this continent.*

> *Running along almost the entire coast of South America, the Andes Mountains form the longest mountain range in this continent.*

2. Scandinavia _____
consists of Norway, Sweden, and Denmark.
Scandinavia is in the northern part of Europe.

3. New Delhi _____
is thickly populated.
New Delhi is the capital of India.

4. Holland _____
has been a nation of sailors for centuries.
Holland lacks natural resources.

5. South America _____
is joined to North America by the Isthmus of Panama.
South America is roughly triangular in shape.

6. Chile _____
stretches along the west coast of South America for 2,600 miles.
Chile is sometimes called the "Shoestring Republic."

7. Israel _____
is a hot and arid land.
Israel lies between Egypt and Jordan on the eastern shores of the Mediterranean.

B. Write five sentences with *which* clauses after the name of your country or a city, river, or mountain in your country. Use commas around each *which* clause.

> EXAMPLE: *The United States, which lies between Canada and Mexico, has a temperate climate.*

C. See how many of the *which* clauses in your sentences can be reduced to *-ing* or *-ed* phrases. Then move the reduced phrase to the beginning of the sentence.

> EXAMPLE: *The United States, lying between Canada and Mexico, has a temperate climate.*
>
> *Lying between Canada and Mexico, the United States has a temperate climate.*

EXERCISE 9: Combining Sentences with Phrases Containing *of which*

A phrase containing *of which* permits two separate sentences to be joined into one.

> SENTENCES: Colombia has twenty-four states.
> All of them are important.

> COMBINATION: Colombia has twenty-four states, *all of which* are important.

In such a sentence, if *of which* is replaced by *of them,* an unacceptable combination is formed.

> COMMA FAULT: Colombia has twenty-four states, *all of them* are important.

Rewrite the following sentences using *of which* to replace a phrase like *of them, of it.* Use a comma before the second part of the sentence. Note which of the sentences given in the exercise have comma faults.

1. There are several mountain ranges, the most important *of them* is the Andes range. *(comma fault)*

   *There are several mountain ranges, the most important **of which** is the Andes range.*

2. We already have small industries, one of the largest *of them* is the textile industry.

3. There are also many other small islands. Some *of them* are gathered in small archipelago fashion.

4. There are many rivers in Venezuela. The most important *of them* are the Orinoco River and the Apure River.

5. Most of Denmark is farmland, about half *of it* is used for grazing.

6. Island groups off the Asian mainland are Japan, the Philippines, and Indonesia. All *of these* have become as important as mainland countries.

7. Asia is very rich in natural resources, many *of them* have not been developed.

8. In Nepal are several of the world's highest mountains. One *of them* is Mt. Everest.

EXERCISE 10: Combining Sentences with Adjectivals and Appositives

Combine each of the following sets of sentences into one sentence.

1. Washington is the capital of the United States.
   It is located in the eastern part of the country.
   It is near the states of Maryland and Virginia.

   Washington, the capital of the United States, is located in the eastern part of the country, near the states of Maryland and Virginia.

2. The longest river in Japan is the Shinano River.
   It is located in the central part of Honshu Island.

3. There are two large lakes in Nicaragua.
   They are Managua and Nicaragua.
   They are linked by the Tipitapa River.

4. The other famous city is Izmir.
   It is an export and import city. (that is, a port)
   It is located on the west coast of Turkey.

5. An important South American river is the Orinoco River.
   This is one of the biggest.
   It comes from the north.

6. The most famous mountain is Mt. Fuji.
   It is very beautiful.
   It's one of the symbols of Japan.

7. One of the highest mountains in Iran is Alborz.
   It is a volcanic mountain.
   It is no longer active. (use _but_)

8. Paraguay has two important rivers.
   They are the Paraná and the Paraguay.
   Both of them make a great contribution to the economy of the nation. (use _of which_)

9. Japan is surrounded by the Pacific Ocean and the Sea of Japan.
   It consists of four islands.
   They are Hokkaido, Honshu, Shikoku, and Kyushu.

10. My country is Malaysia.
    It is an independent and small country.
    It is situated in Southeast Asia.

11. Kyoto is an ancient Japanese city.
    There are many temples and they are magnificent.

12. Venezuela has two important cities. One is Caracas.
    It is the capital of the country.
    Valencia is the other important city.
    Here are located most of the factories.

EXERCISE 11: Reversal of Subject and Verb after Initial
Expressions of Place

Expressions of place at the beginning of sentences often require a reversal of subject and verb.

USUAL ORDER: Canada is to the north of the United States.

REVERSAL: To the north of the United States *is* Canada. (*Canada* is the subject of the sentence.)

USUAL ORDER: The Hawaiian Islands are located in the middle of the Pacific Ocean.

REVERSAL: Located in the middle of the Pacific Ocean *are* the Hawaiian Islands. (*The Hawaiian Islands* is the subject of the sentence. Note that in this reversal the participle *located* is separated from the auxiliary *are*.)

Move the expressions of place to the beginning of the sentence and use a reversal of subject and verb.

1. The island of Sicily is off the southern coast of Italy.

   Off the southern coast of Italy is the island of Sicily.

2. Gold and silver are among the many metals mined in this area of the continent.

3. The Strait of Gibraltar is at the northern shore of Morocco.

4. Iran's rich oil fields are situated near the Persian Gulf. (Start with *situated.*)

5. There are two broad plateaus in the eastern part of South America. (omit *there*)

6. Demavend, Iran's highest peak, is located in the Elburz Mountains. (Start with *located.*)

7. Siberia, the Asian part of Russia, lies to the east of the Ural Mountains.[7]

8. Micronesia, or "little islands," lies in the western Pacific.[7]

9. Three of the continent's great rivers rise in the lake region of Africa.[8]

[7] Begin the sentence with *lying* and use *is* for the verb.

[8] Begin the sentence with *rising* and use *are* for the verb.

EXERCISE 12: Word Forms

Use the correct form of the word in parentheses. (If you need help with the signals that tell whether a noun, verb, adjective, or adverbial form is needed, refer to *Writer's Companion,* Unit 2, in the Grammar Review and Practice section.)

1. New York City is in the (northeast) _____*northeastern*_____ part of the United States.

2. Coal (mine) _____mining_____ is an important industry in the South.

3. People who work on (farm) _____farm_____ are called (farm) _____ .

4. The (cultivate) _____cultivation_____ of crops is very difficult in (mountain) _____mountainous_____ regions.

5. The cost of cattle (raise) _____raised_____ is cheaper if good (graze) _____ land is readily available.

6. The (produce) _____production_____ of coffee is an important industry in Brazil.

7. The Pyrenees Mountains form a natural (bound) _____bound_____ between Spain and France.

8. Texas is in the south (center) _____central_____ part of the United States.

9. (Lie) _____lying_____ in the middle of the Pacific Ocean, Hawaii is considered a place where the East meets the West.

10. Both (agriculture) _____agricultural_____ crops and (manufacture) _____manufactured_____ goods are (produce) _____produce_____ in the eastern part of the United States.

11. Many of the (develop) _____developed_____ countries want to become (industry) _____industrial_____ as rapidly as possible.

12. New York City is both a (commerce) _____comercial_____ and an (industry) _____industrial_____ center.

13. Venezuela's (economic) _____economics_____ has greatly expanded because of the (develop) _____development_____ of its oil industry, but the country continues to have some (economy) _____economical_____ problems.

EXERCISE 13: Sentence Review

Make full sentences from the word groups below, and complete the unfinished words. Make whatever changes or additions are needed, but do not change the word order. Use commas, semicolons, periods, or capital letters wherever necessary.

1. Iberian peninsula / consist / Spain / Portugal.

   The Iberian peninsula consists of Spain and Portugal.

2. United States / bound / north / Canada / and / Great Lakes.

3. London / locate / southeast- / part / England.

4. Suez canal / separate / Africa / from / Asia.

5. north America / south America / situate / West- / Hemisphere.

6. Dairy products / make / from / milk.

7. Cultivat- / crops / be / very difficult / mountain- / regions.

8. Manhattan / be / island / surround / all sides / water.

9. Lima / capital / Peru / situate / west coast.

10. Mexico city / biggest city / my country / locate / centr- / part / Republic of Mexico.

11. Pacific ocean / be / largest ocean / world.

12. Sahara desert / extend / Atlantic ocean / Nile river.

13. My country / have / two important rivers / both / make / great contribu- tion / economy / nation.

EXTRA SPEAKING AND WRITING PRACTICE

EXERCISE 14: Composition: Great Britain

You are going to write a three-paragraph composition based on the two maps of Great Britain that appear with this exercise. Your teacher will ask you to get into pairs or groups first in order to discuss the information that will be required for the composition. Use full sentences in the composition.

GREAT BRITAIN

MAP 1

MAP 2

Maps 1 and 2 adapted from "Great Britain and Northern Ireland," *Encyclopedia Americana,* 1978, 13:266.

(first
paragraph)

I. Countries in Great Britain, and the surrounding area of Great Britain
(Map 1)

   A. Tell which countries Great Britain consists of, and give their location in Great Britain.

B. Give the bodies of water surrounding Great Britain, and give their location.
(B may begin with: Great Britain is surrounded on the _____ by _____ , etc.)

(second
paragraph)

II. Principal cities and rivers in Great Britain
(*Map 1*)

Name the principal cities and rivers and give their location in each country.
(Synonyms for *is located* for geographic areas are: *is situated, lies*)

(third
paragraph)

III. Natural resources in Great Britain
(*Map 2*)

Give the location in their country of some of the natural resources of Great Britain.
(Keep in mind that: animals are raised; crops are produced, raised, grown; minerals are mined, produced, found; dairy products are produced.)

LISTENING–WRITING PRACTICE

EXERCISE 15: Paragraphs for Dictation

Your teacher will dictate each paragraph three times. The first time is for listening only, the second time is for writing, and the third time is for checking what you have written.

Immediately after you give your teacher the dictation you have written, check the dictation in the book for any problems you had in writing it.

DICTATION 1

The United States is bordered on the east and west by the Atlantic and Pacific Oceans, on the north by Canada, and on the south by Mexico and the Gulf of Mexico. The country also includes the outlying states of Alaska and Hawaii. Lying mostly in the temperate zone, the United States has a varied climate and land surfaces. The three principal geographical features are a continuation of those in Canada: the eastern highlands, the broad central plains, and the Rockies and the coastal ranges in the Far West.

Hammond's New Supreme World Atlas, 1965, p. 91.*

DICTATION 2

The mountain region which covers the western third of the United States includes the Rocky Mountains, an area of plateaus and river valleys, and the high Sierra Nevada-Cascade Range. Here is an area of beautiful mountain scenery, spectacular canyons, and broad expanses of deserts. The mountains of the northwest are an important source of lumber, and throughout the area there is considerable mining of copper, silver, gold, lead, zinc, and other minerals. Farming is carried on in the river valleys. In the irrigated areas of the south, citrus fruits, cotton, and winter vegetables are grown. In the north, fruits, sugar beets, and grain are grown.

Hammond's New Supreme World Atlas, 1965, p. 92.*

EXERCISE 16: Dicto-comps

Take notes as your teacher reads each of these dicto-comps to you several times. Then reconstruct the dicto-comp from your notes. The dicto-comp does not need to be written exactly as you heard it, but it should be grammatically correct.

*From *Hammond's New Supreme World Atlas* (Garden City, N.Y.: Doubleday & Co., 1965). Slightly abridged and adapted. Reprinted with permission of C.S. Hammond & Co.

Before you write the dicto-comp, your teacher may ask the class to get together in groups to check with each other on what you heard.

Immediately after you give your teacher the dicto-comp you have written, check the dicto-comp in the book for any problems you had in writing it.

The Geography of the United States

DICTO-COMP 1

My country, the United States, is located in the central part of North America. It is bordered on the north by Canada and the Great Lakes and on the south by Mexico and the Gulf of Mexico. To the east is the Atlantic Ocean and to the west is the Pacific Ocean.

The United States has many large cities. Among the more important are New York, a center of commerce and industry on the East Coast; Chicago in the Middle West; and New Orleans, which is located at the mouth of the Mississippi River in the southeast. Washington, the capital, is in the north central part of the eastern seaboard, between the states of Virginia and Maryland.

The principal mountains are the Appalachian Mountains in the East and the Rocky Mountains in the West. The major river system is the Mississippi River with its tributary, the Missouri. This river system runs from north to south in the east central part of the United States.

DICTO-COMP 2

For nearly three centuries the South was famous as a great agricultural region. Most of the people lived on the land and made a living by farming. They raised big crops of cotton, tobacco, sugar cane, grain, fruits, and vegetables. They shipped foods and raw materials to other regions and other parts of the world.

Today the South is changing. It is becoming a manufacturing region as well as a farming area. The people are moving from the country to factory towns and cities. The factories use the produce of Southern farms, mines, and forests. They make many products which were unknown a few years ago. These include plastics, rayon, nylon, and artificial rubber.

The South has many natural resources and advantages for the farmer and the manufacturer. It is a huge region sweeping westward from the Atlantic coast to the Great Plains of Texas.

"United States—The Land and Its People," *Compton's Encyclopedia*, 1980, 25:56.*

*From "United States—The Land and Its People," *Compton's Encyclopedia*, 1980, Vol. 25, p. 56. © F.E. Compton Company, a division of Encyclopedia Britannica, Inc.

Biography

GRAMMAR AND USAGE

Prepositions of time, place
Expressions of time: *since, for, ago*
Adjective clauses (restrictive)
Punctuation of adjective clauses
    (restrictive and nonrestrictive)
Adjectival phrases
Questions and answers
Time connectives

RHETORIC

Using an outline to guide the composition

DISCUSSION AND COMPOSITION

1. DISCUSSION: Preliminary outline for the composition (prewriting stage)

Subject: *My Autobiography*

Outline *(To Be Placed on the Board)*	Discussion *(Ideas, Grammar and Usage, Vocabulary, Elements of Composition Building)*

I. Childhood (0–12 years)
  A. When and where born
  B. Friends
  C. School
  D. An important event
	Use of the *past* tense
	Verb form: I *was* born
	Prepositions:
	  time: *in,* with a month, year
	      on, with a day
	  place: *to*—go to elementary school
	          BUT enter elementary school

II. Adolescence (12–18 years)
  A. Where lived
  B. Interests and hobbies
	Use of the *past* tense
	Place: *to*—go to high school
	      BUT enter high school
	Transitional time expressions (especially to avoid beginning every sentence with *I*)
	  when I was _____ years old
	  at the age of _____ (years)
	  _____ years later
	  during my adolescence (for a period of time)
	  then, after that, afterwards
	Hobbies: sports, photography, reading, music, dancing, collecting stamps or coins

III. Adulthood (from 18 years)
  A. Age and marital status now
  B. Present studies or work
  C. Ambitions
	Use of the *present* tense
	Verb form: I *am* _____ years (old)
	      I *am* married (or single, or divorced)
	Prepositions:
	  from: to graduate from
	  of: to be a graduate (or alumnus, alumna) of
	  to: go to college
	      BUT go to the university

2. COMPOSITION (to be done before or after the reinforcement practice)

A. WRITING THE COMPOSITION

Place the title of the composition at the top of the page:

My Autobiography

Do not use quotation marks or a period for a title at the top of the page. Use initial capital letters for the first word of the title and for all other words except articles, short prepositions, and short conjunctions.

Write the composition on ''My Autobiography'' following the outline that has been discussed. The right column of the outline pages can be of help to you.

Place each of the three main points in a separate paragraph. If any of these paragraphs is quite long, you may break it in two. Be sure to follow chronological order. Use the *past tense* for points I and II and the *present tense* for point III.

Use 8½ - by 11-inch white paper, with lines for handwritten compositions and without lines for typed compositions. Double-space typewritten papers, and skip lines on handwritten compositions. Write on the front of the paper only, and leave wide margins on *both the left and the right sides* of the paper. Indent the beginning of each paragraph.

Look over your composition carefully before you hand it in.

B. CORRECTING OR REWRITING THE COMPOSITION

When your teacher returns your composition, it will be marked with the symbols from the correction chart on page 257. Make the necessary corrections on the composition and hand it back to your teacher. If you have made many mistakes, you may need to rewrite the composition.

Place the corrections on the correction page, and note down the rule that is involved.

(For more help with problems of writing, consult the Index of Usage and Rhetoric in *Writer's Companion*. The items in this index are arranged in the same alphabetical order as in the correction chart.)

CORRECTION PAGE

Use this page to write down the correction of any mistakes you have made in your composition on "My Autobiography." Include enough of the words surrounding the corrected part to make the meaning clear. (Do not copy down the mistake itself.) If possible, write down the rule that covers the correction you have made.

Review these corrections from time to time in order to avoid making the same mistakes again.

Corrections	Rule
	(See the correction chart if necessary)

REINFORCEMENT PRACTICE

EXERCISE 1: *Prepositions of Time, Place*

TIME	*in*	with a month: *in June* with a year: *in 1976*
	on	with a day: *on June 1, 1976; on Sunday* (*on* is sometimes omitted)
	during	with a period of time: *during the week, during his adolescence*
PLACE	*to*	*go to:* elementary school high school college the university (*but:* enter high school attend the university)
	from	*graduate from* a school
	on	with a street, avenue: *on Main Street* *on Seventh Avenue*
	at	with an address containing the street number: *at 500 Main Street*

Supply a preposition of time or place if necessary.

1. Ludwig van Beethoven was born ___*in*___ 1770 and died ___*in*___ 1827.

2. Abraham Lincoln was born _____ 1809 in Kentucky. He was assassinated in Washington _____ April 15, 1865.

3. Charles Darwin's father wanted him to study medicine, so Charles entered _____ Edinburgh University _____ 1825.

4. The Prime Minister of England usually resides _____ 10 Downing Street.

5. Thoreau, the American writer, entered _____ Harvard College _____ 1833 and graduated _____ this college four years later.

6. Sir Winston Churchill was born _____ November 30, 1874.

7. Albert Camus went _____ public schools in Algiers and then entered _____ the University of Algiers.

8. The American President usually lives in the White House _____ 1600 Pennsylvania Avenue, N.W., Washington, D.C.

9. Tolstoy attended _____ the University of Kazan, but he did not graduate

   _____ this school.

10. Ford's Theater, where Lincoln was shot _____ 1865, is located _____
    511 Tenth Street, N.W., Washington, D.C.

11. Abraham Lincoln became a famous lawyer even though he never graduated

    _____ any law school.

12. In a speech made _____ March 1946, Churchill warned the world about the
    "iron curtain" cutting off Communist Europe from the West.

13. Hemingway arrived[1] _____ Spain _____ February 1937 to write about
    the Civil War for American newspapers.

14. Franklin Delano Roosevelt was President of the United States _____ World
    War II.

EXERCISE 2: Expressions of Time: *since, for, ago*

Since and *for* refer to duration (length) of time, *ago* to one point in the past.

Duration (past to present time) (present perfect tense)		One Point in the Past (past tense)
Since (gives the *beginning of the time*)	*For* (gives the *length of the time* (a quantity)	*Ago* (gives a *quantity of time in relation to the present*
Mr. Chang has lived in the United States *since* 1975.	Mr. Chang has lived in the United States *for* five years.	Mr. Chang came to the United States five years *ago*.

For the following situations, give sentences with *since, for,* and *ago*. Use the present perfect tense with *since* and *for,* and use the past tense with *ago*.

1. Luis began to attend an American university in 1978. It is now 1980 and he is still
   attending the university.

   SINCE   *Luis has attended* (or *has been attending*) *an American university since 1978.*

   Since gives the date when the continuing event began. Note that the progressive form (has been attending) emphasizes the continuing action.

---

[1] After *arrive, in* is used for a large geographic area (continent, country), and *at* for a smaller place
(airport, station, library, etc.).

FOR   *Luis has attended* (or *has been attending*) *an American university for two years.*

For gives the length of time that the event lasts. (In this use, *for* is sometimes omitted.)

AGO[2]   *Luis began to attend an American university two years ago.*

Note that another verb must be used for this completed point in the past.

2. My friend is visiting me. It is now March and he came to visit me in January.

SINCE   _____

_____

FOR   _____

_____

AGO   _____

_____

3. It is now August 5. Dimitri got married on July 5.

SINCE   _____

_____

FOR   _____

_____

AGO   _____

_____

4. It is now December. Anabel became a lawyer in February.

SINCE   _____

_____

FOR   _____

_____

AGO   _____

_____

[2] Do not use *before* for *ago*.

5. My older sister is in the United States. It is now 1980 and she arrived in the United States in 1976.

SINCE _____

_____

FOR _____

_____

AGO _____

_____

6. It is now October 24. I became sick on October 20 and I am still sick.

SINCE _____

_____

FOR _____

_____

AGO _____

_____

7. George is studying medicine. It is now 1980 and he began to study medicine in 1979.

SINCE _____

_____

FOR _____

_____

AGO _____

_____

8. It is now November. Colette became engaged in May.

SINCE _____

_____

FOR _____

_____

AGO _____

_____

EXERCISE 3: Adjective Clauses (Restrictive)

A *clause* contains a subject and a predicate. An *adjective clause* follows a noun and gives more information about the noun. The word beginning the clause depends on the noun the clause refers to.

Noun Referred to	Introductory Word for the Clause	Sentence with an Adjective Clause
a person	who	I really appreciate the teacher **who taught me English.**
a thing	which	I attended the high school **which was near my home.**
a place	where	The high school **where I learned English** was a very good one.

A. Underline the word in parentheses that refers to the noun being described. Replace this word by *who, which,* or *where* used at the beginning of the adjective clause. Then write the complete sentence. (Use the *past tense* for the verbs within the parentheses.)

No commas are required in any part of Exercise 3.

1. The *teacher* (she, teach, me, English) was very strict.
   The teacher (she, teach, me, English) was very strict.

   *The teacher **who** taught me English was very strict.*

2. I'll never forget the *neighborhood* (I, live, there, my childhood).
   I'll never forget the neighborhood (I, live, there, my childhood).

   *I'll never forget the neighborhood **where** I lived during my childhood.*

3. The subject (it, give, me, most trouble) was English.

4. I attended the same *school* (my brother, go, there).

5. I didn't learn much English from the *teacher* (she, be teaching, subject).

6. There were many *friends* (they, come, say, goodbye, me).

7. The *city* (I, born, there) is very beautiful.

8. The *relative* (he, encourage, me, go, university) was my uncle.

9. I had a private *tutor* (he, help, me, learn, English language).

10. The *foreign languages* (they, be taught, my school) were English and French.

11. The *school* (I, study, there, four years) no longer exists.

B. In the kind of clauses above, which are used without commas, *who* or *which* (but not *there*) may be replaced by *that*.

Go over the sentences you made in A to see where *that* can be used instead of *who* or *which*.

> **1.** *The teacher **that** taught me English was very strict.*

C. In sections A and B you made clauses with *who* or *which* as subjects of the clauses. *Who* or *which* may also be *objects* of the verbs in their clauses. As an object, *whom* is the formal equivalent of *who*.

> The girl *whom* (informal, *who*) I married lived next door to me.
> *Whom* (= *the girl*) is the object of *married*.

> I went to the same school *which* my brother attended.
> *Which* (= *the school*) is the object of *attended*.

In these clauses the *whom* or *which* objects may be replaced by *that*.

> The girl *that* I married lived next door to me.

The omission of *whom, that,* or *which* as objects is very common in spoken English.

> The girl I married lived next door to me.
> I went to the same school my brother attended.

Underline the word in parentheses that refers to the noun being described. Replace this word by *whom, that,* or *which* used at the beginning of the adjective clause. Then write the complete sentence. (Use the past tense for the verbs in the parentheses.)

1. The *teacher* (I, respect, her, the most) was my English teacher.
The teacher (I, respect, her, the most) was my English teacher.

> *The teacher **whom** I respected the most was my English teacher.*

2. The *ambition* (I, have, it, a long time) was to be a doctor.

3. The *education* (I, receive, it, high school) was excellent.

4. I still see the *friends* (I, meet, them, elementary school).

5. I finally received the *application form* (I, have to fill out, it).

6. The elementary *school* (I, attend, it) no longer exists.

7. My English *teacher* was the best teacher (I, ever, have, him).

8. The *subject* (I, like, it, the best) was English.

D. Go over the sentences you made in C and omit *whom, that,* or *which*.

> **1.** *The teacher I respected the most was my English teacher.*

E. In clauses that describe nouns, *who* and *which* are not only subjects or objects of verbs, but also objects of prepositions. Only the object form *whom* may be used after a preposition.

> The children with *whom* I played lived on my block.
> I never liked the neighborhood in *which* I lived.

In conversational English the preposition is often placed at the end of the clause.

> The children whom (informal, *who*) I played *with* lived on my block.
> I never liked the neighborhood which I lived *in.*

When this separation of the preposition is made, the *whom* or *which* object may be replaced by *that* (*The children that I played* **with**) or omitted (*The children I played* **with**).

Underline the word in parentheses that refers to the noun being described. Replace this word by *whom* or *which.* Move the preposition plus *whom* or *which* to the beginning of the parentheses. Then write the complete sentence. (Use the past tense for the verbs in the parentheses.)

1. The *person* (I, have to write, to this person) was the Director of Admissions.

> *The person (I, have to write, to this <u>person</u>) was the Director of Admissions.*
>
> *The person* **to whom** *I had to write was the Director of Admissions.*

2. The *teacher* (I, be, most fond, of this teacher) was my English teacher.

3. I would like to visit again the *street* (I, use, live, on this street.)[3]

4. The *teacher* (I, have, most respect, for this teacher) was my history teacher.

5. When I was a child, the only *person* (I, use, have confidence, in this person) was my uncle.

6. For a long time, the only *thing* (I, can, think, about this thing) was becoming a doctor.

7. The *school* (I, go, to this school) was a small but a good one.[3]

8. The only *parties* (I, be invited, to these parties) were children's parties.

9. Everyone would enjoy visiting the *town* (I, come, from this town).[3]

F. Go over the sentences you made in E and move the prepositions to the end of the clauses. Omit *whom* or *which.*

> *The person I had to write* **to** *was the Director of Admissions.*

---

[3] In these sentences, it is also possible to use *where* without the preposition. If the preposition is *from,* however, it is kept with *where.*

EXERCISE 4: Punctuation of Adjective Clauses
(Restrictive and Nonrestrictive)

If the adjective clause *identifies* or *restricts* a noun, no commas are used with the clause.

A mother *who is very strict* can also be very fair.

In the above sentence, *who is very strict* is restrictive: it narrows down the whole class of mothers.

If the adjective clause comes after a noun that is already fully identified, the clause requires commas.

My mother, *who was very strict with me,* was also very fair.

Here, the speaker has only one mother. *Who was very strict with me* is nonrestrictive: it does not identify the mother further.

Commas for nonrestrictive clauses are especially necessary after proper nouns (nouns beginning with capital letters).

Caracas, *where I was born,* has grown very fast.

Make adjective clauses from the words in parentheses. Be careful of the punctuation of restrictive and nonrestrictive clauses. (Use the past tense of the verbs in the parentheses.)

1. My favorite uncle (he, encourage, me, study, English) gave me the money to come to this country.

   My favorite uncle, who encouraged me to study English, gave me the money to come to this country. (The speaker is referring to only one particular uncle.)

2. The person (he, encourage, me, study, English) was my uncle.

   The person who encouraged me to study English was my uncle. (The class word *person* is narrowed down by *who encouraged me* to study English.)

3. The subject (it, give, me, most trouble, high school) was English.

4. English (it, give, me, most trouble, high school) is now very useful to me.

5. Everyone on the block is helping the family (their house, burn down, yesterday). (Use the possessive *whose* for the possessive *their.*)

6. The Johnsons (their house, burn down, yesterday) are being helped by everyone on the block.

7. I attended the same school (my brother, go, there).

8. There were many friends (they, come, say, goodbye, me).

9. The education (I, receive, it, high school) was excellent.

10. I would like to visit again the street (I, use, live, this street).

11. Everyone would enjoy visiting Paris (I, grow up, there).

12. My parents (they, love, me, very much) gave me everything I wanted.

13. A boy (his parents, have money) could afford to go abroad to study.

14. My best friend (his parents, have money) could afford to go abroad to study.

15. The children (I, use, play, with, them) all lived on the same block (I, live, there).

EXERCISE 5: Adjectival Phrases

Part of a sentence, with the subject and a form of *be* omitted, may be used as a phrase after a noun.

Thomas Edison, (he was) famous as the inventor of the phonograph, made many other important inventions.

Commas are required for the adjective phrase in this sentence because the phrase comes after a proper noun.

Change the sentences in parentheses to phrases by omitting the subject and *is* or *was*. Use commas for these phrases.

1. Albert Einstein (he was the most famous scientist in the world) discovered the formula for atomic energy.

   Albert Einstein, the most famous scientist in the world, discovered the formula for atomic energy.

2. Sigmund Freud (he is considered the founder of modern psychoanalysis) had a great influence on modern thought.

3. Karl Marx (he was the greatest revolutionary of all time) did his research for *Das Kapital* in the British Museum.

4. Charles Darwin (he was the originator of the theory of evolution) gathered his information on a five-year boat trip around the world.

5. Martin Luther (he was shocked by the corruption of the Church in his day) finally broke with the established Church and started the Reformation.

6. Henry Wadsworth Longfellow (he is a famous American poet) wrote a poem about "The Courtship of Miles Standish."

7. Niccolo Machiavelli (he was a patriot who wanted to see Italy made strong) outlined the political policy that the end justified the means.

8. John Dewey (he is known as the founder of progressive education) believed that children should "learn by doing."

9. Walt Whitman (he was famous for his poems in *Leaves of Grass*) believed that God existed in man and nature.

EXERCISE 6: Word Forms

Use the correct form of the word in parentheses. You will need auxiliaries with some verbs. (If you need help with the signals that tell whether a noun, verb, adjective, or adverbial form is needed, refer to *Writer's Companion,* Unit 2, in the Grammar Review and Practice section.

1. Helen Keller became deaf and blind in early (child) _____*childhood*_____.

2. The writer Edgar Allan Poe continued to have (infant) _____ fantasies even as an adult.

3. Lolita is the (adolescence) _____ who was made famous in a book by Nabokov.

4. Karl Marx (birth) _____ in Trier, Germany. He (death) _____ in London, England.

5. Edgar Allan Poe (marry) _____ a young cousin of his in 1836. The (marry) _____ lasted until her (die) _____ in 1847.

6. Johnny Appleseed (engage) _____ to a young girl. The (engage) _____ ended when she (dead) _____.

7. Carl Sandburg is the famous (biography) _____ of Abraham Lincoln.

8. Mahatma Gandhi became (engage) _____ at the age of seven. He was (marry) _____ when he was fourteen.

9. When the rate of (born)[4] _____ of people is much higher than the rate of (dead)[4] _____, a country may become over-populated.

10. Most children find friends in their (neighbor) _____.

11. A person's work is his (occupy) _____.

_____
[4] Use plurals for these words.

12. William Shakespeare was (marry) _____ to Anne Hathaway.

13. The vital statistics for a person include his (born) _____,

(marry) _____, and (die) _____.

EXERCISE 7: Sentence Review

Make full sentences from the word groups below. Make whatever changes or additions are needed, but do not change the word order. Use commas, semicolons, or periods where necessary.

1. Karl Marx / born / Germany / 1818 / he / die / London / March 14, 1883.

Karl Marx was born in Germany in 1818. He died (or, *and he died*) *in London on March 14, 1883.*

2. Albert Camus / go / public schools / Algiers / then / enter / University / Algiers.

3. William Shakespeare / famous playwright / be / married / Anne Hathaway / have / three children.

4. Leon Tolstoy / great Russian novelist / attend / University / Kazan but / never graduate / this school.

5. Prime Minister / England / usually / reside / 10 Downing Street / London.

6. Abraham Lincoln / born / 1809 / Kentucky / he / assassinate / Washington / April 15, 1865.

7. Mahatma Gandhi / become / engage / age / seven / he / marry / when / fourteen years.

8. Ford's Theatre / where / Lincoln / shoot / located / Tenth Street / Washington, D.C.

9. Sigmund Freud / founder / modern psychoanalysis / have / great influence / modern thought.

10. Edgar Allan Poe / marry / young cousin / his / 1836 / marriage / lasted / her death / 1847.

11. teacher / teach / me / English / be / very strict.

12. Everyone / would enjoy / visit / town / I / come / from this town.

13. The Johnsons / their house / burn down / yesterday / being helped everyone on the block.

EXTRA SPEAKING AND WRITING PRACTICE

EXERCISE 8: Questions and Answers

A. Working with a partner, take turns asking and answering *wh-* questions based on the following information about three famous people. The answers should be in full sentences.

The two kinds of *wh-* questions that you will be using are:

(1) Questions beginning with the adverbs *when, where, who,* or *how*. These question words are always followed by the same auxiliary as used in a yes–no question.

Statement		Shakespeare was born in 1564.
yes–no question		*Was* Shakespeare born in 1564?
wh- question	When	*was* Shakespeare born?

If the verb does not have an auxiliary (simple present and simple past tenses), an auxiliary from *do* is added for most questions.[5]

Statement		Shakespeare married Anne Hathaway.
yes–no question		*Did* Shakespeare marry Anne Hathaway?
wh- question	When	*did* Shakespeare marry Anne Hathaway?

(2) Questions beginning with the pronouns *who* (for a person), *what* (for a thing), and *which* (for a choice of a person or a thing). With one exception, these question words must also be followed by the same auxiliary that starts a yes-no question.

Statement		Shakespeare married Anne Hathaway.
yes–no question		*Did* Shakespeare marry Anne Hathaway?
wh- question	Who(m)	*did* Shakespeare marry?

[5] An exception is the independent verb *be*. If this verb has no auxiliary, the verb itself is pulled forward to auxiliary position.

Statement:	Shakespeare *was* famous for his plays.
yes–no question:	*Was* Shakespeare famous for his plays?
wh- question:	Why *was* Shakespeare famous?

However, if the question word is the *subject,* it merely replaces the subject, with no change in word order and no addition of an auxiliary.

Statement	*Shakespeare married Anne Hathaway.*
wh- question	*Who* married Anne Hathaway?

1. William Shakespeare

Birth: April 1564; Stratford, England
Marriage: to Anne Hathaway, 1582
Family: three children
Work: by 1592 wrote many famous plays, London
Death: April 23, 1616, Stratford
               52 years old

> EXAMPLE: *When was Shakespeare born?*
> *He was born in April 1564.*
> *Where was Shakespeare born?*
> *He was born in Stratford, England.*

2. Karl Marx

Birth: May 5, 1818; Germany
Education: studied law, history, philosophy
Degree: doctor of philosophy, University of Jena
Marriage: to Jenny von Westphalen, 1843
Family: three daughters
Publications: the *Communist Manifesto,* 1848
                Das Kapital, 1867
Death: March 14, 1883, London
                65 years old

3. Leon Tolstoy

Birth: August 28, 1828; Yasnaya Polyana, Russia
Education: first at home, then at the university; did not graduate
Marriage: to Sofia Andreyevna Behrs, 1862
Family: many children
Novels: *War and Peace,* 1869
                Anna Karenina, 1877
Death: of pneumonia; November 7, 1910; Astapovo, Russia
                82 years old

B. Write a paragraph for each of the men in section A, giving the information about them in full sentences. Try to vary the structure of some of your sentences by beginning them with time expressions.

EXAMPLE: *William Shakespeare was born in April 1564 in Stratford, England.*
In 1582 *he married Anne Hathaway.*

C. Write a short dialog in which an English-speaking person asks you some questions about a famous person in your country and you give the answers in full sentences. The questions might be about the famous person's birth, education, marriage and family, accomplishments, and death. (You may need to check an encyclopedia for some of this information.)

EXERCISE 9: Time Connectives

When you are writing about yourself, it is best not to begin every sentence with *I*. One way to avoid doing this is to move time expressions to the beginning of the sentence. In this way you not only achieve variety of sentence beginnings, but you make clear immediately what the time relations between the statements are.

Here are some time connectives that may be used at the beginning of a sentence.

For a Sequence of Events:

beginning	(at) first, at the beginning
following	later, then, next
	afterward(s)
	after this, after this time (event, etc.)
	after this happened
end	finally

For One Point in Time:

at (the age of) twelve
when I was twelve (years old)

last year (past)
this year (present)
next year (future)
 (Note that no article or preposition is used with these three expressions, but: *the* next or *the* following day.)
a year ago

For a Period of Time that Continues:

during my adolescence
while I was an adolescent
for three years, for a long time
since (the beginning point of a period that continues)

In the following paragraphs, add the omitted time words.

A. _____*During*_____ my childhood, I lived in a small town. _____
I lived there I was very happy. _____ we moved to a large
city. _____ the age of five, I found the city very frightening.
_____ a few months I was very lonesome. The _____
year, _____ I was six years old, I started to attend school.
_____ first I didn't know anybody in my class. But _____
I made some good friends. _____ I began to enjoy my life in the
city.

B. Ever _____ I was a child, I had wanted to study art.
_____ my adolescence, I used to draw whenever I could. Ten years
_____, _____ I was eighteen years old, I came to the
United States. _____ first I studied only English. _____
I went to art school. _____ I began to win prizes for my paintings.
_____ I became very rich.

C. _____ the age of seventeen I fell in love with a beautiful girl in
my school. _____ a long time I was afraid to talk to her.
_____ an opportunity to speak to her came. _____ I was
at a party, I saw her come in. _____ first I was too excited to
move. But _____ I went over to her and asked her to dance.
_____ we were dancing I felt as though I were in heaven. But soon
_____ this, the girl moved to another town. _____
that time I have often regretted having lost her. Perhaps _____
year I'll meet another beautiful girl I can fall in love with.

EXERCISE 10: Questions and Answers: Names

Working with a partner, ask and answer the following questions about the use of names in your country. (American customs are given in the right-hand column.) After you have finished your discussions, write a paragraph or two about customs in your country regarding names. Use the order of the questions as your outline.

Questions	American Customs
1. How do people in your country sign their names?	We first write our first (or given) name, then our last name (or surname, family name). Our last name comes from our father.
2. What are some common first names in your country?	John, Mary, Susan, James, Lily, William, Jane
3. What are some common last names?	Smith, Jones, Williams, Johnson
4. Do you use nicknames (sometimes called pet names, especially for children)?	Jim or Jimmy[6] for James; Bob or Bobby[6] for Robert; Meg or Peggy for Margaret; Bill or Billy[6] for William
5. What are some "nice" first names in your country?	
6. What first names do you like?	
7. Do you have a special name to symbolize a man in your country? A woman?	John Doe; Mr. X for an anonymous man Jane Doe

EXERCISE 11: Questions and Answers: Interview

A. Below is a form that requires some information usually requested when a person applies for a job or for admission to a school. Working with a partner, take turns interviewing each other to get the required information. Begin each question of the interview with the question word to the left of the form.

The interviewer should take down notes in the blank spaces as the person being interviewed answers *in full sentences*.

What   Name_____

Where   Address_____

[6] These names ending in *y* are used especially for children, but they often continue into adult life.

When	Date of birth _____
Where	Place of birth _____
What country	Citizenship _____
What	Marital status (single, married, divorced) _____
How many	Children _____
What schools	Education:
	high school _____
	higher education _____
What	Occupation _____
What	Hobbies _____
How many	Foreign languages _____
How much	Weight _____
How tall	Height _____

EXAMPLE: STUDENT 1: *What is your name?*
STUDENT 2: *My name is* _____.

B. Write up the interview you had with your partner. Begin with: (*"name of your partner"*) told me he lived _____." For this practice, use the past tense (*lived*) because the main verb (*told*) is past (sequence of tenses). However, keep in mind that since most of the information after *told* consists of general statements, the present tense of the verbs in these statements is also appropriate. You may combine some of the information into one sentence (for example, date of birth and place of birth).

EXERCISE 12: Business Letter

Write a letter to a college or university requesting their catalog and an application for admission to their school. Tell them what you want to study and give them your previous education (graduation from high school or the university) so that they may know what your area of specialization is and whether you are applying for undergraduate studies (to get a bachelor's degree) or graduate studies (to get a master's or a doctor's degree).

If you are a foreign student, tell them so.

Use the form on the next page as a model for a business letter. Leave margins on both the left and the right sides of the paper, and on the top and bottom.

```
                                          Your street address
                                          City, state and zip code
                                          February 1, 1982


(4 single spaces down)

Admissions Office
Name of the university
Address of the university

Gentlemen:

  Please send me _____

_____

_____.

    _____

_____

_____

_____.

  Thank you.
                                    Yours truly,


                                    (sign your name)
                   (4 single spaces
                    for your signature)   (print or type your name)
```

In a business letter it is better not to use abbreviations. Write the full name of the state, the month, and the street or avenue.

Note that *Gentlemen* is used in addressing a company or an institution. If you know the name of the Admissions Officer, use it. Then, instead of writing Gentlemen, write Dear Mr. (or Miss, Mrs., Ms.) _____.

It is preferable to use the typewriter for a business letter, but a handwritten letter is acceptable if it is neat and follows the same form as the letter given here.

LISTENING–WRITING PRACTICE

EXERCISE 13: Paragraphs for Dictation

Your teacher will dictate each paragraph three times. The first time is for listening only, the second time is for writing, and the third time is for checking what you have written.

Immediately after you give your teacher the dictation you have written, check the dictation in the book for any problems you had in writing it.

DICTATION 1

Benjamin Franklin labored constantly to improve his mind and character. He taught himself to read French, Spanish, Italian, and Latin. He was a leader in many movements for the benefit of his community. In the midst of his many activities he always found time for the study of science. He developed a theory about the identity of lightning and electricity, and he devised a method to test his theory. In 1752, he attached a key to a kite string during a thunderstorm. When electric sparks came from the key, he had his proof that lightning was an electrical discharge.

"Benjamin Franklin," _Collier's Encyclopedia_, 1968, 10:326–37.*

DICTATION 2

Ernest Hemingway wanted to get into the First World War. When he was turned down by the army because of poor eyesight, he joined an American ambulance unit and later transferred to the Austrian front. After only seven days on the front lines he was seriously wounded. But he was fascinated by war. He reported on the Greco-Turkish War in 1920, the Civil War in Spain in 1937, and the Allied invasion of Europe in 1944. War and death comprise a major part of the subject matter of his books. He also wrote about sports activities that challenged one's manhood—activities such as boxing, bull-fighting, hunting, and fishing.

"Ernest Hemingway," _Cyclopedia of World Authors_, 1958, p. 500.

EXERCISE 14: Dicto-comps

Take notes as your teacher reads each of these dicto-comps to you several times. Then reconstruct the dicto-comp from your notes. The dicto-comp does not need to be written exactly as you heard it, but it should be grammatically correct.

---

*Reprinted with permission from _Collier's Encyclopedia._ © 1968 Crowell Collier Educational Corporation.

Before you write the dicto-comp, your teacher may ask the class to get together in groups to check with each other on what you heard.

Immediately after you give your teacher the dicto-comp you have written, check the dicto-comp in the book for any problems you had in writing it.

DICTO-COMP 1

Thomas Edison is well-known all over the world for his many inventions. Yet he had very little education. When his teachers criticized him for being stubborn and unwilling to learn, his mother decided to teach him herself. She encouraged his natural desire to read and experiment. By the time he was ten years old, he had developed a strong taste for chemistry and made himself a laboratory.

His first inventions were begun during his adolescence. With a little money made from one of his inventions, he started his own manufacturing business in New Jersey. This later developed into a research laboratory. Here he perfected the incandescent lamp, which enabled electricity to replace gas. Here too he first reproduced the sound of the human voice on an instrument called the phonograph.

Constant experimentation played an important part in Edison's success. He slept very little and worked very hard. When people told him he was a genius, he answered, "Genius is 1% inspiration and 99% perspiration."

DICTO-COMP 2

Walt Whitman, the great American poet, was born on Long Island in 1819. At an early age he moved to Brooklyn. He was forced to go to work when he was quite young. However, he read a great deal.

After teaching school for a while, he became a newspaperman and finally the editor of the *Brooklyn Eagle.* Because of his opposition to slavery, he was fired from the newspaper. Then he went to work as a carpenter.

During the Civil War, Whitman volunteered as a male nurse. He supplied the sick men with tobacco, took care of their wounds, and read the Bible to boys who were dying. After the war he worked for the government in Washington. His last days were spent in Camden, New Jersey, where he died in 1892.

His best poems are contained in the volume called *Leaves of Grass.* When this volume was first published, many people criticized it. His poetry did not seem to be poetry at all. It did not rhyme, nor did it have a regular beat or measure. He used the plain, simple words of everyday life. But some people were able to see the greatness of his poetry, which expressed his sincere love for other people. Whitman believed that man and nature were both part of God.

Instructions (How to make or do something)

GRAMMAR AND USAGE

> Passive voice (for a process)
> Conditions: possible and unreal
> Conditions with *otherwise*
> Auxiliaries: *mustn't* versus *don't have to*
> *have* + verb (for instructions)
> Connective adverbs (for sequence of steps)
> Dangling participles
> Subjunctive verbs in *that* clauses

RHETORIC

> Using an outline to guide the composition
> Using an introduction and a conclusion

DISCUSSION AND COMPOSITION

1. DISCUSSION: Preliminary outline for the composition (prewriting stage)

Subject: (Tell what is being made or done)

Outline (To Be Placed on the Board)	Discussion (Ideas, Grammar and Usage, Vocabulary, Elements of Composition Building)

	Give instructions for something you yourself can make or do well.
	
	Subjects for instruction:
	make: the end result is a *thing*
	    make – a bookcase, a table
	            a dress
	            a particular food
	
	do: only an *activity* is involved
	    play – football, tennis, cards (a game)
	          the piano, the guitar (an instrument)
	    collect – stamps, coins
	    plant – flowers, vegetables
	    use – a typewriter, a computer (a machine)
	    bowl, swim, skate, type, dance, drive a car

Introduction: general statements, incentives	Mention what is being made or done.
	Try to catch the interest of the reader in the product or activity you are giving instructions for.
	    easy to make or do
	    quick
	    useful
	    beautiful
	    inexpensive
	    delicious, nourishing (for food)
	    get much pleasure from it
	    relaxing
	    healthy
	    satisfying
	Avoid negative remarks such as "It's hard to do," or "It will take a long time."

I. Tools, materials, equipment (if necessary)	For a recipe, give the ingredients (in exact quantities), and utensils (pot, pan, frying pan, casserole dish, mixing bowl)

Outline (cont.)	Discussion (cont.)
I. Tools, materials, equipment (cont.)	For something to be constructed, specify tools: hammer, nails, saw, pliers, screws, screwdriver
II. Steps in chronological order (Include precautions) (If the instructions are for a game, give the rules here)	Form for giving the steps: imperative: do this, do that with *should:* you should do this, you should do that first person: I do this, I do that (avoid changing from one form to another)
III. IV. V.	Transitions for the steps: then, next, after this; afterward(s); after you do this; after *doing* this, *you* . . . (to avoid a dangling construction)
VI. etc.	Form for precautions: be sure to; be careful not to; you must . . . ; otherwise, . . .
Conclusion: general statements	Refer again to incentives mentioned in the introduction and repeat in other words. Synonyms for adjectives in the introduction: simple: for easy to make or do not time-consuming: for quick practical: for useful attractive: for beautiful economical, money-saving: for inexpensive enjoyment: for pleasure tasty: for delicious nutritious: for nourishing more general comments: You can be proud of your accomplishment. You can enjoy the compliments of your family and friends. You can be satisfied with a job well done.

2. COMPOSITION (to be done before or after the reinforcement practice)

A. ORGANIZING THE COMPOSITION

Before writing your composition, fill in the required information on this Organizational Worksheet. The Worksheet follows the preliminary outline used for the discussion. Suggestions for writing each paragraph are given at the right side of this Worksheet. The pages of the discussion outline provide additional help for the composition.

You may use phrases on this Worksheet except where it calls for full sentences.

ORGANIZATIONAL WORKSHEET
(Preliminary notes for the composition)

Title of the composition _____
(Do not use quotation marks or a period for a title at the top of the page. Use initial capital letters for the first word of the title and for all other words except articles, short prepositions, and short conjunctions.)

Introduction: general statements	Put in a separate paragraph
Opening sentence of paragraph _____	Use the present tense for general statements
_____	Avoid negative remarks like "It's hard to do"
_____	
_____	
Incentives	
_____	
_____	
_____	
_____	

I. Tools, materials, equipment (if necessary)
(For a recipe, give the ingredients here)
Reminder: The recipe is for a dish you know how to make yourself, not a recipe from a book.

New paragraph
Recipe ingredients may be listed in one or two columns

_____
_____
_____
_____
_____
_____
_____
_____
_____

II. Steps in chronological order
Include precautions
(For a game, give the rules here)

New paragraph

Use short paragraphs for the steps (but avoid one-sentence paragraphs)

_____

Make the instructions clear and short, but do not leave out any necessary details

_____

Verbs:

_____
    the imperative: do this, do that

III. _____

_____
Or: you should do this, you must do that

_____
Or: I do this, I do that

IV. _____
Connectives between the steps: then, next, after this, after doing that

_____

_____

V. _____

_____

_____

VI. _____

_____

_____

VII. _____

_____

_____

etc.

Conclusion: general statements
Incentives restated

New paragraph

May be only one or two sentences

_____

Repeat some of the incentives in the introduction, using other words

_____

Use the present tense for general statements

_____

_____

_____

_____

B. WRITING THE COMPOSITION

Write the composition based on your notes on the Organizational Worksheet. Be careful of your paragraphing. Use separate paragraphs for your introduction and your conclusion. (Long paragraphs may be broken in two at appropriate places, but avoid single-sentence paragraphs.)

Use 8½ - by 11-inch white paper, with lines for a handwritten composition and without lines for a typed composition. Double-space a typewritten composition, and skip lines on a handwritten one. Write on the front of the paper only, and leave wide margins on *both the left and the right sides* of the paper. Indent the beginning of each paragraph.

Look over your composition carefully before you hand it in.

C. CORRECTING OR REWRITING THE COMPOSITION

When your teacher returns your composition, it will be marked with the symbols from the correction chart on page 257. Make the necessary corrections on the composition and hand it back to your teacher.

Place the corrections on the correction page, and note down the rule that is involved.

If you have made many mistakes, or if you wish to make some additions to your composition, you may need to write it again. In rewriting the composition, do not make extensive changes or additions without consulting your teacher.

(For more help with your problems in writing, consult the Index of Usage and Rhetoric in *Writer's Companion*. The items in this index are arranged in the same alphabetical order as in the correction chart.)

CORRECTION PAGE

Use this page to write down the correction of any mistakes you have made in your composition on how to make or do something. Include enough of the words surrounding the corrected part to make the meaning clear. (Do not copy down the mistake itself.) If possible, write down the rule that covers the correction you have made.

Review these corrections from time to time in order to avoid making the same mistakes again.

Corrections	Rule *(See the correction chart if necessary)*

REINFORCEMENT PRACTICE

EXERCISE 1: Passive Voice (for a Process)

Instructions can be given in the passive voice if we want to talk about *a process*—that is, *how something is made or done*—rather than how to make or do something.

ACTIVE	*Hold* the fingers lightly over the typewriter keys.
PASSIVE PROCESS	The fingers *are held* lightly over the typewriter keys.
ACTIVE	You *should hold* the fingers lightly over the typewriter keys.
PASSIVE PROCESS	The fingers *should be held* lightly over the typewriter keys.

Note that in the passive sentence the original object (the fingers) becomes the subject.

A. Change the following sentences to the passive voice in order to indicate a process. Begin each passive sentence with the object of the verb in the active sentence. The verbs to be made passive are in italics. Some of the sentences need two passive verbs.

1. *Simmer* the stew for two hours.

   The stew is simmered for two hours.

2. You *should simmer* the stew for two hours.

   The stew should be simmered for two hours.

3. *Plant* the seeds in even rows.

4. You *should sandpaper* the table before you *paint* it.

5. *Throw* the tennis ball high in the air and *serve* it into the proper box of your opponent.

6. You *should preheat* the oven before you *put* the cake in it.

7. You *should drink* plenty of fluids if you have a cold.

8. *Use* a screwdriver to loosen the screws.

9. You *should check* the air in the tires before you start on a long automobile trip.

10. *Mix* all the dry ingredients and *add* them to the others.

11. You *should do* these exercises regularly every morning.

B. You are giving instructions on how to play a particular game (for example, tennis, soccer, Ping-Pong), how to drive a car, how to make a certain dish, or do something else. Write five to ten sentences telling what *should* or *must be done* by the learner who is following your instructions.

> *EXAMPLES:*
>
> MAKING A DISH: *The batter should be well mixed before it is poured into the baking pan.*
>
> PLAYING PING PONG: *The paddle must be held in a special way.*
>
> DRIVING A CAR: *The oil and the water in the car should be checked at regular intervals.*

EXERCISE 2: Conditions: Possible and Unreal

An *if* clause in a sentence may express a possible condition or an unreal one. In instructions, a conditional sentence usually gives advice or suggestions.

> POSSIBLE CONDITION (FUTURE TIME)
> Your cold *will get* better if you *stay* in bed.
> (This kind of condition implies its opposite: *Your cold won't get better if you don't stay in bed.*)
>
> UNREAL CONDITION
> PRESENT TIME
> Your cold *would get* better if you *stayed*[1] in bed.
> (*Real situation:* You're not staying in bed.)
>
> PAST TIME
> Your cold *would have gotten* better if you *had stayed* in bed.
> (*Real situation:* You didn't stay in bed.)

A. The following sentences with possible conditions have been taken from instructions about how to do something. Change these sentences to sentences with *present unreal conditions.*

1. Your cough will not bother you if you take a good cough medicine.

> *Your cough would not bother you if you took a good cough medicine.*

2. You will get rid of your cold if you drink lots of fluids.

3. You will learn faster if you practice every day.

4. The piano will sound better if you have it tuned.

5. The garden will look better if you water the plants every day.

[1] In such sentences, *would* may also occur informally in the *if* clause: Your cold would get better if you would (= were willing to) stay in bed.

6. The car can[2] last a long time if you take good care of it.

7. You can save money if you buy food in season.

8. If you take some driving lessons, you will learn to park the car.[3]

9. If you use an electric typewriter in the office, you can type faster.

10. If you follow these instructions carefully, you will have no trouble.

B. Change the sentences in A to sentences with *past unreal conditions*.

    1. *Your cough wouldn't have bothered you if you had taken a good cough medicine.*

C. Combine these sentences to make *present unreal conditions*. Watch for negative–positive or positive–negative changes.

Real Situation	*The Speaker's Opinion or Advice about This Situation*
1. You aren't staying in bed.	Your cold will not get better.

    If you stayed in bed, your cold would get better.
    (This situation is *unreal now.* Note the negative–positive changes.)

2. You don't practice a lot.	You will not be an excellent pianist.
3. You don't study hard.	You won't become a good student.
4. You don't shop wisely.	You won't save money.
5. You don't watch the road carefully.	You won't become a better driver.
6. You look down at the typewriter keys.	Your typing speed won't improve.
7. You go outside.	Your cold won't get better.

D. Combine these sentences to make *past unreal conditions*.

Real Situation	*The Speaker's Opinion or Advice about This Situation*
1. You didn't stay in bed.	Your cold didn't get better.

    If you had stayed in bed, your cold would have got(ten) better.
    (This situation was *unreal in the past.* Note the negative–positive changes.)

2. You didn't practice a lot.	You weren't an excellent pianist.
3. You didn't study hard.	You didn't become a good student.

[2] *Can* (or *may, might*) may be used instead of *will* in conditional sentences.

[3] Note that an *if* clause may be used at the beginning or the end of the sentence.

4. You didn't shop wisely.   You didn't save money.

5. You didn't watch the road carefully.   You didn't become a good driver.

6. You looked down at the typewriter   Your typing speed didn't improve.
   keys.

7. You went outside.   Your cold didn't get better.

EXERCISE 3: Conditions with *otherwise*

Precautions in instructions are often given in the imperative form of a verb, or with *you should* (advisability) or *you must* (necessity).

> *Learn* (or *you should learn,* or *you must learn*) to drive defensively; *otherwise* you may get hit by another car.

This precaution may also be stated as a condition:

> *If you don't* (or *Unless you*) drive defensively, you may get hit by another car. (Note that this *if* clause is now negative.)

Change the following conditional sentences to their equivalents with *otherwise*. You will need to watch for positive–negative changes. Be sure to use a semicolon before otherwise.[4]

1. Unless you learn to swim with your face in the water, you will never become a good swimmer.

   Learn (or *you should learn,* or *you must learn) to swim with your face in the water; otherwise you will never become a good swimmer.*

2. If the roast isn't basted frequently, it will become dry and tough.

   The roast should (or *must) be basted frequently; otherwise it will become dry and tough.* (The imperative form is not used with a passive.)

3. If you don't pin the pieces of material together carefully, the dress won't come out right.

4. Unless the piano is tuned regularly, it won't sound right.

5. If you don't hold your fingers in the right position over the typewriter keys, you will make mistakes.

6. Unless the typewriter is cleaned and oiled regularly, the keys may not work properly.

---

[4] In sentences with *otherwise,* a period may replace the semicolon, especially if both parts of a sentence are long. Also, a comma is often used **after** *otherwise.*

7. If you don't turn on the ignition in the car with your key, the car won't start.[5]

8. Unless you serve the ball diagonally across into the box of your opponent, the serve doesn't count.[5]

9. If you don't learn to skim in reading, you will never become a fast, efficient reader.

EXERCISE 4: Auxiliaries: *mustn't* versus *don't have to*

Must and *have to* are synonyms when used in the positive. Their negatives, however, have different meanings.

> If you want vegetables to taste right, you *mustn't* let them cook too long.
> (*You mustn't* gives a *warning; mustn't* is a stronger form than *shouldn't*, which gives advice.)

> You don't have to add the wine to this recipe if you prefer not to.
> (*You don't have to* is the equivalent of *you aren't required to, you don't need to*.)

Use *mustn't* or *don't have to* with the verb in parentheses. Keep in mind that *mustn't* is a warning that is stronger than the advice of *shouldn't; don't have to* means *don't need to* or *aren't required to*.

1. You (add) _____*mustn't add*_____ much turpentine to the paint if you want the paint to cover the wood completely.

2. You (add) _____*don't have to add*_____ any turpentine to the paint; the paint is already mixed.

3. You (put) _____ on a second coat of paint if you don't want to.

4. However, if you are going to put on a second coat of paint, you (do) _____ it until the first coat is thoroughly dry.

5. You (leave) _____ on a camping trip until you have thoroughly checked all the equipment and the food supplies.

6. You (take) _____ a tent for a short camping trip; you can take sleeping bags instead.

7. You (drive) _____ in heavy traffic if you are just learning how to drive.

8. In taking care of a cold, you (go) _____ out if you have a fever.

9. You (do) _____ these exercises every day; a few days a week will be enough to get you back in shape.

---

[5] *You should* is not an appropriate choice in these sentences since the conditions express *necessity*.

10. In stamp collecting, you (pick) _____ up the stamps with your fingers.

11. You (be) _____ an expert to enjoy the dance I am going to teach you.

EXERCISE 5: *have* + Verb (for Instructions)

Instructions for a service to be performed are often given with the verb *have*. The service may be expressed in the active or the passive form.

SERVICE EXPRESSED AS ACTIVE:	I had the supermarket *deliver* some groceries. (*Deliver* is the infinitive, without *to*.) The service: The supermarket delivered some groceries.
SERVICE EXPRESSED AS PASSIVE:	I had some groceries *delivered* (by the supermarket). (*Delivered* is the past participle from the passive verb.) The service: Some groceries were delivered by the supermarket.

In this passive use, the *by* phrase is often omitted.

A. Make sentences beginning with *I had* and ending with (1) a service expressed as active, and (2) a service expressed as passive. For the passive the *by* phrase may be omitted.

Instructions to:	Request for Service
1. the maid	Please clean the house.

    (1) ACTIVE: *I had the maid clean the house.*
    (2) PASSIVE: *I had the house cleaned (by the maid).*

2. the druggist	Please fill my prescription.
3. the bank teller	Could you please cash my check?
4. the lawyer	I'd like you to draw up my will.
5. the secretary	Would you mind typing a letter?
6. the shoemaker	My shoes need to be repaired.
7. the auto mechanic	Please change the rear tires.
8. the painter	The whole house needs to be painted.
9. the dressmaker	Would you please lengthen my skirt?

10. the carpenter	Could you please build some book-cases for me?
11. the gardener	You'll trim the hedges, won't you?
12. the handyman	Would you mind replacing the light bulbs?

B. Using one of the forms for requests from A, ask for a service from each of the following people. Then write sentences with *I had* to express the service as (1) active and (2) passive. The *by* phrase may be omitted in the passive.

1. the tailor

> *Please shorten the sleeves of my coat.*
> (1) *I had the tailor shorten the sleeves of my coat.*
> (2) *I had the sleeves of my coat shortened (by the tailor).*

2. the plumber	**7.** the barber
3. the dentist	**8.** the gas station attendant
4. the TV repairman	**9.** the painter
5. the photographer	**10.** the druggist
6. the doctor	**11.** the salesclerk

EXERCISE 6: Connective Adverbs (for Sequence of Steps)

The steps in instructions may be connected with expressions like *then, now, next, after this* (not *after* used alone).

Sometimes a writer uses a connective that repeats too much of what precedes it.

REPETITIOUS
CONNECTIVE: Clean the shoes with a wet rag and let them dry. *After the shoes are dry,* apply a thick coat of the polish.

SHORTER
CONNECTIVE: Clean the shoes with a wet rag and let them dry; *then* apply a thick coat of the polish.

OR

Clean the shoes with a wet rag and let them dry. *Then* (or *After this,*) apply a thick coat of the polish.

Note that if the two steps are put together into one sentence, a semicolon is placed before the connective. Otherwise the connective begins a new sentence.

Replace the long connective with a shorter one like *then, now, next,* or *after this.* Use either a semicolon or a period before the connective.

1. Turn on the electric current. *After this is done,* insert some paper in the typewriter.

> *Turn on the electric current; then insert some paper in the typewriter.*
> OR
> *Turn on the electric current. Then* (or *next, after this,*) *insert some paper in the typewriter.*

2. Place the seeds about three inches apart and cover them with soil. *After the seeds are planted,* give them plenty of water.

3. Brown the chicken in the hot oil for five minutes on each side. *After the chicken has been browned,* drain off the excess oil.

4. Make a list of all the things you will need for your camping trip. *After this list is prepared,* buy the things you don't already have.

5. Step into the car, fasten your safety belt, and make yourself comfortable. *After these things are done,* turn on the ignition.

6. You must serve the ball into the proper box of the tennis court. *After you have made a successful serve,* you are ready for an exciting volley.

EXERCISE 7: Dangling Participles

When an introductory structure does not have its own subject, it often depends on the subject of the main verb for its agent. This is especially true for introductory structures containing the *-ing* participle or the *-ed* participle.

> While *waiting* for the rice to cook, *you* should prepare the gravy.

If the subject of the main verb is not the agent of the *-ing* or *-ed* verb in the introductory structure, this structure is considered as unacceptably "dangling."

> DANGLING: While *waiting* for the rice to cook, *the gravy* should be prepared.
> (*The gravy* is not the agent of *waiting.*)

Underline (1) the *-ing* or *-ed* participle in the introductory structure, and (2) the subject of the main verb that follows. Then correct any dangling constructions in the sentences in one or both of the ways suggested below. (Some of the sentences are correct.)

1 . By practicing every day, your typing speed will improve rapidly.

> *By* <u>practicing</u> *every day,* <u>your typing speed</u> *will improve rapidly.*

CORRECTIONS:

> *By* **practicing** *every day,* **you** *will improve your typing speed rapidly.*

(The subject *you* is now the agent of *practicing*.)

OR

> *If* **you practice** *every day, your typing speed will improve rapidly.*

(*Practice* now has its own subject in the *if* clause and does not depend on the subject of the main verb for its agent.)

2. Once cooked, add the sautéed mushrooms to the chicken.

3. Leaving the pan on a low flame, the whole procedure will take 30 to 40 minutes.

4. After hemming the dress, the last step is ironing it.

5. Once having learned to drive, you will be able to have many enjoyable trips in the country.

6. When doing this dance step, your arms should be placed on your partner's hips.

7. By looking down at the keyboard, your typing speed will be slowed down considerably.

8. Having cut each pattern piece of the dress, the pieces should be pinned together.

9. If carefully constructed and finished, no one will know that you made the table yourself.

10. Before hanging a picture, carefully check the place where the nail is to be hammered in.

11. Prepared in advance, this dish will permit you to enjoy your guests without your having to run into the kitchen all the time.

EXERCISE 8: Subjunctive Verbs in *that* Clauses

Instructions given in the form of advice are often expressed indirectly in *that* clauses after certain verbs. The verbs in such *that* clauses are usually in simple, unchanged form (present subjunctive) *regardless of person or tense.*

In his book *How to Win Friends and Influence People,* Dale Carnegie suggested that a person *be* a good listener. He also recommended that we *become* genuinely interested in other people.

Note that the present subjunctive (*be, become*) are the infinitives without *to*.[6]

Below are some other suggestions given by Dale Carnegie on "How to Win Friends and Influence People." Using one of these verbs—*recommend, advise, suggest, urge, propose, insist*—write sentences expressing Dale Carnegie's advice in *that* clauses. Use *we* as the subject in the *that* clause.

1. Make the other person feel important, and do it sincerely.

   Dale Carnegie advised that we make the other person feel important and that we do it sincerely.

2. Show respect for the other person's opinions.

3. Never tell anyone he or she is wrong.

4. If you are wrong, admit it quickly and emphatically. (change *you* to *we*)

5. Let the other person do a great deal of the talking.

6. Try honestly to see things from the other person's point of view.

7. Be sympathetic to the other person's ideas and desires.

8. Dramatize your ideas. (change *your* to *our*)

9. Call attention to people's mistakes indirectly.

10. Talk about your own mistakes before criticizing the other person. (change *your* to *our*)

EXERCISE 9: Word Forms

Add the correct endings.

1. Something that is *cheap* is <u>econom-*ical*</u>   or <u>inexpen-*sive*</u>.

2. Something that is *useful* is <u>practi-</u>.

3. Something that is *easy* is <u>sim-</u>.

4. Something that is *beautiful* is <u>attrac-</u>.

5. Something that is *tasty* is <u>delic-</u>.

6. Something that is *pleasant* is <u>enjoy-</u>.

[6] Sometimes the auxiliary *should* occurs in such *that* clauses:
   Carnegie suggested that a person *should be* a good listener.

7. Something that is *nourishing* is nutri-_____.

8. Something that is *lightly fried* is saut-_____.

9. Something that is *slowly cooked on low heat* is sim-_____.

10. A *safety measure* is a precau-_____.

11. *Something that encourages us to action* is an incent-_____.

12. *Any of the things that are mixed together* is an ingred-_____.

13. *Something that we do* is an activ-_____.

14. *Something that we do well and take pride in* is an accomplish-_____.

15. *Something that is done by a tailor to make our clothes fit better* is called an altera-_____.

EXERCISE 10: Sentence Review

Make full sentences from the word groups below, and complete the unfinished words. Use the correct form of the verb, together with any auxiliaries that might be required (especially *must, should, would, had*). Do not change the word order. Use commas, semicolons, and periods wherever necessary.

(These sentences are taken from Exercises 1,2,3,4,8. If you are in doubt about any of the sentences, check against the proper exercise.)

1. Air / in tires / check / before / you / start / on / long / trip. (passive)

    The air in the tires should be checked before you start on a long trip.

2. screwdriver / use / loosen / screws. (passive)

3. piano / sound / better / if / you / have / it / tune- _____ .
    (Note: The piano isn't tuned now.) (unreal conditional)

4. car / last / long / time / if / you / take / care / it.
    (Note: You aren't taking care of it now.) (unreal conditional)

5. if / you / practice / every day / you / learn / faster.
    (Note: You *didn't practice* every day *last year*.) (unreal conditional)

6. your cold / get / better / if / you / stay / bed.
    (Note: You *didn't stay* in bed *last week*.) (unreal conditional)

7. unless / typewriter / clean and oil / regular- _____ / keys / not work / proper- _____ .

8. you / learn / skim / in read- _____ / otherwise / you / never / become / fast / effici- _____ / reader.

9. you / turn on / ignition / in car / otherwise / car / not start.

10. you / not add / much turpentine / if / you / want / the paint / cover / wood / complete- _____ .

11. Dale Carnegie / advise / we / make / other person / feel / important. (Use a *that* clause after *advise*.)

12. Dale Carnegie / recommend / we / dramatize / our / ideas. (Use a *that* clause after *recommend*.)

EXTRA SPEAKING AND WRITING PRACTICE

EXERCISE 11: Composition: Adding an Introduction: Recipe

The following recipe for a Potato and Vegetable Casserole comes from *The Complete Book of Vegetable Cookery.* Look it over to see why you would want to recommend it to a friend.

1 ½ pounds potatoes, peeled and sliced thin
2 cups chopped tomatoes
1 ½ cups thinly sliced carrots
1 cup chopped onion
2 cloves garlic, minced
¼ cup chopped parsley
1 ½ teaspoons salt
½ teaspoon freshly ground black pepper
1 ½ cups water
¼ cup olive oil

In a buttered baking dish, spread the potatoes. Mix together the tomatoes, carrots, onion, garlic, parsley, salt, and pepper; spread over the potatoes. Add the water; bake in a 375-degree oven for 45 minutes. Pour the oil over the top; bake 15 minutes longer. Serve hot or cold. Serves 4 to 6.*

Note that in this kind of recipe, only the essential information is given. The simple imperative form of the verb is used, and there are no transitions to connect steps.[7]

Write a short introduction for this recipe. Give your reasons why the reader would want to make this vegetable dish. You might use some of the reasons already suggested for making something: it is easy to make, economical, tasty, nutritious. You might also refer to the idea of variety: this is an unusual way to serve vegetables, especially for those who don't like vegetables or for those who are vegetarians.

To catch the attention of the reader more easily in the introduction, you might put one or more of these reasons in the form of questions.

* From *The Complete Book of Vegetable Cookery* by Myra Waldo. Copyright © 1962 by Myra Waldo. Reprinted by permission of Bantam Books, Inc. All rights reserved.

[7] In short instructions, articles and pronouns are also often omitted.

EXERCISE 12: Composition: Adding the Body and a Conclusion:
How to Take Care of a Cold

The following is an introduction to a composition giving instructions on how to take care of a cold.

How to Take Care of a Cold

You've all had colds at some time and know how miserable a cold can make you feel. Your nose runs, your throat hurts, you're sneezing, you have a headache, and you may have a fever. Doctors don't know just what causes a cold, but they know what should be done to get rid of it. Here is some of the advice they give.

First, discuss as a class, or in groups, the remedies for taking care of a cold. Then copy the introduction given above and continue the composition. In full sentences arranged in paragraphs, tell the readers what they must do to take care of a cold. Some of the things to consider are rest, food, drink, medications, clothes to wear outdoors.

Also tell the readers what they mustn't do—for example, go outdoors when it is very cold, overeat, take too much medication, get too close to other people who can catch your cold.

Add a brief conclusion.

LISTENING-WRITING PRACTICE

EXERCISE 13: Paragraphs for Dictation

Your teacher will dictate each paragraph three times. The first time is for listening only, the second time is for writing, and the third time is for checking what you have written.

Immediately after you give your teacher the dictation you have written, check the dictation in the book for any problems you had in writing it.

DICTATION 1

The dictionary can be a very valuable tool for anyone who is studying English. Everyone knows that it gives the meaning and the spelling of words, but many people are not aware of its usefulness for grammar and pronunciation. For example, the dictionary can help you with any grammatical irregularity. See for yourself. If you look up the noun *crisis,* you will observe that the plural is *crises.* If you look up the verb *fall,* you will note that the past is *fell* and the past participle is *fallen.* Also, if endings like *-s* and *-ed* affect the spelling of a word, this information is given. Thus, with the word *arch* will be its plural form *arches;* with the verb *occur* will be its past form *occurred.*

DICTATION 2

If you want to determine the pronunciation of a word, check the information in parentheses right after the word. Within these parentheses, the word is rewritten phonetically with symbols for the sounds and with stress marks for the accented syllables. In an American dictionary, the symbols are mainly letters of the alphabet. Because there are many more vowel sounds than the five vowel letters, special marks above these letters differentiate the sounds. At the bottom of the dictionary page you will find illustrations of the sounds of each symbol. If two pronunciations are given for a word, for example, *direction,* this means that either pronunciation is acceptable.

EXERCISE 14: Dicto-comps

Take notes as your teacher reads each of these dicto-comps to you several times. Then reconstruct the dicto-comp from your notes. The dicto-comp does not need to be written exactly as you heard it, but it should be grammatically correct.

Before you write the dicto-comp, your teacher may ask the class to get together in groups to check with each other on what you heard.

Immediately after you give your teacher the dicto-comp you have written, check the dicto-comp in the book for any problems you had in writing it.

DICTO-COMP 1

How to Make Curried Chicken and Rice (Simplified American Style)

Curried chicken and rice is one of the easiest dishes to prepare. It requires very few ingredients and makes a tasty meal with your favorite salad. Here is all you need.

    4 good-sized chicken parts
    ½ cup brown rice
    1 heaping tablespoon mild curry (the next time you may want more or less
        curry depending on your taste)
    1 tablespoon salt
        This recipe will serve four people.

Wash the chicken parts and place them in a pot with enough water to cover them. Add the curry and the salt; then cover the pot. When the water boils, add the rice, and then lower the heat. Stir occasionally to prevent the rice from sticking to the bottom of the pan. Continue cooking on a low flame for 45 minutes or until both the rice and the chicken are done. If the water is absorbed before the rice is done, add a little more water. If there is too much water, raise the heat and cook un-covered until most of the water has evaporated.

You are now ready to serve your curried chicken and rice dish with the salad you have prepared. If you have followed the simple instructions given in this recipe, you will get many compliments from your family or guests for a delicious meal that was very easy to prepare and didn't cost a great deal.

DICTO-COMP 2

Here are a few of the most important rules of reading hygiene.

First, get expert help in relieving eyestrain. Get eyeglasses if you are near-sighted or farsighted or have other defects of vision.

Second, hold your book up when you read. Don't let your head bend over a book that is lying flat on your desk or table. Hold the book vertically in your hand or propped up on the desk at the best distance for you. For most persons the best distance is about fourteen inches from the eyes.

Third, read in a good light. Avoid reading in bright sunlight and be careful to turn on the light before twilight falls. Sit with your back to the light. The light should fall over the left shoulder (or the right, if you are left-handed). In this way you keep out of your own light and avoid having a bright light shining into your eyes.

Ruth Strang, *Study Types of Reading Exercises,* 1951, p. 74.*

* From Ruth Strang, *Study Types of Reading Exercises* (New York: Teachers College Press, 1951). Copyright 1951 by Ruth Strang. Abridged by permission of the publisher.

Holidays

GRAMMAR AND USAGE

Prepositions of time: *in, on, at*
Definite article (*the*)
Noun phrases: *the* + verbal noun + *of*
Agreement between subject and verb
Passive voice
much–many, (a) little, (a) few
Questions and answers
Spelling: Noun plurals in *-es*

RHETORIC

Using an outline to guide the composition
Using an introduction and a conclusion
Using a transitional lead-in to the body of the composition

DISCUSSION AND COMPOSITION

1. DISCUSSION: Preliminary outline for the composition (prewriting stage)

Subject: *The Celebration of* (name of holiday)
in (name of your country)

Outline (To Be Placed on the Board)	Discussion (Ideas, Grammar and Usage, Vocabulary, Elements of Composition Building)
Introduction: general comments about kinds of holidays, including those in your country	Possible comments: My country, like all other countries, has many holidays. Some are national, some religious, some social. (An example of each may be given.) Some are days when people get off from work or school, some are not.
Transitional lead-in: connection with your subject of *one* holiday	Possible transitions: One of the holidays I enjoy the most is a national (or religious, social) one. *Or* My favorite holiday is a national (or religious, social) one. *Or* The national (or religious, social) holiday I always look forward to is _____ .

I. Date of the holiday, and background (if possible)	Points of usage:
	1. prepositions of time:
	    in—season, year, month, part of the day
	    at—noon, midnight, time of the day
	    on—days of the week, dates, holidays
	2. Initial capitals: holidays, days of the week, months
	3. No *the* with the name of a holiday

II. What people do to celebrate this holiday III. IV. V. VI.	Possible activities: have a vacation from work or school clean the house wear special clothes or costumes go to a place of worship: a church, temple, synagogue, mosque watch parades listen to speeches shoot off firecrackers

Outline (cont.)	Discussion (cont.)
VII. etc.	watch fireworks put out flags place wreaths on graves have parties, dances eat special foods go to the beach or to the country decorate homes, stores, streets
Conclusion: general statements	Possible comments: enjoyment of the holiday looking forward to the next year's celebration or end with an interesting final detail or a personal anecdote

2. COMPOSITION (to be done before or after the reinforcement practice)

A. ORGANIZING THE COMPOSITION

Before writing your composition, fill in the required information on this Organizational Worksheet. The Worksheet follows the preliminary outline used for the discussion. Suggestions for writing each paragraph are given at the right side of this Worksheet. The pages of the discussion outline provide additional help for the composition.

You may use phrases on this Worksheet except where it calls for full sentences.

ORGANIZATIONAL WORKSHEET
(Preliminary notes for the composition)

Title of the composition _____
(Do not use quotation marks or a period for a title to the top of the page. Use initial capital letters for the first word of the title and for all other words except articles, short prepositions, and short conjunctions.)

Introduction: general statements Opening sentence of paragraph _____ _____ _____	Put in a separate paragraph Use the present tense for general statements Keep this paragraph short

Kinds of holidays

_____

_____

_____

_____

Transitional lead-in connecting the general state-ments of the introduction to the specific subject of *one* holiday

Do not use *the* with the name of a holiday

Full sentence _____

_____

_____

_____

I. Date and background of the holiday

Keep this short—may be in-cluded in the paragraph with the transition

_____

_____

Be careful of your use of prepositions, initial capitals

_____

_____

II. What people do to celebrate this holiday

Use chronological order

This is the main part of the composition

_____

_____

Use several paragraphs, but avoid one-sentence para-graphs

_____

III. _____

_____

_____

IV. _____

_____

_____

V. _____

_____

_____

VI. _____

   _____

   _____

   _____

VII. _____

   _____

   _____

   _____

etc. _____

   _____

   _____

Conclusion: general statements   New paragraph
                                            The conclusion may simply be
   _____   an interesting final detail re-
                                            garding the celebration of the
   _____   holiday.

   _____

   _____

   _____

   _____

   _____

   _____

   _____

B. WRITING THE COMPOSITION

Write the composition based on your notes on the Organizational Work-sheet. Be careful of your paragraphing. Use separate paragraphs for your introduction and your conclusion. (Long paragraphs may be broken in two at appropriate places, but avoid single-sentence paragraphs.)

Use 8½ - by 11-inch white paper, with lines for a handwritten composition and without lines for a typed composition. Double-space a typewritten composition, and skip lines on a handwritten one. Write on the front of the paper only, and leave wide margins on *both the left and the right sides* of the paper. Indent the beginning of each paragraph.

Look over your composition carefully before you hand it in.

C. CORRECTING OR REWRITING THE COMPOSITION

When your teacher returns your composition, it will be marked with the symbols from the correction chart on page 257. Make the necessary corrections on the composition and hand it back to your teacher.

Place the corrections on the correction page, and note down the rule that is involved.

If you have made many mistakes, or if you wish to make some additions to your composition, you may need to write it again. In rewriting the composition, do not make extensive changes or additions without consulting your teacher.

(For more help with your problems in writing, consult the Index of Usage and Rhetoric in *Writer's Companion*. The items in this index are arranged in the same alphabetical order as in the correction chart.)

CORRECTION PAGE

Use this page to write down the correction of any mistakes you have made in your composition on "The Celebration of (*name of holiday*) in (*name of your country*)." Include enough of the words surrounding the corrected part to make the meaning clear. (Do not copy down the mistake itself.) If possible, write down the rule that covers the correction you have made.

Review these corrections from time to time in order to avoid making the same mistakes again.

Corrections

Rules
(See the correction chart if necessary)

REINFORCEMENT PRACTICE

EXERCISE 1: Prepositions of Time: *in, at, on*

The following are the most common prepositions for a point in time.

in	with seasons	in (the) spring, in (the) summer in (the) fall, in (the) winter
	with years	in 1976
	with months	in February
	with certain parts of the day	in the morning, in the afternoon, in the evening
at	with certain parts of the day	at night, at noon, at midnight
	with the time of the day	at five o'clock
on	with days	on Sunday (day of the week) on February 22 (date) on Labor Day, on New Year's Eve (holiday) — *on* may be omitted except at the beginning of the sentence

Note that names of days of the week and names of months begin with capital letters. Initial capital letters are also required for every word in the name of a holiday (*Independence Day, Christmas Eve*). Note also that *the* is not used with names of holidays.

A. Use the time expression *in, at,* or *on*.

1. The Declaration of Independence was signed _*on*_ July 4, 1776.

2. Thanksgiving Day is observed _____ the fall.

3. Catholic people go to church _____ Christmas Eve.

4. Santa Claus is supposed to arrive _____ night to put presents under the Christmas tree.

5. Columbus Day celebrates the discovery of America _____ 1492.

6. _____ Independence Day, it is customary to have firework displays _____ the evening.

7. Mother's Day is observed _____ May, Father's Day _____ June.

8. _____ New Year's Eve, parties often begin late, _____ ten or eleven _____ night.

9. May Day is observed _____ May 1.

10. Many holidays that occur _____ Sunday are celebrated _____ the following Monday.

B. In full sentences, give the dates of five holidays in your country. Use capital letters for the word *Day* if it is part of the name of the holiday. Use capital letters for the name of the day or the month. Do not use *the* with the name of the holiday.

> *Independence Day is observed* (or, *is celebrated*) *on July 4.*

EXERCISE 2: Definite Article (*the*)

The is usually required with ordinal numbers: the first, the second, the third.

Labor Day is observed on *the first* Monday in September.

The also occurs with other words that establish a sequence: the next, the following, the last.

New Year's Eve is celebrated on *the last* day of the year.

The next day begins the New Year.

The is not used when *next* or *last* simply marks a point that is future or past from the present.

PRESENT: The store is having a sale *this* week.

FUTURE: The store will have a sale *next* week.

PAST: The store had a sale *last* week.

(Note that no preposition of time appears with these points of time.)

Dates are usually written as cardinal numbers but are spoken as ordinals. Thus the written date *May 1* is spoken as May *first* or May *the first.* If the date is written *1 May,* it is spoken as *the first* of May.

Use *the* where required. If cardinal numbers are given, change them to ordinals.

1. Thanksgiving Day is celebrated on (four) ____*the fourth*____ Thursday of November.

2. St. Valentine's Day falls on February 14 __(spoken form) *(the) fourteenth*__ .

3. A holiday that falls on a Sunday is celebrated on _____ following Monday.

4. Memorial Day is observed on _____ last Monday in May.

5. In _____ next few years we may have more holidays than we

   had _____ last year.

6. April Fool's Day, which occurs on April 1 (spoken form) _____ , is the day
   we play tricks on each other.

7. Many people stay up late on New Year's Eve. On _____ next
   day they are very tired.

8. Washington's Birthday is commemorated on (three) _____
   Monday in February.

9. Christmas Day falls on December 25 (spoken form) _____ .

10. Election Day occurs on _____ first Tuesday after _____
    first Monday in November.

EXERCISE 3: Noun Phrases: *the* + Verbal Noun + *of*

By changing the verb in a predicate phrase to a noun, we can sometimes
use the entire phrase as a noun.

Subject	**Predicate**
Americans	celebrate Thanksgiving.
The celebration of Thanksgiving	is a family tradition.

Note that the verbal noun *celebration* requires *the* before it; its object, *Thanksgiving,* requires *of* before it.

In the following sentences, change the words in parentheses to noun phrases
following the pattern: *the* + verbal noun + *of.* If the verbal noun has a subject,
place the subject in possessive form or in a *by* phrase. If the original subject is
included in the noun phrase, it is either in possessive form (*Americans' celebration of Thanksgiving*) or in a *by* phrase (*celebration of Thanksgiving by Americans*).

1. (decorate their homes for Christmas) takes some people a long time.

   The decoration of their homes for Christmas takes some people a long time.

2. On the second Monday in October, (Columbus discovered America) is commemorated.

   On the second Monday in October, Columbus' discovery of America (OR the discovery of America by Columbus) is commemorated.

3. (children enjoy holidays) is greatest at Christmas time.

4. Thanksgiving Day commemorates (the Pilgrims celebrated the good harvest of 1621).

5. On Election Day, certain public places, especially schools, are used for (elect government officials).

6. In the United States, (declare Independence) was signed in 1776.

7. At Christmas time, (exchange gifts) around the Christmas tree is a popular custom.

8. (Americans observe Memorial Day) takes place on the last Monday in May.

EXERCISE 4: Agreement between Subject and Verb

The verb in a sentence must agree with the subject in number. This kind of agreement is especially required with verbs in the simple present tense.

The girl remembers. (A singular noun requires a verb ending in -s.)
The girls remember. (A plural noun requires a verb that has no -s.)

Agreement is also needed with those auxiliaries that have different forms for the singular and plural:

Singular	Plural
is	are
was	were
has	have
does	do

If the subject is long, the verb agrees with the main word in the subject.

The *atmosphere* during the Christmas holidays *is* very festive.

Subjects used with *each* or *every* require singular verbs.

Everyone *enjoys* getting the day off from work on a holiday.
Each holiday *is* celebrated in a different way.

Where *there* is used in subject position, the verb (usually *be*) agrees with the noun that follows it.

There *is* one *holiday* that I especially love.
There *are* some *holidays* that I especially love.

Underline the form in parentheses that agrees with the subject.

1. Everybody (like, likes) to have a holiday from work.

   Everybody (like, likes) to have a holiday from work.

2. Memorial Day (commemorate, commemorates) the servicemen who (was, were) killed in past wars.

3. At a New Year's party, each guest (wear, wears) a funny hat and (have, has) a noisemaker.

4. The work which a housewife (have, has) to do to prepare for some holidays often (take, takes) a long time.

5. There (is, are) a lot of noise on New Year's Eve.

6. The children in every family (enjoy, enjoys) Christmas time.

7. Everyone (is, are) sad on Labor Day because it (mark, marks) the end of the summer vacation.

8. There (is, are) few people who (do, does) not enjoy getting off from work.

9. Every woman who (get, gets) a valentine on St. Valentine's Day (is, are) pleased.

10. People who often (do, does) not attend church during the year (go, goes) there for the solemn ceremonies at Easter time.

11. The police (is, are) needed to preserve order during a parade. (*Police* is always plural.)

12. On January 1 everybody (wish, wishes) each other a Happy New Year.

13. My country, like all other countries, (have, has) many holidays.

14. The size of the box of Valentine chocolates (depend, depends) on how much money the boy (have, has) or on how much he (care, cares) for the girl.

15. Traditional food prepared with special ingredients (is, are) served.

16. Each of his children (get, gets) an expensive gift for Christmas.

EXERCISE 5: Passive Voice

Change the following sentences to the passive. Start the passive sentence with the original object, and omit the subject *people*.

1. People send greeting cards at Christmas time.

   Greeting cards are sent at Christmas time.

2. People commemorate the dead servicemen on Memorial Day.

3. People wear new clothes on Easter Sunday.

4. People eat turkey on Thanksgiving Day.

5. People drink much liquor on New Year's Eve.

6. People give presents for Christmas.

7. People ring bells in church during some holidays.

8. People observe many holidays on Mondays.

9. People decorate store windows for the Christmas holidays.

10. People sometimes spend a lot of money to prepare for a holiday.

11. People blow horns on New Year's Eve.

12. People hear solemn music in church at Easter time.

13. People put a wreath on the Tomb of the Unknown Soldier on Memorial Day.

14. People sing Christmas carols during the Christmas holidays.

15. People leave gifts for children under the Christmas tree.

16. People can see Santa Claus's "helpers" inside and outside the big stores.

17. People make New Year's resolutions on December 31.

EXERCISE 6: *much–many, (a) little, (a) few*

Adjectives generally do not change their form when they are used with plural nouns. Exceptions are *much* and *little*. These two adjectives occur only with noncountable nouns. With plural countable nouns, *much* becomes *many*, and *little* becomes *few*.

Noncountable Noun	Plural Countable Noun
Much music was played.	*Many* songs were sung.
(A) *Little* music was played.	(A) *Few* songs were sung.

A little and *a few* stress the *presence* of something in a small quantity (*I have a little money; I have a few friends*); *little* and *few* stress the *absence* of almost all quantity (*I have little money; I have few friends*).

Underline the correct form.

1. Christmas dinner is served in (much, many) restaurants.

   Christmas dinner is served in (much, many) restaurants.

2. Even though their hosts had made elaborate preparations for the Halloween party, (few, a few) children came, because of the bad weather.

3. (Much, many) people go to the beach on Independence Day.

4. Too (much, many) noise is heard on July 4.

5. Everyone was happy that only¹ (few, a few) speeches were made.

6. Not (much, many) work gets done on a holiday.

7. (Few, a few) people came to the parade because of the heat.

8. Even after cleaning all day, she still had (little, a little) more housework to do to prepare for the holiday.

9. Only (little, a little) turkey was left from their Thanksgiving dinner.

10. Very (little, a little) turkey was left from their Thanksgiving dinner.

11. Very (few, little) people work on New Year's Day.

12. They spent (much, many) money on Christmas presents, so now they have (little, few) money in the bank.

EXERCISE 7: Word Forms

Use the correct form of the word in parentheses and complete the unfinished words.

(If you need help with the signals that tell whether a noun, verb, adjective, or adverbial form is needed, refer to *Writer's Companion,* Unit 2, in the Grammar Review and Practice section.)

1. The (observe) _____*observation*_____ of Labor Day takes place on the first Monday in September.

2. It is (custom) _____ for families to eat Thanksgiving dinner together.

3. On St. Patrick's Day the Irish commemorate the day of St. Patrick's (die) _____.

4. Many (religion) _____ services are held at Easter time.

5. During Christmas the brightly (decorate) _____ stores make the shopping areas look very (festival) _____.

¹ *Only* requires the form with *a:* **Only a** *few days are left before Christmas.*

6. Sometimes children are puzzled by the (appear) _____ of many Santa Clauses on the streets at Christmas time.

7. The exchange of gifts adds to the (enjoy) _____ of the Christmas holidays.

8. On the Fourth of July, Americans express their (proud) _____

   in their great (inherit) _____.

9. Christmas is a time for (gay) _____ and (merry) _____

   _____.

10. Memorial Day (commemor- _____ the dead servicemen of all wars.

11. During the Carnival in New Orleans, there are many joyous (festiv- _____

   _____ that take place.

12. The valentine sent on St. Valentine's Day (symbol) _____ the love we feel for the one who receives it.

13. Christmas (origin- _____ celebrated the (born) _____

   of Christ. Now the Christmas (celebrate) _____ has (wide)

   _____ to include many (enjoy) _____

   activ- _____.

14. Some holidays are (basic) _____ religious. Others are (gen-

   eral) _____ observed by everyone in the country, (especial)

   _____ the (nation) _____ holidays.

EXERCISE 8: Sentence Review

Make full sentences from the word groups below, and complete the unfinished words. Make whatever changes or additions are needed, but do not change the word order. Use commas, semicolons, or periods wherever necessary.

1. Santa Claus / suppose / arrive / night.

   Santa Claus is supposed to arrive at night.

2. Mother's Day / observe / May, / Father's Day / June.

3. Many holidays / occur / Sunday / celebrate / following / Monday.

4. It is / custom- / families / eat / Thanksgiving dinner / together.

5. Exchange / gifts / add / enjoy- / Christmas holidays.

6. Memorial Day / observe / last Monday / May.

7. Decorate / their homes / take / some people / long time.

8. Everybody / like / have / holiday / work.

9. There / be / few people / who / not enjoy / holidays.

10. Few / people / came / parade / because / heat.

11. In / United States / Election Day / occur / first Tuesday / after / first Monday / November.

12. There / be / lot / noise / New Year's Eve.

13. Each / his children / get / expensive gift / Christmas.

14. Lot / money / spend / prepare / for / holiday.

15. Some / holiday / be / basic / religious / others / be / general / observe / everyone in the country.

EXTRA SPEAKING AND WRITING PRACTICE

EXERCISE 9: Questions and Answers: Holidays

A. Below is some information about holidays. One of them, Thanksgiving, is an American holiday only. The other three holidays are celebrated in many parts of the English-speaking world and elsewhere.

Working with a partner, take turns asking and answering questions about the information given for each holiday. The answers should be in full sentences.

Halloween

Date:	October 31
Time began:	in pre-Christian England
Activities (what people do):	(1) no vacation from school or work
	(2) masquerade parties for children and adults; costumes and masks worn as disguises
	(3) children in costume go from door to door saying "Trick or treat" (treat: candy, fruit, coins)
Decorations:	(1) harvest fruit and vegetables
	(2) paper images of witches on broomsticks, black cats, skeletons
	(3) lighted pumpkins (called jack-o'-lanterns)
	(4) colors of decorations are black and orange
Example:	
Question:	*When is Halloween? or When does Halloween take place? or When is Halloween celebrated? or What is the date of Halloween?*
Answer:	*Halloween is October 31. or Halloween takes place on October 31. or Halloween is celebrated on October 31. or The date of Halloween is October 31.*

Thanksgiving

Date:	fourth Thursday of November
Commemorates:	the Pilgrims' good harvest of 1621
Activities (what people do):	(1) vacation from school or work
	(2) family reunions
	(3) festive dinners: turkey, sweet potatoes, cranberry sauce, pumpkin pie or mince pie
Decorations:	harvest fruit and vegetables (especially yellow or orange ones)

Christmas

Date: December 25
Commemorates: birth of Christ
Activities (what people do):   (1) vacation from school or work
                                 (2) go to church for solemn services, beautiful music
                                 (3) sing Christmas carols
                                 (4) go to stores to shop for clothes and gifts
                                 (5) exchange gifts (small children believe Santa Claus brings them gifts)
                                 (6) send greeting cards
                                 (7) wish each other Merry Christmas
Decorations: (1) Christmas trees with lights and ornaments—in homes, stores, streets
                                 (2) store windows decorated, many elaborately

New Year's

Date: January 1
Purpose: (1) say goodbye to the old year
                                 (2) greet the new year
Activities (what people do):   (1) vacation from school or work
                                 (2) send greeting cards
                                 (3) have big parties on New Year's Eve
                                        much drinking
                                        stay up to midnight to greet the new year
                                        at midnight, kiss each other, wish each other Happy New Year
Decorations: elaborate decorations for New Year's Eve parties at home and in restaurants, with confetti, streamers, noisemakers, funny hats

B. Using the information given in A, write one paragraph for each of the four holidays.

C. Write a short dialog in which an English-speaking person asks you questions about a holiday in your country and you give the answers. (Do not use the holiday you wrote about in your composition.)

The questions can be about: the date of the holiday
                               what the holiday celebrates
                               what people do:
                                    parties, dancing
                                    religious activities
                                    special clothes worn
                                    special foods eaten
                                    decorations
                               public activities:
                                    speeches, parades, demonstrations, fireworks, pageants

EXERCISE 10: Spelling: Noun Plurals in -es

The regular plural ending for a noun is -s.

games, symbols, tricks

However, after certain letters, -es is added:
(1) after sybilants, spelled *ch, sh, s, x*

churches, dishes, classes, boxes

(2) after nouns ending in *y* preceded by a consonant. The *y* is changed to *i* before the *es*.

countries, activities

If a vowel comes before *y*, only *s* is added.

holidays.

Many one-syllable nouns ending in -*f* or -*fe* in the singular end in -*ves* in the plural.

leaves, knives

Use -*s* or -*es* for the plural of the nouns in parentheses. Make whatever change is necessary before adding the plural ending.

1. Many (festivity) _____*festivities*_____ take place during the Christmas (holiday) _____*holidays*_____.

2. (Box) _____ of candy are given to (sweetheart) _____
   _____ on St. Valentine's Day.

3. During the summer vacation, many (bus) _____ take people
   to the different (beach) _____.

4. Halloween takes place when the (leaf) _____ are falling from
   the (tree) _____.

5. On festival (day) _____, many (housewife) _____
   _____ use their best (dish) _____.

6. Halloween is based on some old pagan (belief) _____.(This is
   an exception to the rule.)

7. At Thanksgiving time, the (church) _____ are full of people
   giving (prayer) _____ of thanks for their (blessing) _____
   _____.

8. At Halloween (party) _____ people wear (costume) _____

   _____ and play (game) _____.

9. On New Year's Day, no (class) _____ are held and all (busi-

   ness) _____ are closed.

10. On Halloween, (witch) _____ are (symbol) _____

    of evil.

11. Good (wish) _____ are exchanged on New Year's Day.

12. On Memorial Day, people visit the (cemetery) _____ to place

    (wreath) _____ on the (grave) _____ of the
    dead.

13. On Independence Day, we can hear many (speech) _____

    and see many (parade) _____.

LISTENING-WRITING PRACTICE

EXERCISE 11: Paragraphs for Dictation

Your teacher will dictate each paragraph three times. The first time is for listening only, the second time is for writing, and the third time is for checking what you have written.

Immediately after you give your teacher the dictation you have written, check the dictation in the book for any problems you had in writing it.

DICTATION 1

On March 17, many Americans, Irish or not, wear something green to honor Patrick, the patron saint of Ireland. That day is not his birthday, but the day of his death in 493 A.D. The first celebration of St. Patrick's Day in the United States took place in Boston in the eighteenth century, probably because Boston had a large Irish population. The idea spread to other cities also, with religious services, dinners, and parades commemorating the day. The most famous parade is in New York, when thousands of marchers and scores of bands from local schools and organizations parade down Fifth Avenue.

Arthur E. Albrecht, *Here and There,* "It's a Great Day for the Irish," March 1974.*

DICTATION 2

The custom of hiding eggs at Easter began in Ireland. During Holy Week, children made nests of stones in which they hid their eggs. In the Slavic countries, Easter eggs were decorated with exquisite designs symbolic of good fortune, good health, fulfillment of wishes, and love. Egg-rolling began in the Germanic countries. In the United States, the annual egg-rolling party on the White House lawn is nationally famous. Children come from all parts of the country to roll gaily colored, hard-boiled eggs down the terraced lawn. Then the children themselves roll down the lawn, shrieking with laughter.

Arthur E. Albrecht, *Here and There,* "The Legend of the Easter Egg," April 1976.

EXERCISE 12: Dicto-comps

Take notes as your teacher reads each of these dicto-comps to you several times. Then reconstruct the dicto-comp from your notes. The dicto-comp does not need to be written exactly as you heard it, but it should be grammatically correct.

Before you write the dicto-comp, your teacher may ask the class to get together in groups to check with each other on what you heard.

* *Here and There* is a publication of English in Action.

Immediately after you give your teacher the dicto-comp you have written, check the dicto-comp in the book for any problems you had in writing it.

DICTO-COMP 1

Labor Day

Labor Day is one of the important holidays observed in all the states in the United States. This day honors American workers. It dates back to 1884, when a parade in New York City was held by several unions. They wanted to call attention to the contributions of workers to the American economy.

Labor Day is observed on the first Monday in September. The day not only honors American workers but it marks the end of most summer activities. Beaches, summer camps, and summer cottages are closed until the following year. Highways are crowded with returning vacationers, and parents look forward to the opening of school within the next few days.

Soon after Labor Day, businesses, department stores, theaters, schools, and other organizations begin their fall activities.

Arthur E. Albrecht, *Here and There,* "An All-American Holiday," September 1973.

DICTO-COMP 2

Thanksgiving

People in many parts of the world have offered thanks for their blessings, especially at harvest time. In the United States we have a day set apart for this purpose. The first Thanksgiving Day in this country was celebrated by the Pilgrims in the fall of 1621, a year after they landed in Massachusetts. The day was one of religious observation and feasting. Wild turkeys, geese, corn, and other foods were abundant. Friendly Indians joined that first day of celebration.

As time passed, Thanksgiving began to be celebrated in other parts of New England. However, there was no country-wide observance until 1863. This is when President Abraham Lincoln issued the first proclamation calling for a national day of thanksgiving. Since that time, each president has followed Lincoln's precedent. Thanksgiving is now celebrated on the fourth Thursday in November.

The day is marked by religious services, by family reunions, and by festive dinners. A traditional meal includes roast turkey, cranberry sauce, vegetables in season such as squash and sweet potatoes, fruits, nuts, and mince pie or pumpkin pie.

Arthur E. Albrecht, *Here and There,* "Did You Know That . . . ," November 1973.

UNIT 6

Telling Stories

GRAMMAR AND USAGE

Direct and indirect statements
Direct and indirect questions
Direct and indirect requests
Exclamations
Double objects in indirect statements and requests
Indirect statements, questions, requests (review)
Adjective structures after nouns

RHETORIC

Using an outline to guide the composition
Using an introduction and a conclusion
Using a transitional lead-in to the body of the composition

DISCUSSION AND COMPOSITION

1. DISCUSSION: Preliminary outline for the composition (prewriting stage)

Subject: (*Name of Story*—a fairy tale, folk tale, myth, or legend)

Outline (To Be Placed on the Board)	Discussion (Ideas, Grammar and Usage, Vocabulary, Elements of Composition Building)
	Note: The kind of story being discussed is a fairy tale. Students who want to write about a folk tale, myth, or legend can get information for a definition in Exercise 7 or can consult a dictionary.
Introduction: general statements, including a definition of fairy tale	*The process of telling a story* Definition of a fairy tale: a simple narrative that deals with supernatural beings and is told for the amusement of children
	A fairy tale often reflects the values, beliefs, and customs of a society.
	Kinds of persons, other creatures, and magical things in fairy tales: fairy godmother, wicked stepmother and stepsisters, kings and queens, princes and princesses, magicians fairies, witches, giants, dwarfs, mermaids, monsters, dragons enchanted animals, fish enchanted castles, forests magic lamps, rings, carpets, mirrors
The main topic	Themes in fairy tales: moral—often good wins out over evil takes place far away and long ago impossible tasks to perform magical spells—transformation of a person into an animal breaking an enchantment through kindness and love help is given the good person by a creature with magical powers third and youngest son succeeds where the first two fail third and youngest daughter is the most beautiful and the most virtuous

Outline (cont.)	Discussion (cont.)
	Themes in fairy tales (cont.):
	jealousy of older brothers and sisters wickedness of the stepmother (not the natural mother)
Transitional lead-in: connecting the general statements of the introduction to the *one* story you are going to talk about	One of my favorite fairy tales is . . .
	Let me tell you about the fairy tale I like best.
	A fairy tale I remember from my childhood is . . .
	A fairy tale that my mother (or grandmother) often told me is . . .
	A fairy tale that is very famous in my country is . . .
I. What happened in the story (use chronological order)	Opening sentence of first paragraph begins: Once upon a time . . . A long time ago . . . Many years ago . . .
	Direct speech:
II.	(1) use of quotation marks for the actual words spoken
	(2) Use of a comma to separate *said, told, asked,* etc. from the spoken words
	Indirect speech:
III.	(1) sequence of tenses (past verbs after a past main verb): The wicked fairy *told* the Queen that her daughter *would* die when the girl *was* fifteen.
IV.	(2) normal word order in indirect questions: direct: How *can* I go to the ball? indirect: Cinderella asked her fairy godmother how *she could* go to the ball.
V.	(3) use of *if* or *whether* to introduce indirect yes–no questions direct: Can I go to the ball? indirect: Cinderella asked her fairy godmother *whether* (or *if*) she could go to the ball.
VI.	(4) change in pronouns
	(5) *said to* becomes *told* in indirect speech.
VII.	
etc.	

Outline (cont.)	Discussion (cont.)
Conclusion: general statements	Can end with the end of the story, a natural conclusion (often, They lived happily ever after) or a general comment about good conquering evil (or any other moral)

2. COMPOSITION (to be done before or after the reinforcement practice)

A. ORGANIZING THE COMPOSITION

Before writing your composition, fill in the required information on this Organizational Worksheet. The Worksheet follows the preliminary outline used for the discussion. Guidance for writing each paragraph is given at the right side of this Worksheet. The pages of the discussion outline provide additional help for the composition.

You may use phrases on this Worksheet except where it calls for full sentences.

ORGANIZATIONAL WORKSHEET
(Preliminary notes for the composition)

Title of the composition _____
(Do not use quotation marks or a period for a title at the top of the page. Use initial capital letters for the first word of the title and for all other words except articles, short prepositions, and short conjunctions.)

Introduction: general statements

Opening sentence of paragraph _____

_____

_____

_____

_____

Put in a separate paragraph
Use the present tense for general statements
(For a definition of a folk tale, myth, or legend, see Exercise 7 or consult a dictionary.)

Include a definition of fairy tale (or other type of story)

_____

_____

_____

_____

_____

Transitional lead-in connecting the general statements of the introduction to the *one* story you are going to write about _____

New paragraph
The story can begin in this same paragraph

_____

_____

_____

_____

_____

I. What happened in the story

_____

_____

_____

II. _____

_____

_____

III. _____

_____

_____

IV. _____

_____

_____

V. _____

_____

_____

VI. _____

_____

_____

VII. _____

_____

_____

Use chronological order

Use the past tense for these past events

Separate these events into paragraphs at natural points; avoid long paragraphs

Use the correct forms of direct and indirect speech

etc. _____

_____

_____

(Not all the events need to be listed in this worksheet.)

Conclusion: general statements

_____

_____

_____

_____

_____

_____

(may be omitted if the end of the story provides a natural conclusion)

New paragraph

Use the present tense for general statements

B. WRITING THE COMPOSITION

Write the composition based on your notes on the Organizational Worksheet. Be careful of your paragraphing. Use separate paragraphs for your introduction and your conclusion. (Long paragraphs may be broken in two at appropriate places, but single-sentence paragraphs should be avoided.)

Use 8½ - by 11-inch white paper, with lines for a handwritten composition and without lines for a typed composition. Double-space a typewritten composition, and skip lines on a handwritten one. Write on the front of the paper only, and leave wide margins on *both the left and the right sides* of the paper. Indent the beginning of each paragraph.

Look over your composition carefully before you hand it in.

C. CORRECTING OR REWRITING THE COMPOSITION

When your teacher returns your composition, it will be marked with the symbols from the correction chart on page 257. Make the necessary corrections on the composition and hand it back to your teacher.

Place the corrections on the correction page, and note down the rule that is involved.

If you have made many mistakes, or if you wish to make some additions to your composition, you may need to write it again. In rewriting the composition, do not make extensive changes or additions without consulting your teacher.

(For more help with your problems in writing, consult the Index of Usage and Rhetoric in *Writer's Companion*. The items in this index are arranged in the same alphabetical order as in the correction chart.)

CORRECTION PAGE

Use this page to write down the correction of any mistakes you have made in your composition on a fairy tale (or folk tale, legend, or myth). Include enough of the words surrounding the corrected part to make the meaning clear. (Do not copy down the mistake itself.) If possible, write down the rule that covers the correction you have made.

Review these corrections from time to time in order to avoid making the same mistakes again.

Corrections	Rule
	(See the correction chart if necessary)

REINFORCEMENT PRACTICE

EXERCISE 1: Direct and Indirect Statements

Statements in direct speech become noun clause objects in indirect speech.

DIRECT STATEMENT: The Beast said to (or told) Beauty, "I love you."

INDIRECT STATEMENT: The Beast told Beauty that he loved her.
(The word *that* may be omitted in indirect speech.)
(*Say* may be used without an object. *Tell* requires an object.)

Note these changes from direct to indirect speech:

The past main verb (*told*) requires a past verb (*loved*) in the indirect statement. (sequence of tenses)

Told replaces *said to* in indirect speech.

The pronouns change in indirect speech: *I* becomes *he, you* becomes *her.*

There is no comma before the indirect statement.

A. Rewrite the sentences, changing the quoted statements to indirect speech.

1. The fairy godmother said to Cinderella, "You're also going to go to the ball."

    The fairy godmother told Cinderella that she was also going to go to the ball.

2. Cinderella said to her stepsisters, "I will help you get ready for the ball."

3. Rumpelstiltskin said to the maiden, "I'll spin the gold if you'll give me your first-born child."

4. The Beast said to Beauty, "You forgot your promise, and so I decided to die, for I could not live without you."

5. Beauty replied, "I do not wish you to die, but to live to become my husband."

6. The fairy said to Beauty, "You have chosen well, and you have your reward."

7. Bluebeard said to his wife, "You will die at once because you have disobeyed me."

8. Sleeping Beauty said to the prince, "I have waited for you for a long time."

B. Change the indirect statements to direct speech. Use a comma after *said,* and use the correct form of the pronouns and verbs.

1. The weavers said that they could weave the finest cloth in the world.

   The weavers said, "We can weave the finest cloth in the world."

2. They said that clothes made of this cloth were invisible to a stupid person.

3. The emperor said that if he wore such clothes he could distinguish the clever people from the stupid.

4. The emperor said that he had to have this cloth woven for him immediately.

5. The people who saw the emperor in the procession said that he looked marvelous in his new clothes.

6. A little child said that the emperor had nothing on at all.

7. All the people finally said that the emperor was not wearing any clothes at all.

EXERCISE 2: Direct and Indirect Questions

Questions in direct speech become noun clause objects in indirect speech.

Yes-No Question

DIRECT: Cinderella asked, "Can I go to the ball?"

INDIRECT: Cinderella asked *whether}* / *if}* she could go to the ball.

Wh- Question

DIRECT: Cinderella asked, "How can I go to the ball?"

INDIRECT: Cinderella asked *how* she could go to the ball.

Note these changes from direct to indirect questions:

The sentence ends with a period, not a question mark (unless the whole sentence is a question).

The past main verb (*asked*) requires a past verb (*could*) in the indirect question. (sequence of tenses)

Whether or *if* introduces a noun clause object made from the yes–no question.

The pronouns in the indirect questions are changed—*I* becomes *she*

Normal subject–verb order is used in the indirect questions.

No comma sets off the indirect question from the word of asking.

A. Rewrite the sentences, changing the quoted questions to indirect speech. Be careful of the punctuation and the subject–verb order. Use the correct form of the pronouns and the verbs.

1. Her stepsisters asked Cinderella mockingly, "Do you want to go to the ball?"

   Her stepsisters asked Cinderella mockingly whether (or if) she wanted to go to the ball.

2. Cinderella asked her stepsisters, "Did you enjoy yourselves at the ball?"

3. The genie of the lamp asked Aladdin, "What is your wish?"[1]

4. Bluebeard asked his wife, "Why is there blood on the key?"

5. The two thieves asked the emperor, "Isn't it a beautiful piece of cloth?"

6. The emperor asked, "Doesn't my suit fit me marvelously?"

7. A little child who was watching the procession asked, "Why isn't the emperor wearing any clothes?"

8. At the ball, all the people asked, "Who is that beautiful girl?"[1]

B. Rewrite the sentences, changing the indirect questions to direct questions.

1. The weavers asked the prime minister if he did not admire the exquisite patterns and the beautiful colors.

   The weavers asked the prime minister, "Don't you admire the exquisite patterns and the beautiful colors?"

2. The emperor asked himself whether he was unfit to be the emperor because he could not see the clothes.

3. Aladdin asked the magician why they had come to the cave.

4. The Sultan asked his minister whether he had ever seen such precious jewels.

5. Rumpelstiltskin asked the princess what his name was.

6. The princess asked the old lady what she was doing at the spinning wheel.

7. Bluebeard asked his wife where the key was.

8. The sultan asked what had become of Aladdin's palace.

---

[1] In this sentence, the verb is placed at the *end* of the indirect question.

EXERCISE 3: Direct and Indirect Requests

Requests in direct speech often become infinitive phrase objects in indirect speech.

DIRECT REQUEST:	Beauty asked (or, told) her father, "Bring me a red rose when you return from your voyage."
INDIRECT REQUEST:	Beauty asked (or, told) her father to bring her a red rose when he returned from his voyage.
DIRECT REQUEST (negative):	Bluebeard said to (or told) his wife, "Don't open the door to one room."
INDIRECT REQUEST (negative):	Bluebeard asked (or, told) his wife not to open the door to one room.

Note these changes from direct to indirect requests:

The verb that begins the request (*bring*) becomes an infinitive (*to bring*).

The negative request (*don't open*) becomes the negative infinitive (*not to open*).

The pronoun *me* becomes *her*.

Common verbs used in making requests are *request, ask, tell* (= *say to*). Stronger verbs are *beg, entreat, beseech, implore, urge, warn*.

In formal usage, these verbs can also be followed by *that* clauses.

Beauty asked that her father bring her a red rose.

(See Exercise 8 in Unit 4 for practice with such clauses.)

Rewrite the sentences, changing the quoted requests to indirect speech with infinitives.

1. Cinderella's fairy godmother said to her, "Run into the garden and get a pumpkin."

   Cinderella's fairy godmother told her to run into the garden and get a pumpkin.

2. Her fairy godmother warned Cinderella, "Do not stay out after midnight."

3. Cinderella begged the messenger, "Let me try on the slipper."

4. The Moroccan magician urged Aladdin, "Put on my magic ring and go into the cave."

5. The magician warned Aladdin, "Do not touch any of the walls of the cave or you will die."

6. The bear said to Snow White and Rose Red, "Let me come with you and don't be afraid."

7. The weavers told the emperor, "Take off your clothes and try on the new clothes."

EXERCISE 4: Exclamations

Exclamations begin with *what* or *how*.

		Exclamatory Phrase		Balance of Sentence
what	*with nouns*			
	singular (countable)	What a	magnificent *castle* . .	this is.
	singular (noncountable)	What	exquisite *food*	this is.
	plural	What	luxurious *things*	this castle has.
how	*with adjectives and adverbs*			
	adjective	How	*kind*	the owner of the castle is.
	adverb	How	*mysteriously*	all the food has appeared.

An exclamation may end with a period or an exclamation mark.

Use the information given below to make exclamations. Begin the exclamation with *what, what a,* or *how.* Use normal subject-verb order after the exclamatory phrase.

1. When Little Red Riding Hood saw her "grandmother," she exclaimed:
   a. You have big teeth

   What big teeth you have. (or!)

   b. Your ears are long

   How long your ears are. (or!)

   c. You have big legs
   d. You are behaving strangely

2. When Snow White came to the dwarfs' cottage, she exclaimed:
   a. This is a clean cottage
   b. The beds look small

    c. This food tastes good
    d. I am tired and sleepy
    e. I have gone very far

3. When the prince saw Snow White, he exclaimed:
    a. I am lucky to see such a beautiful girl
    b. She is beautiful
    c. She is a beautiful girl
    d. She has a beautiful face

4. The thieves exclaimed to the emperor:
    a. It is a beautiful piece of cloth
    b. This is fine cloth
    c. The cloth is a beautiful color
    d. The clothes fit well
    e. Your new clothes are magnificent

EXERCISE 5: Double Objects in Indirect Statements and Requests

Two kinds of information may appear after a verb of speaking: (1) the person who is addressed, and (2) what is said. The preposition *to* may appear before the person addressed. What is said may begin with *that* or *an infinitive.*

	Person Addressed	What is Said
The magician explained	*to* Aladdin	*that* the ring had great powers.
The magician told	Aladdin	*that* the ring had great powers.
The magician urged	Aladdin	*to go* into the cave.

(Informally, the word *that* may be omitted from sentences like the above.)

In the sentences that follow, the words in parentheses contain information about the person who is addressed and what is said. Use this information to construct full sentences *in indirect speech.* Do not change the order of the words. (For some sentences, two choices are possible.) Keep in mind that after verbs like *suggest, ask* (= request), and *urge, that* clauses require the simple form of the verb (the subjunctive).

  1. Cinderella promised (her fairy godmother—she, return, home, midnight). (two possibilities)

    Cinderella promised her fairy godmother that she would return home at midnight.
    Cinderella promised her fairy godmother to return home at midnight.

2. The magician suggested (princess—give, him, her old lamp, for, new one).

3. Her fairy godmother told (Cinderella—return, home, midnight).

4. Bluebeard told (his wife—die, at once, because, she, disobey, him).

5. Cinderella begged (the messenger—let, her, try on, shoe).

6. The old woman explained (Beauty—spinning wheel, make, thread).

7. Bluebeard warned (wife—not open, door).

8. The magician urged (Aladdin—go, into, cave). (two possibilities)

9. The mirror told (queen—Snow White, be, most beautiful girl, of all).

10. Aladdin asked (magician—help, him, get out, cave). (two possibilities)

EXERCISE 6: Indirect Statements, Questions, Requests (Review)

Rewrite the sentences, changing the quoted statements, questions, or requests to indirect speech. Observe the sequence of tenses. Use the simple form of the verb in *that* clauses after verbs like *ask* (= request), *request, suggest, urge, beg*.

1. The magician said to Aladdin, "The ring will preserve you from all danger."

    The magician told Aladdin that the ring would preserve him from all danger.

2. Aladdin asked his uncle, "Help me get out of the cave."

    Aladdin asked his uncle to help him get out of the cave.
    OR
    Aladdin asked that his uncle help him get out of the cave.

3. Aladdin's mother urged him, "Sell the enchanted lamp right away."

4. The Moroccan magician asked the princess, "Do you have any old lamps to exchange for new ones?"

5. Cinderella's fairy godmother implored her, "Do not stay at the ball past midnight."

6. Her stepsisters asked Cinderella, "Help us dress for the ball."

7. The prince told his messengers, "Find the girl who wore the glass slipper."

8. The stepmother said to Hansel and Gretel's father, "There's not enough food for everyone."

9. In "The Water of Life," each brother met a dwarf who asked, "Where are you going?"

10. The two elder brothers answered rudely, "It's none of your business."

11. Rumpelstiltskin said to the princess, "If you guess my name in three days, you may keep your child."

12. The queen asked the magic mirror, "Who is the most beautiful woman?"

13. Beauty begged her father, "Bring me back only one red rose."

EXERCISE 7: Adjective Structures After Nouns

A noun may be modified by several grammatical structures that follow it. This kind of modification is especially common in _definitions_.

> _Definition:_   A fairy tale is a simple narrative of folk origin dealing with supernatural beings which is told for the amusement of children.

The adjective structures that modify the noun _a simple narrative_ are:

of folk origin	_prepositional phrase_
	begins with a preposition
dealing with supernatural beings	_participial phrase_
	begins with an -_ing_ or -_ed_ participle
which is told for the amusement of children	_adjective clause_
	begins with the pronoun _which, that,_ or _who_

The adjective structures usually follow the order given above: prepositional phrase, then participial phrase, then adjective clause.

Working with a partner, combine each group of sentences into one sentence that gives a definition of a particular kind of story. Use the structures given at the right of each group. (Some definitions will have only two of these structures, and others will have two of the same structure that will need to be joined by _and._)

1. A folk tale is:
Noun: _a story_

It is about ordinary people.	_prepositional phrase_
It forms part of an oral tradition.	_participial phrase_ (use a comma at the beginning of the phrase)
It reveals the customs and beliefs of a particular group of people.	_participial phrase_ (connect with _and_)

> _Sentence:_   A folk tale is a story about ordinary people, forming part of an oral tradition and revealing the customs and beliefs of a particular group of people.

2. A fable is:

Noun: *a fictitious narrative*

It is intended to teach some moral truth.
participial phrase

In a fable animals act like human be-ings.
adjective clause
(begin the clause with *in which*)

3. A legend is:

Noun: *an oral narrative*

It is about some wonderful event.
prepositional phrase

It has been handed down for genera-tions among a people.[2]
participial phrase
(use a comma at the beginning of the phrase)

It is popularly believed to have a histor-ical basis.
participial phrase (connect with *and*)

4. A myth is:

Noun: *a traditional story*

It is about gods and heroes.
prepositional phrase

It serves to explain some natural phenomenon, the origin of man, or the customs and institutions of a people.[2]
participial phrase (use a *comma* at the beginning of the phrase)

5. An epic is:

Noun: *a long narrative poem*

It is in very dignified style.
prepositional phrase

It celebrates episodes of a people's[2] heroic tradition.
participial phrase

EXERCISE 8: Word Forms

Use the correct form of the word in parentheses, and complete the unfinished words.

(If you need help with the signals that tell whether a noun, verb, adjective, or adverbial form is needed, refer to *Writer's Companion,* Unit 2, in the Grammar Review and Practice section.)

1. Fairy tales are (imagine) <u>*imaginary* (also *imaginative*)</u> stories dealing with magic

   and the supernatur-_____<u>al</u>_____.

2. The words "Once upon a time" are often (find) _____ at the

   (begin) _____ of fairy tales.

---

[2] *A people* is used here in the singular to refer to a particular group of persons—racial, national, or religious. Only in this sense does the word have the plural, *peoples.*

3. Fairies are (diminu-_____ creatures with magic powers.
   They are (rare-_____ (harm) _____, but
   some of them are (mischief) _____.

4. In some fairy tales, the hero (final) _____ wins the
   (hero-_____, either through his great (strong) _____
   or his (clever) _____, or through the (assist) _____
   of magical powers.

5. We expect the hero in a fairy tale to be (attract) _____ in (appear) _____. He often marries a (love) _____
   and (virtue) _____ (prince-_____.

6. In some fairy tales, troubles are (cause-_____ by the
   (jealous) _____ of (wick-_____ sisters or
   brothers.

7. Snow White and the Seven Dwarfs is a (favor) _____ movie of
   many people both old and young.

8. Snow White had great (pure) _____ and (innocent) _____
   _____.

9. Cinderella was so (beauty) _____ that the prince fell in love
   with her (immediate) _____.

10. Hansel and Gretel were (abandon-_____ in the woods by their
    father and their stepmother.

11. Bluebeard killed many of his wives because of their (disobey) _____
    _____. They all opened a door which was (forbid-_____ to
    them.

12. Aladdin, the lazy son of a (China) _____ tailor, was enticed by
    a (magic-_____ from Morocco to enter a cave and obtain a
    lamp for him.

EXERCISE 9: Sentence Review

Make full sentences from the word groups below. Make all the verbs *past* except those in direct speech. Make whatever changes or additions are needed, but do not change the word order. Watch the punctuation.

1. Beast / tell / Beauty / he / love / her.

   The beast told Beauty (that) he loved her.

2. Cinderella / say / her stepsisters / "I / help / you / get ready / ball."

3. Fairy godmother / tell / Cinderella / she / also / be going / ball.

4. Weavers / say / they / can / weave / finest / cloth / world.

5. All / people / finally / say / emperor / not wear / clothes / at all.

6. Bluebeard / ask / his wife / "Why / blood / on / key?"

7. Genie / ask / Aladdin / "What / your / wish?"

8. Sultan / ask / his minister / he / ever / see / such / precious / jewels.

9. Aladdin / ask / magician / why / they / come / to cave.

10. Bluebeard / say / wife / "Don't / open / door / one room."

11. Weavers / tell / emperor / "Take off / your clothes / and try on / new clothes."

12. When / prince / see / Snow White / he / exclaim / "beautiful / girl / she / is!"

13. Aladdin / ask / his uncle / "Help / me / get out / cave."

14. Queen / ask / magic mirror / "Who / most / beautiful / woman?"

EXTRA SPEAKING AND WRITING PRACTICE

EXERCISE 10: Composition: Cinderella

Your teacher will read this story about Cinderella aloud to you once or twice. You may look at the story during this reading if your teacher wishes you to do so.

Then on the next page you will be asked to make questions that will help you reconstruct the story without looking at its written form.

A long time ago there lived a little girl called Cinderella. The name of the girl comes from *cinders,* meaning ashes from the fire. Cinderella's wicked stepmother made her do all the housework. The only place where the girl could stay was near the kitchen fire.

One day the king announced that there would be a great ball. Cinderella helped her stepsisters dress for the ball. When she was alone by the fire she began to cry. Just then her fairy godmother appeared. She gave Cinderella a beautiful gown so she could go to the ball. She changed some animals and vegetables into a coach and horses for Cinderella. She told the girl she had to be back by midnight. At that time everything would change back to what it was before.

At the ball, the prince was charmed by Cinderella's beauty and splendor. But at a quarter to twelve, Cinderella rushed away. The next night of the ball, however, Cinderella forgot the time. When the clock struck twelve, she ran away quickly, but dropped one of the glass slippers she was wearing.

The prince, who had fallen in love with Cinderella, sent messengers throughout the kingdom to find the girl whom the glass slipper would fit. A messenger tried the shoe on Cinderella's foot and it fit. She then produced the other shoe. After this the prince married Cinderella and they lived happily ever after.

A. Complete the questions below, which are based on the story your teacher has just read to you. Do *not* look at the original story. Use the past tense for past events.

(For this part of the exercise, disregard the information under Connectives.)

Connectives
(for Exercise B only)

When	Cinderella live ?	
What	her name	mean ? (Use present tense for a general statement)
What	her wicked stepmother	make her do ?
Where	only place she	could stay ?

133

¶ One day   What   king   announce ?

                   How   Cinderella   help   her stepsisters ?

                   When   she   begin   cry ?

Just then   Who   appear ?

⎡ What   she   give   Cinderella ?

⎣ Why   she   do   this ? (Use *so* in your answer for
                                   Exercise B)

                   What   she   change   into   coach,
                   horses   for Cinderella ?

                   What   the warning   her fairy godmother
                   give   Cinderella ?

¶ At the ball,   How   Prince   feel   about   Cinderella's
                   beauty, splendor ?

But   When   Cinderella   rush away ?

The next night   What   Cinderella   forget ?
of the ball, however,
                   ⎡ At what time   she   run away   quickly ?

But. . . . . ⎣ What   she   drop ?

                   ⎡ Who   fall in love   Cinderella ? (use the past perfect
                                                           tense)

                   ⎢ Who   he   send   throughout   kingdom ?

                   ⎣ Why   he   send out   they ?

¶   ⎡ Who   try   shoe   Cinderella's foot ?

                   ⎣ What   happen ?

Then. . . . . What   Cinderella   produce ?

After this   ⎡ Who   marry   Cinderella ?

                   ⎣ How   they   live ?

B. Working with a partner, answer the questions in A. (Do not look at the original story.) Then write the story of Cinderella by joining these answers with the connectives listed in the Connectives column.

Combine into one sentence the answers to those questions that are linked together with brackets. Start new paragraphs where you see the symbol ¶.

LISTENING–WRITING PRACTICE

EXERCISE 11: Paragraphs for Dictation

Your teacher will dictate each paragraph three times. The first time is for listening only. The second time is for writing, and the third time is for checking what you have written.

Immediately after you give your teacher the dictation you have written, check the dictation in the book for any problems you had in writing it.

DICTATION 1

Although a fairy tale is told for the amusement of children, it usually reflects the customs, beliefs, and values of a society. It may deal with supernatural beings such as fairies, witches, and dragons. There may be enchanted forests, castles, and animals in the story. Human beings may have magic powers, superhuman strength, or great wisdom. The good characters are beautiful or handsome, and their goodness defeats the wickedness of the evil characters. The language in a fairy tale is usually old-fashioned. Often the story begins with "Once upon a time" and ends with "They lived happily ever after."

DICTATION 2

The early American movies of the twenties and thirties had many elements of a fairy tale. It was always clear which characters were the "good guys" and which were the "bad guys." The hero was very handsome—his jaw was square and his face was clean-shaven. The villain was slightly foreign-looking, often with a mustache (in the days when most American men didn't wear mustaches). As in a fairy tale, the wicked villain created a series of obstacles which the hero had to overcome. Of course the hero finally defeated the villain and won the beautiful heroine. The movie ended with the final embrace of the hero and the heroine, which suggested the fairy-tale ending—that they would live happily ever after.

EXERCISE 12: Dicto-comps

Take notes as your teacher reads each of these dicto-comps to you several times. Then reconstruct the dicto-comp from your notes. The dicto-comp does not need to be written exactly as you heard it, but it should be grammatically correct.

Before you write the dicto-comp, your teacher may ask the class to get together in groups to check with each other on what you heard.

Immediately after you give your teacher the dicto-comp you have written, check the dicto-comp in the book for any problems you had in writing it.

DICTO-COMP 1

Little Red Riding Hood

One day a pretty little girl called Red Riding Hood was going through the woods to take some cake to her grandmother. On the way she met a wolf, who asked her where she was going. "To my grandmother's house," she said. "It is the first in the village over there."

The wolf ran ahead by a shorter road and reached the grandmother's house first. He knocked on the door.

"Who's there?" asked the grandmother.

"It's your granddaughter, Red Riding Hood," said the wolf, disguising his voice.

She told him to come in. As soon as he was inside, he quickly ate her up.

Soon Red Riding Hood came to her grandmother's house and entered. She was surprised at the way her grandmother looked.

"Grandmother, dear," she exclaimed, "what big arms you have!"

"The better to embrace you, my child."

"Grandmother, dear, what big legs you have!"

"The better to run with, my child!"

"Grandmother, dear, what big ears you have!"

"The better to hear you with, my child!"

"Grandmother, dear, what big eyes you have!"

"The better to see you with, my child."

"Grandmother, dear, what big teeth you have!"

"The better to eat you with!"

And the wicked wolf leaped upon Little Red Riding Hood and was ready to eat her up. Just then a hunter came into the house and killed the wolf. He cut open the wolf's stomach and rescued the grandmother.

DICTO-COMP 2

Snow White and the Seven Dwarfs

Once upon a time there was a queen who had a magic mirror. She used to stand in front of it and say,

"Mirror, mirror on the wall
Who is the fairest one of all?"

And the mirror would answer, "You are the fairest of them all."

When her stepdaughter, Snow White, was seven years old, the queen asked the mirror the same question. But this time the mirror said,

"Queen, you are very fair, it's true,
But Snow White is now fairer than you."

The queen was very jealous and decided to get rid of Snow White. She asked a hunter to take Snow White into the woods and kill the girl. But when they were in the woods, the hunter took pity on her and left her there.

The frightened girl ran through the woods until she came to a small house. In it she found a table set for seven. She took a little food and drink from each plate and cup and then went to sleep in one of the beds.

When the seven dwarfs who lived in the house came home, they discovered Snow White asleep. In the morning they asked if she would stay and keep house for them. She consented gladly.

Many years later, when the queen found out that Snow White was still alive in the woods, she decided to again try to kill the girl. The queen came to the girl's house as an old lady and offered her an apple. Snow White took one bite and fell to the earth as dead. When the dwarfs returned they could not revive Snow White. They were very sad and put her in a glass coffin in the mountain, where they could look at her.

One day the king's son was riding in the mountains and saw the coffin. He begged so long for the girl in the coffin that the dwarfs consented to let him have her.

While the king's servants were carrying the coffin over their shoulders, they stumbled over a bush. The shaking of the coffin made the bit of poisoned apple fall out of Snow White's mouth. She awoke, to the great joy of the prince. They were married soon after and lived happily ever after.

Superstitious Beliefs

GRAMMAR AND USAGE

Cause–result with *if* clauses
Cause–result with *if* clauses or gerund phrases
Unreal conditions
Conjunctive adverbs: *therefore, however, otherwise*
Articles: definite (*the*) and indefinite (*a, an*)
most, most of the, the most

RHETORIC

Using an outline to guide the composition
Using an introduction and a conclusion
Using a transitional lead-in to the body of the composition
Using transitions between paragraphs

DISCUSSION AND COMPOSITION

1. DISCUSSION: Preliminary outline for the composition (prewriting stage)

Subject: *Superstitious Beliefs in* (name of your country)

Outline (To Be Placed on the Board)	Discussion (Ideas, Grammar and Usage, Vocabulary, Elements of Composition Building)
Introduction: general statements, including a definition of superstition	Definition of superstition: an unreasonable belief that supernatural forces can cause good or bad things to happen Results from ignorance and fear of the unknown Often involves magic and witchcraft May have a religious origin
Transitional lead-in to the kinds of superstitions that will be discussed	Final sentence of introductory paragraph may mark a transition to the main points of the composition: Superstitions are often attached to numbers, animals and birds, and things
I. Superstitions about numbers	Possible opening sentences and connectives within the paragraph: There are several superstitions about numbers in my country. For example, we have one about number 13.... Another one is about .... Or for the second sentence: The most common one concerns (or, is about) number 13. luck, lucky: Number 13 will bring bad *luck.* Number 13 is *unlucky.* Number 13 is an *unlucky* number.
II. Superstitions about animals and birds (may include insects)	Possible opening sentence of paragraph and connectives within the paragraph: We also have a few (some, many) superstitions about animals and birds. One is about the owl.... Another (or, a second) concerns ....

Outline (cont.)	Discussion (cont.)

II. Superstitions about animals and birds (cont.)	Vocabulary
	  omen, sign, symbol(ize)
	  a good luck (or, a lucky) charm
	  the cry of an owl
	  the cry of a crow, raven (black birds)
	  a rabbit's foot
	  a black cat crossing your path
	
	In sentences with *if:* present tense in the *if* clause, future with the main clause
	  If you *hear* the cry of an owl (or, a crow), a death *will occur* in the family.

III. Superstitions about things	Possible opening sentence of paragraph:
	  We have still other superstitions about (or, concerning) things.
	
	Coherence may be established through parallel *if* clauses beginning sentences.
	
	If you: break a mirror
	          walk under a ladder
	          find a four-leaf clover
	          spill salt on the table
	          light three cigarettes with one match
	          open an umbrella in the house
	          put a horseshoe over your door

Conclusion: general statements	People who still believe in these superstitions:
	  mostly older, less educated people
	  people in the country
	Your own belief

2. COMPOSITION (to be done before or after the reinforcement practice)

A. ORGANIZING THE COMPOSITION

Before writing your composition, fill in the required information on this Organizational Worksheet. The Worksheet follows the preliminary outline used for the discussion. Guidance for writing each paragraph is given at the right side of this Worksheet. The pages of the discussion outline provide additional help for the composition.

You may use phrases on this Worksheet except where it calls for full sentences.

ORGANIZATIONAL WORKSHEET
(Preliminary notes for the composition)

Title of the composition _____
(Do not use quotation marks or a period for a title at the top of the page. Use initial capital letters for the first word of the title and for all other words except articles, short prepositions, and short conjunctions.)

Introduction: general statements, including a definition of superstition

Opening sentence of paragraph _____

_____

_____

_____

Put in a separate paragraph

Use the present tense for the general statements in this paragraph and in the rest of the composition

Definition of superstition

_____

_____

_____

_____

_____

Transitional lead-in connecting the general statements of the introduction to the kinds of superstitions that will be discussed

May be included at the end of the introductory paragraph

Full sentence _____

_____

_____

_____

_____

I. Superstitions about numbers

Opening sentence of paragraph _____

_____

_____

_____

New paragraph

Mention the subject *numbers*

Examples: _____

_____

_____

_____

Expressions for examples:
for example, for instance
or, one example is . . .
another example is . . .

II. Superstitions about animals and birds
Opening sentence of paragraph _____

_____

_____

New paragraph
Mention the subject *animals*
and *birds* (or only one of these)

Examples: _____

_____

_____

_____

III. Superstitions about things
Opening sentence of paragraph _____

_____

_____

New paragraph

Mention the subject *things*

Examples: _____

_____

_____

_____

Conclusion: general statements

_____

_____

_____

New paragraph

B. WRITING THE COMPOSITION

Write the composition based on your notes on the Organizational
Worksheet. Be careful of your paragraphing. Use separate paragraphs for
your introduction and your conclusion. (Long paragraphs may be broken in
two at appropriate places, but single-sentence paragraphs should be avoided.)

Use 8½- by 11-inch white paper, with lines for a handwritten composition and without lines for a typed composition. Double-space a typewritten

composition, and skip lines on a handwritten one. Write on the front of the paper only, and leave wide margins on *both the left and the right sides* of the paper. Indent the beginning of each paragraph.

Look over your composition carefully before you hand it in.

C. CORRECTING OR REWRITING THE COMPOSITION

When your teacher returns your composition, it will be marked with the symbols from the correction chart on page 257. Make the necesssary corrections on the composition and hand it back to your teacher.

Place the corrections on the correction page, and note down the rule that is involved.

If you have made many mistakes, or if you wish to make some additions to your composition, you may need to write it again. In rewriting the composition, do not make extensive changes or additions without consulting your teacher.

(For more help with your problems in writing, consult the Index of Usage and Rhetoric in *Writer's Companion*. The items in this index are arranged in the same alphabetical order as in the correction chart.)

CORRECTION PAGE

Use this page to write down the correction of any mistakes you have made in your composition on "Superstitious Beliefs in (*name of your country*)." Include enough of the words surrounding the corrected part to make the meaning clear. (Do not copy down the mistake itself.) If possible, write down the rule that covers the correction you have made.

Review these corrections from time to time in order to avoid making the same mistakes again.

Corrections	Rule
	(See the correction chart if necessary)

REINFORCEMENT PRACTICE

EXERCISE 1: Cause-Result with *if* Clauses

A conditional *if* clause often represents a cause. The rest of the sentence (the main clause) is the result.

> CAUSE: If you *hear* the cry of an owl or a raven,
> RESULT: there *will be* a death in the family. (main clause)

The verb in the *if* clause is in the *present tense;* the verb in the main clause is in the *future tense* with *will.* [1]

Combine each group of words about superstitions so that the cause is placed in an *if* clause. Use the present tense in the *if* clause and the future tense with *will* in the main clause.

1. Cause: a bridesmaid (catch) the bridal bouquet
   Result: she (be) married herself soon

   If a bridesmaid catches the bridal bouquet, she will be married herself soon.

2. Result: a young girl (be) an old maid
   Cause: she take the last piece of bread or cake

   A young girl will be an old maid if she takes the last piece of bread or cake. (no comma before the final *if* clause)

3. Cause: someone (get) a gift of a knife
   Result: he (avoid) bad luck by giving a coin in exchange

4. Cause: a woman (want) to have a baby boy
   Result: she (wear) blue colors during her pregnancy

5. Result: a young couple (not get) married in May
   Cause: they (want) to have a successful marriage

6. Result: a man (carry) his bride over the doorstep of their new home
   Cause: he (want) to avoid the evil spirits that are gathered outside every threshold

7. Cause: your left hand (itch)
   Result: you (receive) money

8. Result: you (give away) money
   Cause: your right hand (itch)

---

[1] *Be going to* can also be used in the main clause: If you hear the cry of an owl or a raven, there is *going to be* a death in the family.

9. Cause: you (wear) green
    Result: your relatives soon (wear) black

10. Cause: a bat (fly) low and (touch) you
     Result: some misfortune (happen) to you

EXERCISE 2: Cause–Result with *if* Clauses or Gerund Phrases

A cause may be expressed not only in a conditional *if* clause, but in a gerund phrase.

	Cause	*Result*
1. A conditional *if* clause	*If you break a mirror,*	you will have seven years' bad luck.
2. A gerund phrase	*Breaking a mirror*	will bring you seven years' bad luck.

Combine the word groups so that the *cause* is expressed once in an *if* clause and once in a gerund phrase.

1. Cause: carry a rabbit's foot
    Result: good luck

    IF CLAUSE: *If you carry a rabbit's foot, you will have good luck.*

    GERUND PHRASE: *Carrying a rabbit's foot will bring you good luck.*

2. Cause: walk under a ladder
    Result: bad luck

3. Cause: light three cigarettes on one match
    Result: bad luck

4. Cause: spill salt on the table
    Result: bad luck

5. Cause: find a four-leaf clover
    Result: good luck

6. Cause: find a penny
    Result: good luck all day

7. Cause: a black cat crosses your path
    Result: bad luck
         (for the gerund phrase, begin with: *A black cat's . . .*)

8. Cause: open an umbrella in the house
    Result: bad luck

9. Cause: break off the bigger end of the wishbone
    Result: good luck because your wish will be granted

EXERCISE 3: Unreal Conditions

The form of verbs in a conditional sentence can indicate that the fact stated in the sentence is not real. Such verb forms may refer to present or past time.

Present Time		*Verb Forms*
(Real fact:	No one is sneezing now.)	
Unreal fact:	If someone *sneezed,*	past tense
	I *would say,* "God bless you."	auxiliary *would*
Past Time		
(Real fact:	No one sneezed.)	
Unreal fact:	If someone *had sneezed,*	past perfect tense
	I *would have said,* "God	auxiliary *would have*
	bless you."	

A. Use the correct forms of the verbs to make conditions about facts that are unreal at the present time.

1. If I (spill) _____*spilled*_____ salt on the table, I (throw) ___*would throw*___
some over my left shoulder to avoid bad luck.

2. If I (give) _____ a woman a present of a purse, I (put) _____
_____ a good luck penny in the purse.

3. If a black cat (try) _____ to cross my path, I (get) _____
_____ out of the way fast.

4. If I (decide) _____ to get married, I (not have) _____
_____ the wedding on Friday the thirteenth.

5. If my sister (get) _____ married, at the wedding she (wear)
_____ "something old, something new, something borrowed, and something blue."

6. If a friend (give) _____ me a present of a knife, I (give) _____

_____ him a coin to avoid cutting our friendship.

7. If someone (step) _____ between me and another person as

we were walking together, I (say) _____ "bread and butter."

B. Use the correct forms of the verbs in A to make conditions about facts that were unreal in the past time.

> **1.** *If I **had spilled** salt on the table, I **would have thrown** some over my left shoulder to avoid bad luck.*

EXERCISE 4: Conjunctive Adverbs: *therefore, however, otherwise*

A sentence with *therefore, however,* or *otherwise* can be joined to the preceding sentence by a semicolon.

> A friend gave me a present of a knife; therefore(,) I gave him a coin to avoid cutting our friendship.

A comma after a word like *therefore* depends on whether the writer would pause at that point in speaking.

Words like *therefore* may also appear in other positions in the second part of the combined sentence.

> A friend gave me a present of a knife; I therefore gave him a coin to avoid cutting our friendship.

Replace the words in italics with *therefore, however,* or *otherwise,* and join the sentences with a semicolon. See if these words can go in other positions than the beginning of the second part of each sentence. However, make sure that the semicolon remains where the period was.

1. He spilled some salt on the table. *For this reason* he will have bad luck.

> *He spilled some salt on the table;* **therefore**(,) *he will have bad luck.* AND . . . *; he will* **therefore** *have bad luck.*

2. He spilled some salt on the table. *But* if he spills salt over his left shoulder, he can avoid bad luck.

> *He spilled some salt on the table;* **however,** *if he spills salt over his left shoulder, he can avoid bad luck.*
> AND . . . *; if he spills salt over his left shoulder,* **however,** *he can avoid bad luck.*

3. He must spill salt over his left shoulder. *If he doesn't,* he'll have bad luck.

> *He must spill salt over his left shoulder;* **otherwise**(,) *he'll have bad luck.*
> AND . . . *; he'll have bad luck* **otherwise.**

4. I put a horseshoe over my door. *As a result of this,* I expect to have good luck.

5. You mustn't walk under a ladder. *If you do,* some misfortune will befall you.

6. They live on the thirteenth floor. *In spite of this,* they don't expect any bad luck.

7. Don't let a black cat cross your path. *If you do,* you'll have bad luck.

8. I broke off the bigger end of the wishbone. *For this reason,* my wish will be granted.

9. People believe that a crow is a sign of death. *But* I think this belief is only a superstition.

10. He always carries a rabbit's foot with him. *For this reason,* he thinks he can avoid bad luck.

11. You mustn't open an umbrella in the house. *If you do,* something bad will happen.

EXERCISE 5: Articles: Definite (*the*) and Indefinite (*a, an*)

A. The most basic rule about articles is that *a* or *the* is required with a *singular countable noun.*

She spilled salt on *the* table. (*the* means a *known* person or object)

She broke *a* mirror. (*a* means *any one* person or object)[2]

Because of its basic meaning of *one, a* occurs mostly with a singular countable noun.

A plural noun does not usually require an article.

She doesn't believe in *ghosts.*

The is not used with a noncountable noun when this noun stands alone.

Many people believe in *magic.*

However, *the* precedes most nouns, countable or noncountable, singular or plural, *if they are followed by modifiers.*

NONCOUNTABLE NOUN:	Many people believe in *the* magic *performed by their witch doctors.*
COUNTABLE NOUN:	*The* number *which we consider unlucky* is thirteen. (With countable nouns, *a* meaning *one* may also be used in such a sentence.)

---

[2] The only exception to this rule occurs when another determiner (such as *this, her, any, some*) is used: She broke *her* mirror.

Use *a, an, the,* or nothing. (In some cases there are two possibilities.)

1. ___*The*___ house where he used to live is haunted by _____ ghosts.

2. Breaking ___*a*___ mirror will cause you _____ trouble.

3. ___*A*___ crow is ___*a*___ symbol of _____ death.

4. He knocked on ___*X*___ wood so that nothing bad would spoil ___*the*___ plan he had made.

5. There was once ___*the*___ belief that _____ gold could be made by _____ man.

6. _____ superstitions, which I remember, were told to me by _____ my grandfather.

7. _____ superstitions are ___*the*___ result of _____ fear and _____ ignorance.

8. Walking under ___*a*___ ladder will bring _____ bad luck.

9. ___*The*___ house, which is supposed to be haunted by ___*a*___ ghost is hard to sell.

B. The definite article *the* is generally used for someone or something *known:*

Known because it is already mentioned	*A* black cat was walking toward him. He crossed the street so that *the* black cat would not come near him.
Known because it is a familiar person or object in the environment immediate environment	He was worried because *the* mirror had fallen off *the* wall in *the* bedroom.
more distant environment	Some people feel that *the* sun, *the* moon, and *the* stars affect our daily lives.

Use *a, an, the* or nothing.

1. If you spill _____ salt on ___*the*___ table, you can avoid _____ bad luck by throwing _____ some salt over your left shoulder.

2. Yesterday my friend gave me _____ horseshoe for _____ good luck. I'm putting _____ horseshoe over _____ door of _____ my house.

3. When _____ moon is full, _____ evil spirits wander over _____ earth.

4. Opening _____ umbrella in _____ house will bring you _____ bad luck.

5. She always wears _____ good luck charm. _____ charm was given to her by _____ friend of hers.

6. On Halloween you may see _____ witch flying on _____ broomstick. _____ witch will be accompanied by _____ black cat.

C. Use _a, an, the,_ or nothing. Keep in mind that _a_ or _an_ refers to _one_ and is used only with singular countable nouns. Remember also that _an article must be used with a singular countable noun._

1. ___*A*___ rabbit's foot is carried by __*a or the*__ person who wants to have _____ good luck.

2. _____ young woman usually likes to have _____ wedding in _____ month of June.

3. _____ man will carry his bride over _____ threshold of their new house to avoid _____ evil spirits that are gathered there.

4. If you see _____ crow, _____ misfortune will befall you.

5. _____ number thirteen is _____ unlucky number.[3]

6. _____ superstition is _____ unreasonable belief in _____ super-natural.[4]

7. It is often _the_ ignorant and _the_ uneducated who believe that _the_ lives of _____ men are affected by _____ supernatural forces.

8. _an_ uneducated person often believes in _____ magic and _____ witchcraft.

9. In some countries, _____ number four is avoided in buildings because _____ number is unlucky.

---

[3] Articles are usually omitted with cardinal numbers (one, two, three, etc.): _Number thirteen is an unlucky number._ But: _No one likes to live on_ **the thirteenth floor.**

[4] Adjectives used as nouns are usually preceded by _the_: _Superstition results from a fear of the_ **unknown.**

EXERCISE 6: *most, most of the, the most*

The has different uses with *most*, depending on whether *most* has the meaning of quantity or whether it is the *superlative* of an adjective or an adverb.

Most as Quantity (part of a whole)

most Most educated people do not believe in superstition.
(*Most* without *of* is used mainly with plural nouns.)

most of the Most of the educated people in my country do not believe in superstition.
(If *of* follows *most, the* (or another determiner) is usually required after *of*.)

Most as a Superlative

the most Only *the most* superstitious people believe in magic and witchcraft.
(*The* is used before *most* only with superlatives.)

A. In the following sentences, supply *the* wherever it is required with *most*. Be sure to use *the:* (1) after *most of* and (2) before *most* as a superlative.

1. At _____ most _____ weddings, rice is thrown at the married couple as they leave the church.

2. _____ most of ___*the*___ wedding guests threw rice at the married couple as they left the church.

3. ___*The*___ most _____ expensive gown was worn by the bride.

4. _____ most of ___*the*___ time, people avoid getting married on Friday the thirteenth.

5. _____ most ___*the*___ brides carry a bouquet of roses for good luck.

6. _____ most of ___*the*___ young women I know prefer to get married in June.

7. ___*the*___ most _____ attractive man at the wedding was the best man.

8. _____ most _____ people will avoid lighting three cigarettes with one match.

9. _____ most of _____ farmers who lived in Europe before the twentieth century did not start anything new when the moon was waning.

10. ___*the*___ most _____ widespread superstition of all is the one about number thirteen.

11. Some people believe that _____ most _____ accidents happen in threes.

12. _____ most of _____ accidents that happened here occurred in threes.

13. _____ most of _____ superstitions that people believe in arise out of ignorance.

14. _____ most _____ superstitions that people believe in arise out of ignorance.

15. _____ most of _____ actors in the play are superstitious.

16. _____ most _____ actors are superstitious about the opening night of their play.

B. Sometimes it is possible to use either *most* or *most of the.* Write *two* sentences for each of the following by inserting first *most,* then *most of the* at the beginning of the sentence. (Do *not* use *the* in front of *most.*)

1. _____ young people I know do not believe in superstition.

   _____*Most young people I know do not believe in superstition.*_____

   _____*Most of the young people I know do not believe in superstition.*_____

2. _____ superstitions in my country are very old ones.

   _____

   _____

3. _____ beliefs about signs or omens that affect our future are superstitions.

   _____

   _____

4. _____ people who have superstitions about Friday the thirteenth do not get married on that day.

   _____

   _____

EXERCISE 7: Word Forms

Complete the words in the following sentences. Some words are already complete.

1. Anyone who belie-_____*ves*_____ in supersti-_____*tion*_____ is supersti-_____*tious*_____ .

2. Supersti-_____ is an unreason-_____ belie-
_____ in the supernatur-_____.

3. It often origin-_____ because of ignor-_____
of natur-_____ cause-_____.

4. It may come from a fear-_____ of the unknown-_____
_____ and the myster-_____.

5. Many sign-_____ and omen-_____ symbol-
_____ good luck-_____ or bad luck-_____
_____.

6. Primit-*ive*_____ or ignor-_____ people have
many supersti-_____ belie-_____.

7. Number thirteen is an unluck-_____ number.

8. See-*ing*_____ a crow is a sign-_____ of dea-
*th*_____.

9. Misfort-*une*_____ can result from break-*ing*_____ a
mirror.

EXERCISE 8: Sentence Review

Make full sentences from the word groups below. Make whatever changes or
additions are needed, but do not change the word order. Use commas,
semicolons, or periods wherever necessary.

1. If / you / walk / under / ladder / you / have / bad luck.

   If you walk under a ladder, you will have bad luck.

2. If / black cat / cross / your path / you / be / unlucky.

3. Break / mirror / bring / you / bad luck.

4. If / young girl / took / last piece / bread / she / be / old maid.

5. If / bridesmaid / had caught / bridal bouquet / she / become / bride / herself /
within / following / year.

6. If / someone / sneeze / I would say / "God / bless / you."

7. If / I / decide / get / marry / I would not have had / wedding / Friday / 13.

8. He / was / worry / because / mirror / fall / off / wall / in / bedroom.

9. Superstition / be / result / fear / unknown.

10. House / where / he / used to / live / haunt / ghosts.

11. Tradition / has / preserve / many / superstition.

12. There / be / once / belief / gold / can / be / make / man.

13. See / crow / be / sign / death.

14. Most / expensive / gown / was / wear / bride.

15. Most / young women / I / know / prefer / get / marry / June. (give two possibilities)

EXTRA SPEAKING AND WRITING PRACTICE

EXERCISE 9: Writing About Personal Characteristics

Astrologers feel that a person's character is determined by the date of birth. They divide the year into the twelve signs of the zodiac[5] and they describe the characteristics of persons born under each of these signs. Some people feel that this kind of analysis of a person's character is pure superstition; others feel that many of the things the astrologers say are quite accurate.

Following is a list of personal qualities that astrologers say are characteristic of people born under each of the twelve signs. Discuss these characteristics as a class or in groups to see how true each one is for you. Look up the words that are unfamiliar to you.

Next write a short composition choosing one or two personal characteristics included under your sign and *give examples to show why you agree or disagree with this description.*

Begin the composition with: "According to the astrologers, persons born under my sign, _____, are . . . (or, have . . .)." (Give only the characteristics you will agree or disagree with, and write about only one characteristic at a time.) You may include statements like: "I (dis)agree with that. . . ." or "This characteristic is certainly (not) true for me. For example, . . ."

Signs of the Zodiac—Personal Characteristics[6]

ARIES 3/21–4/19   (*Mars*[7]—rules energy, courage, aggressiveness, action, ambition, pioneering)

has initiative, courage, drive, enthusiasm
resourceful, self-confident, impulsive, imaginative
dynamic—a doer who wants to be first in everything
independent, restless—wants challenges and adventures
outgoing, enjoys competition in work but not monotony
a natural organizer with executive ability
faults: impatient, not persistent, thoughtless, selfish, quick-tempered

---

[5] The *Zodiac* is the narrow path in which the sun, the moon, and the planets travel in the heavens. The zodiac is divided into twelve equal parts.

[6] Not all sources show exactly the same beginning or ending day for each sign.

[7] The name in parentheses after each sign of the zodiac is the heavenly body (sun, moon, or planet) that dominates the sign.

TAURUS 4/20–5/20   (*Venus*—rules art, beauty, love, peace and harmony, perfection)

stubborn determination, slow starter, persistent, courageous
kind, but with a violent temper when pushed too far
sense of material values—talent for acquiring money
has great vitality and sensuality, love of beauty
conservative, very practical, methodical, shrewd
faults: hard to adapt to change, moody, carries grudges (doesn't forget or forgive), greedy, overly possessive, extremely conservative

GEMINI 5/21–6/21   (*Mercury*—rules the mind, communication)

lighthearted, whimsical, talkative, witty conversationalist
alert, changeable, a quick and intelligent thinker with an excellent sense of humor
has need for novelty and variety, versatile and adaptable, skilled with hands
faults: superficial, lacks warmth, fickle, easily bored, restless, nervous, not persistent, careless about money

CANCER 6/22–7/22   (*Moon*—rules moods, emotions, intuition, change, domesticity)

tenacious, versatile, moody, sensitive, idealistic
possessive, very changeable, home-loving, protective of the family
romantic, affectionate, gentle
faults: overpossessive, jealous, tends to accumulate, emotionally insecure, inconsistent.

LEO 7/23–8/22   (*Sun*—rules the will, drive, executive power)

a born leader, bold, energetic, ambitious, honest, enthusiastic
generous, loyal, optimistic, cheerful, sympathetic, self-confident
a strong personality—wants to be noticed and admired
emotionally intense, melodramatic—favors dramatic gestures
faults: arrogant, vain, self-centered, dictatorial, bossy, thoughtless, vulnerable to flattery

VIRGO 8/23–9/22   (*Mercury*—rules the mind, communication)

intellectual, logical and analytical mind, levelheaded
methodical, meticulous, master of detail, hard-working, practical
dependable, enjoys routine work, perfectionist
modest, neat, loyal, reserved
faults: fanatic about neatness and order, emotionally cold, nervous, critical and nagging, faultfinding, insecure, intolerant of ignorance

LIBRA 9/23–10/22   (*Venus*—rules art, beauty, love, peace and harmony, perfection)

poised, diplomatic, peace-loving, imaginative, fair-minded, intellectual
hates arguments, can see both sides, never totally committed

dislikes hard work, romantic but not sensual
loves beauty—especially beauty of human relationships
has artistic talent, good at working with people
faults: indecisive, gets discouraged easily, hesitant, not practical, careless in
money matters

SCORPIO 10/23–11/21   (*Pluto*—rules power, intensity, everything beneath the
surface and behind the scenes)

strong drive, magnetic personality, great vitality
hard worker, has great patience and power of concentration, ambitious
realistic, practical, sensible, courageous, self-assured, loyal
unshakable determination of the kind that makes martyrs and fanatics
competes to win, not for the fun of it
subtle and secretive—manipulates people from the background
very sensual (the sexiest sign of the Zodiac)
faults: lacks control over the emotions, ruthless and unfair, suspicious, jealous,
overly possessive, selfish, arbitrary

SAGITTARIUS 11/22–12/21   (*Jupiter*—rules sociability, kindness, enthusiasm,
generosity, optimism)

warm, friendly, tolerant, good-natured, honest, curious
talkative, extrovert—fun to have around
restless and independent—needs action, travel, adventure
likes sports, but plays for enjoyment
not very domestic—doesn't like to be tied down
faults: fickle, not persistent, extravagant, impatient, forgetful, depends too much
on luck.

CAPRICORN 12/22–1/19   (*Saturn*—rules self-discipline, hard work, responsibil-
ity, patience, cautiousness)

works hard but wants it to count, wants to rise to the top
ambitious, authoritative, industrious, self-disciplined
conservative but forceful, practical, orderly, cautious
excellent organizer—plans large-scale ventures
values honor and respectability
faults: single-minded in pursuing success, gloomy, pessimistic, impatient, dis-
trustful

AQUARIUS 1/20–2/18   (*Uranus*—rules originality, invention, freedom, individ-
ualism)

independent thinker but unpredictable, nonconformist
intellectual, rational, objective, fair-minded, tolerant
inventive, progressive, thinks in large-scale terms
friendly, good-humored, kind, spontaneous
faults: impersonal, resists intimate contact, impractical, eccentric, irresponsible

PISCES 2/19–3/20   (*Neptune*—rules vagueness, confusion, creativity, illusion, changeability)

imaginative, original, sympathetic, generous, honest
unrealistic, highly emotional, intuitive, impressionable
creative in all arts, also mathematics and science
faults: jealous, possessive, gloomy, lacks confidence, impractical, easily led

EXERCISE 10: Word Forms

Use the correct word form for the following characteristics of people born under each of the twelve signs of the zodiac.

(If you need help with the signals that tell whether a noun, verb, adjective, or adverbial form is needed, refer to *Writer's Companion,* Unit 2, in the Grammar Review and Practice section.)

1. The Capricorn person:
   (12/22–1/19)

   is (ambition) _____ *ambitious* _____

   (order) _____

   (caution) _____

   (self-discipline) _____

   lacks (origin) _____ *originality* _____

   (self-confident) _____

   Is a (material) _____ *materialist* _____

   a (plan) _____

   an (organize) _____

2. The Aquarius person:
   (1/20–2/18)

   is (friend) _____

   (not predict) _____

   has (good-humored) _____

   (object) _____

   lacks (aggressive) _____

   resists (intimate) _____

   is a (not conforming) _____

3. The Pisces person:
   (2/19–3/20)

   is (imagination) _____

   (change) _____

   (no organization) _____

has (subtle) _____

(creative) _____

lacks a sense of (secure) _____

and (real) _____

4. The Aries person:
   (3/21–4/19)

is (courage) _____

(energy) _____

(impulsive) _____

has (aggressive) _____

(initiate) _____

lacks (patient) _____

(persist) _____

5. The Taurus person:
   (4/20–5/20)

is (determine) _____

(depend) _____

(conserve) _____

has (vital) _____

lacks (adapt) _____

6. The Gemini person:
   (5/21–6/21)

is (talk) _____

(adapt) _____

(superficiality) _____

has (versatile) _____

lacks (warm) _____

7. The Cancer person:
   (6/22–7/22)

is (possess) _____

(change) _____

(jealousy) _____

has (intuitive) _____

lacks emotional (secure) _____

8. The Leo person:
   (7/23–8/22)

is (cheer) _____

(dictator) _____

has (arrogant) _____

(generous) _____

lacks (thoughtful) _____

is an (ideal) _____

    an (optimism) _____

9. The Virgo person: is (modesty) _____
    (8/23–9/22)

    (diligence) _____

has (dependable) _____

is a (fanaticism) _____ about
neatness

10. The Libra person: is (hesitate) _____
    (9/23–10/22)

    (intellect) _____

    (fair-mindedness) _____

is not (emotion) _____

    (argument) _____

lacks (commit) _____

11. The Scorpio person: is (patience) _____
    (10/23–11/21)

    (suspect) _____

has (determine) _____

    (loyal) _____

12. The Sagittarius person: is (friend) _____
    (11/22–12/21)

    (enthusiasm) _____

has (optimistic) _____

lacks (persist) _____

EXERCISE 11: Composition for Similarities and Differences: Western and Eastern Zodiacs

Pages 164 and 165 give the charts of the Western zodiac and the Oriental animal cycle. As a class or in groups, discuss the similarities and the differences between the two. Then write three paragraphs about these similarities and differences. Use the following outline:

First paragraph   *Introduction:* general statements (keep this short)

Second paragraph   I. *Similarities*
                                (use an opening sentence that tells the reader you are
                                going to discuss the similarities)
                                expressions for similarity:
                                    similar to . . . in that
                                    like (or alike) . . . in that
                                    both
                                    one similarity between . . .
                                    another (or a second) similarity
                                    the same as, or the same _____as

Third paragraph   II. *Differences*
                                (use an opening sentence that tells the reader you are
                                going to discuss the differences)
                                expressions for difference:
                                    different from . . . in that
                                    but; however; on the other hand
                                    while, whereas
                                    one difference between . . .
                                    another (or a second) difference

Wherever possible, give *examples* for the similarities or differences you point
out.

As you look for similarities and differences between the two zodiacs, you might
consider the following:

  the shape of each zodiac
  the divisions of each zodiac
  the center of each zodiac[8]
  the period of time covered by each zodiac
  the symbols used in each zodiac
  the relation to people's lives of each zodiac

[8] *Duality* (double character or nature) at the center of the Oriental animal cycle:

Yang	*Yin*
heaven	earth
active	passive
positive	negative
male	female
firm	yielding
strong	weak
light	dark

The two together (yang and yin) represent the whole universe.

Western Zodiac

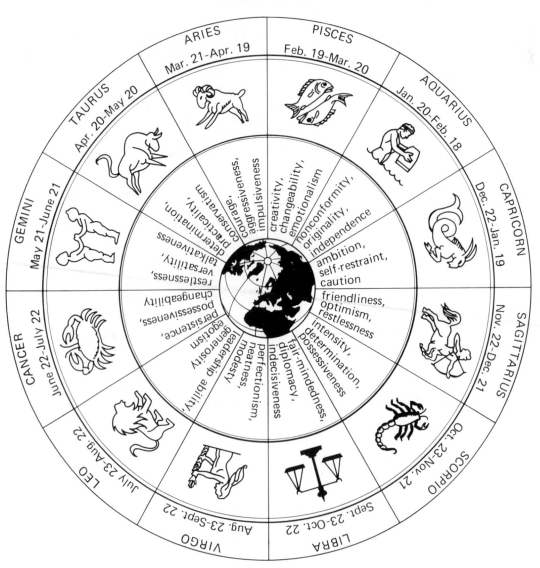

ARIES
Mar. 21–Apr. 19

PISCES
Feb. 19–Mar. 20

AQUARIUS
Jan. 20–Feb. 18

TAURUS
Apr. 20–May 20

CAPRICORN
Dec. 22–Jan. 19

GEMINI
May 21–June 21

SAGITTARIUS
Nov. 22–Dec. 21

CANCER
June 22–July 22

SCORPIO
Oct. 23–Nov. 21

LEO
July 23–Aug. 22

LIBRA
Sept. 23–Oct. 22

VIRGO
Aug. 23–Sept. 22

creativity, changeability, emotionalism

nonconformity, originality, independence

ambition, self-restraint, caution

friendliness, optimism, restlessness

intensity, determination, possessiveness

fair-mindedness, diplomacy, indecisiveness

perfectionism, neatness, modesty

leadership ability, generosity, egotism

persistence, possessiveness, changeability

restlessness, versatility, talkativeness

determination, practicality, conservatism

aggressiveness, courage, impulsiveness

Oriental Animal Cycle

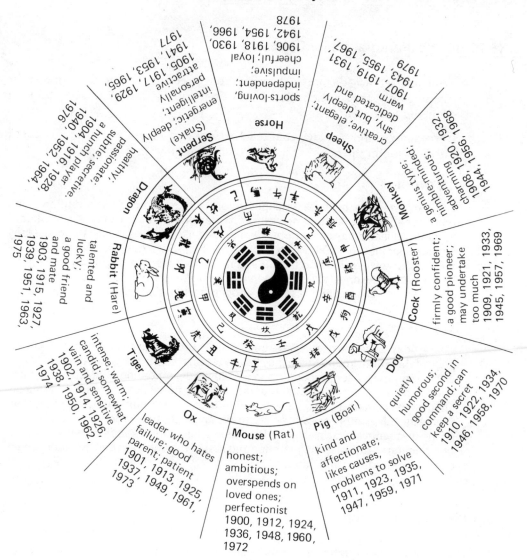

Horse
sports-loving,
independent;
impulsive;
cheerful; loyal
1906, 1918, 1930,
1942, 1954, 1966,
1978

Serpent (Snake)
attractive
personally
intelligent;
energetic; deeply
1905, 1917, 1929,
1941, 1953, 1965,
1977

Dragon
healthy;
passionate;
subtle; secretive:
a hunch player
1904, 1916, 1928,
1940, 1952, 1964,
1976

Sheep
creative; elegant;
shy, but deeply
warm and
dedicated and
1907, 1919, 1931,
1943, 1955, 1967,
1979

Monkey
charming
nimble-minded;
adventurous;
a genius type:
1908, 1920, 1932,
1944, 1956, 1968,

Rabbit (Hare)
talented and
lucky;
a good friend
and mate
1903, 1915, 1927,
1939, 1951, 1963,
1975

Cock (Rooster)
firmly confident;
a good pioneer;
may undertake
too much
1909, 1921, 1933,
1945, 1957, 1969

Tiger
intense; warm;
candid; somewhat
vain and sensitive
1902, 1914, 1926,
1938, 1950, 1962,
1974

Ox
leader who hates
failure; good
parent; patient
1901, 1913, 1925,
1937, 1949, 1961,
1973

Mouse (Rat)
honest;
ambitious;
overspends on
loved ones;
perfectionist
1900, 1912, 1924,
1936, 1948, 1960,
1972

Pig (Boar)
kind and
affectionate;
likes causes;
problems to solve
1911, 1923, 1935,
1947, 1959, 1971

Dog
quietly
humorous;
good second in
command; can
keep a secret
1910, 1922, 1934,
1946, 1958, 1970

Oriental animal cycle chart © 1972/1976 by The New York Times Company. Reprinted by permission.

LISTENING-WRITING PRACTICE

EXERCISE 12: Paragraphs for Dictation

Your teacher will dictate each paragraph three times. The first time is for listening only, the second time is for writing, and the third time is for checking what you have written.

Immediately after you give your teacher the dictation you have written, check the dictation in the book for any problems you had in writing it.

DICTATION 1

Anyone who believes in superstition is superstitious. Superstition is an unreasonable belief in the supernatural. It often originates because of ignorance of natural causes. It may come from a fear of the unknown and the mysterious. Many signs and omens symbolize good luck or bad luck. For example, if you carry a rabbit's foot you will avoid bad luck. If you find a four-leaf clover you will have good luck. Hearing the cry of a crow is a sign of death. Misfortune can result from breaking a mirror, walking under a ladder, or opening an umbrella in the house.

DICTATION 2

Today, because people have become more educated and have greater knowledge of the world around them, they have a rational basis for connecting cause and effect. For this reason, superstitions are slowly disappearing. But, although many educated people now say that superstitions are nonsense, they are still uneasy about some of them. For example, they continue to avoid doing important things on Friday the thirteenth. They still refuse to live on the thirteenth floor or to get married on the thirteenth day of the month. It will take a long time to eradicate superstitions that originated because of ignorance and fear of the unknown and that still persist because of tradition and habit.

EXERCISE 13: Dicto-comps

Take notes as your teacher reads each of these dicto-comps to you several times. Then reconstruct the dicto-comp from your notes. The dicto-comp does not need to be written exactly as you heard it, but it should be grammatically correct.

Before you write the dicto-comp, your teacher may ask the class to get together in groups to check with each other on what you heard.

Immediately after you give your teacher the dicto-comp you have written, check the dicto-comp in the book for any problems you had in writing it.

DICTO-COMP 1

The Friday the 13th Club gathered on its big day yesterday to hear a New York University professor speak—not always seriously—about the irrational fear of the number 13.

"It's a fairly solemn subject, you know," Professor Owen S. Rachleff said. "New York stores will lose about $250,000 worth of business today because people are afraid to venture out. They should know that most disastrous accidents happen at home."

Mr. Rachleff, who is the author of a new book called "The Secrets of Superstition," said one of the things that disturbed him most about the fear of the number 13 was the practice of many landlords to call the thirteenth floor of their buildings the fourteenth.

Mr. Rachleff continued his lecture by recklessly smashing a small mirror ("When you break it, you're supposed to break your soul"), throwing salt over his left shoulder ("It's supposed to get in Satan's eyes"), and lighting three cigarettes on one match ("An unlucky practice because it supposedly gives Satan more time to snatch you").

Judy Klemesrud, "Triskaidekaphobes: Are You One of Them?" *The New York Times,* August 14, 1976, p. 23.*

DICTO-COMP 2

Found in many cultures throughout the world, a fetish may have the form of an animal or human statuette, an Indian medicine bundle, a picture, a buffalo horn, or a sword. It is different from other magical objects because it is supposed to have human thoughts and feelings. It may also be the home of a spirit or other supernatural being.

An example of a fetish comes from a Cambodian legend. There was once a king who possessed a sword containing a spirit. If the king were to draw the sword a few inches out of its sheath, the sun would hide its face and all men and animals would fall into a deep sleep. If the king were to draw the sword out completely, the world would come to an end.

What is interesting about the sword is not its power, but the behavior of people toward it. The sword was clothed in the most costly silks and linens and annually presented with gifts of pigs, chickens, and buffalo. In return it was expected to bring rain to the country. The sword was the dwelling place of a powerful spirit on whose goodwill the prosperity of the people depended.

Adapted from Arthur S. Gregor, *Amulets, Talismans and Fetishes.* New York: Charles Scribner's Sons, © 1975, pp. 77–78.†

Rules of Etiquette (Politeness)

GRAMMAR AND USAGE

Verb–preposition combinations
Separable verb–preposition combinations
Pronouns in general statements
Negative prefixes

RHETORIC

Using an outline to guide the composition
Using an introduction and a conclusion
Using a transitional lead-in to the body of the composition
Using transitions between paragraphs

DISCUSSION AND COMPOSITION

1. DISCUSSION: Preliminary outline for the composition (prewriting stage)

Subject: *Rules of Etiquette in* (name of your country)

Outline *(To Be Placed on the Board)*	Discussion *(Ideas, Grammar and Usage, Vocabulary, Elements of Composition Building)*
Introduction: general statements Purpose of rules of etiquette	Possible comments: Every country has its own rules of etiquette. Etiquette is polite social behavior that makes life easier and more pleasant. It helps people to get along with each other. It often reflects a country's social values and beliefs.
Kinds of rules: 1. conventional 2. social	Example: serving and eating food Example: respectful behavior toward older people and toward women
Transitional lead-in to suggest that both types of rules will be discussed	This composition will deal with both types of rules of etiquette in my country. *Or* I want to discuss both types. . . . *Or* I would like to give examples of both types. . . .
I. Conventional rules—serving and eating food	Opening sentence of paragraph: mention the subject, conventional rules about serving and eating food
A. serving the food	Time when meals are served Number and order of courses served Eating utensils used and their place on the table (place setting)
B. eating the food	Behavior of the people at the table (table manners)
II. Social rules—respectful behavior	Opening sentence of paragraph: mention the subject, rules about respectful social behavior
A. toward older people	Behavior of children toward grown-ups Behavior of students toward teachers
B. toward women	Examples: (U.S.) dining in a restaurant

Outline (cont.)	Discussion (cont.)
B. toward women (cont.)	introductions opening doors in buildings, cars walking in the street Note: this point may have to be reversed (respect shown by women to men) in some cultures
Conclusion: general statements	Possible comments: Changing customs—more informality now Influence of Western customs Rules of etiquette not so strictly observed now, especially by the younger generation The women's liberation movement is causing the breakdown of some of these rules about respectful behavior.

2. COMPOSITION (to be done before or after the reinforcement practice)

A. ORGANIZING THE COMPOSITION

Before writing your composition, fill in the required information on this Organizational Worksheet. The Worksheet follows the preliminary outline used for the discussion. Guidance for writing each paragraph is given at the right side of this Worksheet. The pages of the discussion outline provide additional help for the composition.

You may use phrases on this Worksheet except where it calls for full sentences.

ORGANIZATIONAL WORKSHEET
(Preliminary notes for the composition)

Title of the composition _____
(Do not use quotation marks or a period for a title at the top of the page. Use initial capital letters for the first word of the title and for all other words except articles, short prepositions, and short conjunctions.)

Introduction: general statements Opening sentence of paragraph_____ _____ _____ _____	Put in a separate paragraph Use the *present tense* for the general statements in this paragraph and in the rest of the composition

Purpose of rules of etiquette _____

_____

_____

_____

_____

Kinds of rules (conventional and social, with examples)

_____

_____

_____

_____

Transitional lead-in connecting the general statements of the introduction to the two kinds of rules of etiquette

Full sentence _____

_____

_____

_____

May be the conclusion of the introductory paragraph, or may begin the paragraph that follows it

I. Conventional rules—serving and eating food)
   Opening (or second) sentence of paragraph

_____

_____

_____

New paragraph
Mention the subject, conventional rules about serving and eating food

A. Serving the food

_____

_____

_____

_____

_____

_____

B. Eating the food

_____

_____

_____

_____

_____

_____

II. Social rules—respectful behavior

Opening sentence of paragraph_____

New paragraph

Mention the subject, rules about respectful social behavior

_____

_____

_____

_____

A. Respect shown to older people

_____

_____

_____

_____

_____

B. Respect shown to women

(Or respect shown to men by women)

_____

_____

_____

_____

_____

Conclusion: general statements   New paragraph

_____

_____

_____

_____

_____

_____

_____

B. WRITING THE COMPOSITION

Write the composition based on your notes on the Organizational Worksheet. Be careful of your paragraphing. Use separate paragraphs for your introduction and your conclusion. (Long paragraphs may be broken in two at appropriate places, but single-sentence paragraphs should be avoided.)

Use 8½ - by 11-inch white paper, with lines for a handwritten composition and without lines for a typed composition. Double-space a typewritten composition, and skip lines on a handwritten one. Write on the front of the paper only, and leave wide margins on *both the left and the right sides* of the paper. Indent the beginning of each paragraph.

Look over your composition carefully before you hand it in.

C. CORRECTING OR REWRITING THE COMPOSITION

When your teacher returns your composition, it will be marked with the symbols from the correction chart on page 257. Make the necessary corrections on the composition and hand it back to your teacher.

Place the corrections on the correction page, and note down the rule that is involved.

If you have made many mistakes, or if you wish to make some additions to your composition, you may need to write it again. In rewriting the composition, do not make extensive changes or additions without consulting your teacher.

(For more help with your problems in writing, consult the Index of Usage and Rhetoric in *Writer's Companion*. The items in this index are arranged in the same alphabetical order as in the correction chart.)

CORRECTION PAGE

Use this page to write down the correction of any mistakes you have made in your composition on "Rules of Etiquette in (*name of your country*)." Include enough of the words surrounding the corrected part to make the meaning clear. (Do not copy down the mistake itself.) If possible, write down the rule that covers the correction you have made.

Review these corrections from time to time in order to avoid making the same mistakes again.

Corrections	*Rule* *(See the correction chart if necessary)*

REINFORCEMENT PRACTICE

EXERCISE 1: Verb–Preposition Combinations

Many combinations of verbs and prepositions have meanings that are different from each of their two parts. For example, *get up* = awake, *keep on* = continue, *take after* = resemble.

Replace the verb in parentheses with a verb–preposition combination. Use the proper verb form. (If you have any difficulties with this vocabulary, consult the list of verb–preposition combinations at the end of this exercise.)

1. Rules of etiquette are (transmit) ____*handed*____ ____*down*____ from generation to generation to help people (be in harmony) ____*get*____ ____*along*____ with each other.

2. Parents should (raise) ____*bring*____ ____*up*____ their children to have good manners so that when the children (mature) *grow* ____*up*____ *breed* they will be well-bred. *having good manner*

3. If you plan to (visit) ____*Call*____ ____*on*____ friends, it's more polite to (telephone) ____*Call*____ ____*up*____ first.

4. A gentleman (remove) ____*Takes*____ ____*off*____ his hat in the elevator of a residence building or a hotel when a lady (enter) *Come* ____*into*____ the elevator.

5. At a social gathering, it is best not to (raise) *bring* *up* unpleasant or very controversial subjects.

6. Good manners should be observed whether you (have food at home) *eat* ____*in*____ or (have food in a restaurant) *eat out.*

7. In a restaurant the man helps the woman (remove) ____*Take*____ ____*off*____ her coat if the waiter doesn't do it. Also, when they leave the restaurant, the man helps the woman (don) *put* ____*on*____ her coat.

8. It's better taste for a woman not to (put on cosmetics) *make* ____*up*____ in public.

good manner. don ≠ doff

9. A gentleman (rise from his seat) ___Stands___ ___up.___

when a lady (enter) ___come into___ the room.

10. In the United States, the fork is (lift) ___picked up___ with the right hand.

11. It is not polite to (appear) ___turn up___ at a party without an invitation.

12. The polite person (extinguish) ___put___ ___out___ his or her cigarette when entering a no-smoking area.

Verb–Preposition Combinations for Exercise 1

bring up (a child), *raise*
bring up (a subject), *raise*
call on, *visit*
call up, *telephone*
come into, *enter*
eat in, *have food at home*
eat out, *eat in a restaurant*
get along with, *be in harmony with*
get (stand) up, *rise from one's seat*

grow up, *mature*
hand down, *transmit*
make up, *put on cosmetics*
pick up, *lift*
put on (clothing), *don*
put out (something that is burning), *ex-tinguish*
take off (clothing), *remove*
turn up, *appear*

EXERCISE 2: Separable Verb–Preposition Combinations

Many verb–preposition combinations are separable: their objects may appear either after the combination or between the two parts. However, a pronoun object appears *only between* the two parts.

NOUN OBJECT: You should call up *your friends.*
OR
You should call *your friends* up.

PRONOUN OBJECT: You should call *them* up.

Other verb–preposition combinations are *nonseparable:* the noun or pronoun object comes *only after* the two parts.

NOUN OBJECT: You should call on *your friends.*

PRONOUN OBJECT: You should call on *them.*

Use pronouns for the italicized words along with the proper form of the verb–preposition combinations for the verbs in parentheses. (If you have any difficulties with this vocabulary, consult the list of verb–preposition combinations at the end of this exercise.)

1. I just received an invitation, but the *date* is illegible. I can't (understand)
_____*make*_____ _____*it*_____ _____*out*_____.
(separable combination)

2. She's wearing a beautiful *dress*, but nothing else that she has on (harmonize)
_____*goes*_____ _____*with*_____ _____*it*_____.
(nonseparable combination)

3. When her boyfriend made her an *offer of marriage*, she (reject) _____turn_____
_____him_____ _____down_____ — as kindly as possible.

4. You should write a *thank-you note* to your hostess. It's not polite to (postpone)
_____put_____ _____it_____ _____off_____.

5. They are worried about *their son*. They're afraid that they (not raise) _____have_____
not _____brought_____ _____him_____ _____up_____
as well as possible. (several possibilities for the verb tense)

6. If a friend is in the hospital with an *illness*, we often send him a card wishing
badly, that he will (recover) _____get_____ _____over_____ _____it_____
_____ soon.

7. He never wears *clothes* that suit the occasion. He doesn't know how to (choose)
_____pick_____ _____them_____ _____out_____. He
is so impetuous that he (not test for fit or appearance) _____does_____
does thing without _____not_____ _____try_____ _____them_____
thinking _____on_____.

8. He has some *friends* in Washington. If he plans to (visit) _____Call_____
_____on_____ _____them_____, it would be more polite to
(telephone) _____Call_____ _____them_____ _____up_____
first.

9. If you are smoking a *cigarette* you should (extinguish) _____put_____
_____it_____ _____out_____ before you enter an elevator.

10. When a young man dates a *girl*, he should (come to get) _____Call_____
_____for_____ _____her_____ when he (escort somewhere)
_____take_____ _____her_____ _____out_____.

11. The *concert* never took place. They had to (cancel) _____Call_____
_____it_____ _____off_____ because the singer became ill.

Separable combinations are marked (S); nonseparable combinations are marked (NS).

bring up (a child), *raise* (S)
call for (someone or something), *come to get* (NS)
call off (something), *cancel* (S)
call on (someone), *visit* (NS)
call up (on the telephone), *telephone* (S)
get over (an illness), *recover from* (NS)
go with (something, usually clothes), *harmonize with* (NS)
make out (some writing), *understand* (S)

pick out (something), *choose* (S)
put off (something), *postpone* (S)
put out (something that is burning), *extinguish* (S)
take out (someone), *escort somewhere* (S)
try on (an item of clothing), *test for fit or appearance* (S)
turn down (a person or an offer), *reject* (S)

EXERCISE 3: Pronouns in General Statements

Personal pronouns are often used in general statements to represent everybody that the statement is about.

WE: In my country, *we* often eat dinner very late.

YOU: In my country, *you* must respect your elders.

ONE: *One* learns *one's* (or *his* or *her*) manners at home at an early age.

In using these pronouns for general statements, we must be consistent. If we start with *we,* we must continue using this pronoun and not shift to one of the others.

PRONOUN SHIFT: *We* should not forget that the rules of etiquette depend on the culture where *you* are.

Correct the faulty pronoun shifts used in the following general statements about customs in different countries. (The verbs that follow the pronouns may also need to be corrected.)

1. Good manners should be observed whether one eats in a restaurant or whether you eat at home.

    *Good manners should be observed whether **one** eats in a restaurant or whether **one** eats at home.* (or use *you* in both places instead of *one*)

2. We say a prayer to ask God to bless the food. Then one also thanks Him for the food.

3. After we finish eating, we put the fork and the knife to the right. But if you put one to the right and one to the left, this means you are not finished eating.

4. First, we serve soup and vegetables, and then we usually eat sashimi and drink rice wine. Finally you eat some dessert.

5. When one is invited to dinner, the hostess expects you to arrive on time. (in this sentence, change the first pronoun)

6. When we sit at the table, we must wait for everyone to start eating. Sometimes you have to wait until the head of the family begins eating.

7. One should not talk about unpleasant subjects at a social gathering. Also, you should avoid any subject that might hurt the feelings of the people you are with.

EXERCISE 4: Negative Prefixes

Words may be made negative by adding the prefixes *in-* (*im-* before *p* or *m*), *un-*, *dis-*, or *mis-*.

Use the correct form of the negative.

1. It is (not pleasant) _____*unpleasant*_____ to be with people who are (not courteous) _____*discourteous*_____ and always do the (not correct) _____*incorrect*_____ thing.

2. (Not obedient) ___disobedient___ children who (not behave) ___misbehave___ _____ have not been brought up well by their parents.

3. It is (not polite) ___impolite___ to be (not respectful) ___disrespectful___ _____ to one's elders.

4. People who are (not considerate) ___inconsiderate___ or (not decent) ___indecent___ will gain the (no approval) ___disapproval___ of others.

5. If we are (not accustomed) ___unaccustomed___ to the ways of another culture, we may behave in an (not acceptable) ___unacceptable___ way and possibly commit an (no propriety) ___impropriety___ (not following the rule correctly)

6. It was once considered (not modest) ___immodest___ for a lady to use the words *stomach* and *leg*.

7. It is bad taste to make (not appropriate) ___inappropriate___ or (not proper) ___improper___ remarks to others.

8. A person who is (not able) ___unable___ to like other people often has the (no ability) ___inability___ to be polite to them.

9. No one likes to be with people who are (not courteous) _____

   or (not pleasant) _____.

10. A hostess will (not approve) _disapprove_ of a guest who (not

    regard) _disregard_ the social amenities.

    misbehave

EXERCISE 5: Word Forms

Use the correct form of the word in parentheses. In sentences with choices,
select the correct word.

(If you need help with the signals that tell whether a noun, verb, adjective, or
adverbial form is needed, refer to *Writer's Companion*, Unit 2, in the Grammar
Review and Practice section.)

1. Rules of etiquette have long been in (exist) _existence_ in (social)

   society to make life more (please) _pleasant_

   and more (harmony) _harmonious_.   pieces left over

2. Some of our rules of etiquette are remnants of (Middle Ages) _Medieval_
   (50-60 century)

   _____ customs when knights were very (chivalry) _Chivalrous_ to
   the ladies.   male politeness

3. The person who follows the rules of etiquette has (good manners). He is

   Well-mannered. If he does not follow these rules, he is _bad-_

   manner-ed. (both words are hyphenated)

4. We also say that a person who follows the rules of etiquette has (good breed-

   ing). She is _Well-bred_. If she does not follow the rules, she is

   bad _ill-bred_. (both words are hyphenated)

5. The rules of etiquette tell us what kind of (behave) _behavior_ is

   (courtesy) _Courteous_ and what kind is (not polite) _impolite_.

   _____

6. The person who observes the rules of etiquette shows (courteous) _Courtesy_

   _____ and (consider) _Consideration_ toward others. He always

   (behavior) _behaves_ with (proper) _Propriety_ and

   (decent) _decency_.

   ill nature = bad manner.

7. To be (social) _Socially_ acceptable, a person must observe the (custom) _Customary_ rules of etiquette.

8. Some parents today have been too (permit) _permissive_ and have not trained their children in the rules of (polite) _politeness_ and common (courteous) _Courtesy_.

9. In the United States, an (obey) _Obedient_ and (respect) _respectful_ child will ask for his or her parents' (permit) _permission_ to leave the dinner table.

10. A gentleman (raises, rises) _rises_ from his (sit, seat) _seat_ when he is (introduce) _introduced_ to a lady. A lady remains (seat) _Seated._ when an (introduce) _introduction_ is made.

Causative

11. It was once (custom) _Customary_ for a gentleman to (rise, raise) _raise_ his hat when he passed a female (acquaint) _acquaintance_ on the street.

12. In a restaurant, a woman does not leave her purse (lying, laying) _lying_ on the table.

13. In an (introduce) _introduction_, a man is (present) _presented_ to a woman, and a younger person is (introduce) _introduced_ to an older one.

14. RSVP (from the French "*Répondez s'il vous plaît*") means "Please reply." You should reply (prompt) _promptly_ to an (invite) _invitation_.

15. Also, you should arrive (punctual) _punctually_ when you are (invite) _invited._ to dinner.

punctual : on time

EXERCISE 6: Sentence Review

Make full sentences from the word groups that follow. Make whatever changes or additions are needed, but do not change the word order. Be careful of the punctuation.

puncture : put a hole in something

A. For the verbs in parentheses, use verb–preposition synonyms. If these combinations have objects, put the objects in the correct position.

1. If / you / plan / (visit) / friends / it's / more polite / (telephone them) / first.

   If you plan to call on friends, it's more polite to call them up first.

2. Parents / should / (raise) / their children / have / good manners / so that / when / children / (mature) / they / be / well-bred.

3. Date / this invitation / be / illegible / I / can't / (understand it).

4. They / be / worried / their son / they / be / afraid / they (not raise him) / well. (several possible verb tenses)

5. Gentleman / (rise from his seat) / when / lady / (enter) / room.

6. She / wear / beautiful dress / but / nothing else / that / she / have on / (harmonize) / it.

B. As you make these sentences, add the correct negative prefixes or the correct word endings.

1. It / be / (not) -polite / be / (not) -respectful / one's / elders.

2. Person / who / be / (not) -able / like / other / people / often / have / the / (no) -ability be / polite / them.

3. It / be / (not) -pleasant / be / with / people / who / be / (not) -courteous.

4. They / have / (not) -obedient / children / who / (not) -behave.

5. Rules / etiquette / tell / us / what kind / behav-_____ / be / courte-_____ / and / consider-_____.

6. You / should / arrive / punctual-_____ / when / you / be / invite-_____ / dinner.

EXTRA SPEAKING AND WRITING PRACTICE

EXERCISE 7: Summary: Place Setting

Your teacher will give you some time to read the following description of the way a table is set for a formal dinner in the United States. Study the illustration carefully.

Note that the first paragraph gives a general description of the placement of silverware to the left and right of the dinner plate. The second paragraph gives us the exact order of the eating utensils moving from left to right. The third paragraph describes the items above these, moving from right to left. Thus a complete circle is followed in the description.

When we set the table in the United States, we follow two rules. First, we place the forks, knives, and spoons to the left or right of the dinner plate according to the hand that will pick these items up. Then we determine the order of the items of silverware on the left and right by the rule "begin at the outside and eat in." For example, since it is the American custom to eat the salad before the main dish, the salad fork is the outside fork on the left.

The diagram below illustrates a typical place setting. On the extreme left we find the folded napkin. To the right of the napkin are the salad fork, the fork, and the dinner plate. Then to the right of the plate are the knife, with the cutting edge toward

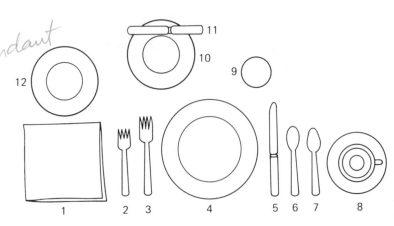

1. Napkin. 2. Salad fork. 3. Fork. 4. Plate. 5. Knife
6. Dessert spoon. 7. Teaspoon. 8. Cup and saucer.
9. Glass. 10. Bread-and-butter plate. 11. Butter knife.
12. Salad plate.

Diagram from *Mind Your Manners,* by Betty Allen and Mitchell Pirie Briggs (J. B. Lippincott), p. 69. Copyright © 1964 by Betty Allen and Mitchell Pirie Briggs. Reprinted by permission of Harper & Row, Publishers, Inc.

the plate, the dessert spoon and finally the teaspoon. (If soup is being served, the soupspoon would be next.) To the right of the spoons are the cup and saucer.

Above the knife we find the glass (if a wine glass is used, it is to the right of the water glass). Above the forks is the bread-and-butter plate, on which is placed the butter knife. Moving further leftward, we find the salad plate above the napkin.

Work together in groups to reconstruct the three paragraphs about a table setting in the United States. Use the illustration but do not refer back to what you have read.

Remember that the first paragraph gives an explanation of the general order in which the silverware is placed, the second paragraph gives the order of the tableware items from left to right, and the third paragraph gives the order of the items above these from right to left.

EXERCISE 8: Skit: Dinner in an American Restaurant

Work with two other students to act out and then write a skit (a short play) about dining in an American restaurant.

Use the information in the left column for your skit. This column tells what the characters in the skit do or say. Use the present tense for the action.

The right column is for your information only. It explains some American customs about dining in a restaurant. You may incorporate some of this information within the skit.

There are two main characters in the skit: John, a young American man, and Maria, a girl from your country who is now living in the United States. (You may use another name for the girl, one that is common in your country.) The third student plays all the other characters.

The skit must include both the directions for the actions, and the dialog that gives the actual words spoken. The skit is begun for you at the end of this introductory section.

DINNER IN AN AMERICAN RESTAURANT

What Is Being Said and Done	*Explanation of American Customs*
It's 6:00 P.M. Maria and John enter the restaurant. The hostess approaches. She asks whether he has a reservation. He replies that he does and he gives his name. They follow the hostess to the table, Maria going first.	A young man usually calls for the young woman at her home to escort her to the restaurant. At a popular restaurant, especially a small one, it's customary to make a reservation in order to be sure of getting a table at the desired time.

John helps Maria to her seat. He asks her whether he may help her with her coat. She answers yes.

A man (called a captain) or a woman (the hostess) leads diners to their table. The woman diner precedes the man.

The waiter or the woman's escort helps to seat her and helps her with her coat. In many large or expensive restaurants the man checks his coat; he may or may not check the woman's.

The cocktail waitress approaches. She asks if they want to order a drink.

John asks Maria whether she would like a drink. She says yes, tells him what she wants, and he orders for both of them. The waitress brings the drinks.

Some typical drinks before dinner:
    martini (gin and vermouth)
    Manhattan (whiskey and vermouth)
    Scotch—with water or soda or on the rocks (with ice cubes)
    whiskey sour (whiskey, lemon juice, sugar)

They place their napkins on their laps, leaving them half folded. The waiter comes over. He greets them, hands them menus, and leaves.

John asks Maria what she would like to order.

Maria looks over the menu.
    (Note: Use the menu at the end of this exercise.)

She asks a few questions about American terms she's not sure of.

John supplies the answers.
    (Note: Consult the dictionary if necessary to answer Maria's questions.)

Maria tells John what she will have.

The waiter approaches to take their order. John orders the appetizers, salads and entrées from the full course dinner. He gives Maria's order first.

The menu at the end of this exercise is a short but typical American menu. The price of the entrée (main course) includes the whole dinner. The courses in a full dinner are: appetizer, salad, entrée, dessert, and beverage. The same restaurant may also serve food *à la carte,* which means each course has a separate charge.

If steak or roast beef is ordered, you must tell the waiter whether you want the meat rare (not cooked much), medium, medium rare, or well done.

The appetizers, the salads, and the entrées are brought to their table at appropriate intervals. During this time John asks Maria a few questions about differences between the eating customs in her country and those in the United States. Maria gives the answers.

Some American eating customs:
    A popular time to come to a restaurant is between 6 and 7 P.M., especially if the diners are going afterward to the theater (which usually starts at 8 P.M.). In the cities it is considered more fashionable to dine later.

    The salad is served before the main course.

Some U.S. table manners:
  using the same hand to cut the food
  with the knife and to pick up the
  food with the fork
not cutting up all one's food at once
breaking off only a small piece of
  bread at a time and buttering it
not putting elbows on the table
not smoking until after dessert

At the end of the main course the waiter removes the plates and the silver.

The waiter shows them the menus again. He asks them what they would like to order for the beverage and dessert. John asks Maria what she would like to have.

He orders for both of them.

They finish the dessert.

John asks Maria if she would like a cigarette. She says yes. He offers it to her and lights it for her.

Soon he suggests that they'd better leave so that they can get to the theater on time.

He asks the waiter for the bill.

He checks the bill, then puts money down for the waiter.

John and Maria leave the restaurant.

The diner indicates that he has finished eating the main course by placing the knife and fork in the middle of the plate. (This custom is often disregarded.)

A usual tip in a restaurant is 15 percent. In very elegant restaurants, 20 percent may be given.

Beginning of the Skit

DINNER IN AN AMERICAN RESTAURANT

It's 6:00 P.M. Maria and John enter the restaurant.
The hostess approaches.
HOSTESS: Good evening. Do you have a reservation?
JOHN: Yes, I have a reservation for two for six o'clock in the name of John Smith.
HOSTESS: Yes, Come with me please.
      (Continue the skit. Supply both action and the conversation.)

John and Maria have gone to a moderately priced restaurant serving simple American food. The price of the entrée is the price of the whole dinner (appetizer, salad, entrée, dessert, beverage).

AMERICAN RESTAURANT

DINNER MENU

Appetizers

Fresh fruit in season   Fruit cocktail   Half grapefruit
Juice (tomato, orange, grapefruit)
Soup du jour[1]
Shrimp cocktail ($1.00 extra)

Salads

Tossed salad   Hearts of lettuce   Sliced cucumber
Dressing: French, Russian, oil and vinegar, Roquefort

Entrées

Roast chicken	8.25
Pot roast	7.50
Baked ham	8.25
Lamb stew	8.00
Fried liver	7.75
Sirloin steak	10.50
Roast beef	10.50
Sautéed filet of sole	8.25
Broiled halibut	8.75
Baked flounder	8.75
Fried shrimp	8.50
Seafood platter	9.00

Vegetables (choose two)

Potatoes (baked, mashed, or French fried), Corn, Peas, Carrots, Cabbage, Squash,
Stewed tomatoes, String beans

Desserts

Assorted French pastries
Chocolate cake
Strawberry shortcake ($.50 extra)
Apple pie, Blueberry pie, Cherry pie (à la mode, $.50 extra)[2]
Banana cream pie
Ice cream or sherbet
Fresh fruit salad
Cheese and crackers

Beverages

Coffee, Sanka, Tea, Milk

[1] Each day a different soup is served. The diner must ask the waiter what the soup is for that day.

[2] *A la mode* means with a scoop of ice cream. (used for pie or cake)

LISTENING-WRITING PRACTICE

EXERCISE 9: Paragraphs for Dictation

Your teacher will dictate each paragraph three times. The first time is for listening only, the second time is for writing, and the third time is for checking what you have written.

Immediately after you give your teacher the dictation you have written, check the dictation in the book for any problems you had in writing it.

DICTATION 1

Every country has its own rules of etiquette. Etiquette is polite social behavior that makes life easier and more pleasant so that people can get along with each other. Some of the rules of etiquette are merely conventional and arbitrary. They deal with the manner in which certain things are done, such as the serving and eating of food. Other rules reflect more deeply the values of a society: for example, the rules about respectful behavior toward older people or toward women. Today, because of the freer lifestyle of the younger generation, some of these rules are ignored. Even polite society does not insist on as many of the social amenities as it once did.

DICTATION 2

Good manners form the basis of modern etiquette. Its component parts are courtesy, promptness, a sense of decorum, good taste, and—most important—consideration of and respect for others. The Golden Rule applies: "Do unto others as you would have them do unto you." These attitudes and their application are essential to the functioning of society at every level, whether it is social, business, or diplomatic.

Etiquette must be learned. The child, self-centered and demanding, must be taught the rudimentary social graces which will equip him for living in harmony with others.

"Etiquette," *Encyclopedia International,* 1967, Vol. 6, p. 544.*

EXERCISE 10: Dicto-comps

Take notes as your teacher reads each of these dicto-comps to you several times. Then reconstruct the dicto-comp from your notes. The dicto-comp does not need to be written exactly as you heard it, but it should be grammatically correct.

Before you write the dicto-comp, your teacher may ask the class to get together in groups to check with each other on what you heard.

* Reprinted by permission of Grolier Incorporated.

Immediately after you give your teacher the dicto-comp you have written, check the dicto-comp in the book for any problems you had in writing it.

DICTO-COMP 1

Here are some things you should not do at the dinner table.*

1. Never butter a whole slice of bread at once. Break off and butter one rather small piece at a time.
2. Never sprawl your legs out far enough under the table to encroach upon the territory of others.
3. Never gulp water. Sip from the glass quietly between bites.
4. Never let your plate look messy.
5. Never help yourself too generously.
6. Never talk or drink with food in your mouth.
7. Never scratch your head, yawn, stretch, or slouch at the table.
8. Never load your fork or spoon too heavily.
9. Never monopolize the conversation or sit in gloomy silence.
10. Never tip your chair back so that it rests on only two legs.
11. Never reach across the table or in front of anyone.
12. Never serve yourself with your own silver.
13. Never blow on your food to cool it.
14. Never cut up all your food before beginning to eat.
15. Never use a toothpick in the presence of others.

DICTO-COMP 2

The manners expected of a gentleman are clearly defined. A gentleman stands when a woman, a member of the clergy, or an older man enters the room or comes up to him to begin a conversation. In a public place a gentleman helps a woman remove her coat and then hangs it up or checks it for her. If he smokes, he offers the woman he's with a cigarette and lights it for her if she accepts.

A gentleman walks on the curb side of the street, a custom that supposedly began in horse-and-buggy days when a man walked nearer to the roadway to shield the woman's clothes from mud. He removes his hat in apartment house elevators, but not in lobbies or elevators of public buildings.

A woman's manners are much less clearly defined. While a man's manners are protective, the lady's object is to seem worthy of protection. She gives him time to open doors, to help her with her coat, to light her cigarette. If, however, it becomes obvious that the man is not going to perform these courtesies, she opens the door, shrugs off the coat, or lights the cigarette without calling attention to his inattention.

"Etiquette," *Collier's Encyclopedia,* 1968, Vol. 9, pp. 363–64.†

* Abridged and adapted from *Mind Your Manners* by Betty Allen and Mitchell Pirie Briggs (J. B. Lippincott), pp. 75–77. Copyright © 1964 by Betty Allen and Mitchell Pirie Briggs. Reprinted by permission of Harper & Row, Publishers, Inc.

† Reprinted with permission from *Collier's Encyclopedia.* © 1968 Crowell Collier Educational Corporation.

Vacations

GRAMMAR AND USAGE

Participles in main verbs: *-ing* and *-ed*
Participles as adjectives
Participles in reduced adjective and adverbial clauses
Gerunds after verbs
would rather versus *had better*
Noun structures after *suggest, recommend,* etc.
Spelling: doubling final consonants before added vowels

RHETORIC

Using an outline for a friendly letter of persuasion
Using an introduction and a conclusion in the letter
Using a transitional lead-in to the body of the letter
Using transitions between paragraphs of the letter

DISCUSSION AND COMPOSITION

1. DISCUSSION: Preliminary outline for the composition (prewriting stage)

Subject: *An Invitation to Visit* (name of your country)
(This is a letter recommending that an American friend
or a classmate visit your country)

Outline (To Be Placed on the Board)	Discussion (Ideas, Grammar and Usage, Vocabulary, Elements of Composition Building)
	Note: the address and the date are on the top right side of the paper
Opening of the letter: Dear _____,	This opening begins on the left-hand margin. A comma is used with the opening of a friendly letter.
Introduction: greeting	Suggestions: give some friendly greeting such as: Hi, How are you? *Or* refer to a letter received from your friend.
Transitional lead-in from the greeting to the visit you are suggesting Invitation to your country	I would like to invite you to visit my country. *Or* I would enjoy having you come to my country.
Suggestion that your friend visit you too	Explain that you will be in your country at the time of the suggested visit. Please come to see me. You can be my guest. I will accompany you for all or part of your trip.
I. Tell why your friend would enjoy visiting your country	Opening sentence of paragraph: mention the subject, *enjoyment of your country* Keep this paragraph general (the specific details will go with the next main point) People: friendly, hospitable, helpful, unhurried Natural attractions: good climate mountains, beaches, lakes, waterfalls, canyons, volcanoes

Outline (cont.)	*Discussion* (cont.)

I. Tell why your friend would enjoy visiting your country (cont.)	Recreational attractions:
	    sports: swimming, boating, fishing, camping, hunting
	Historical and religious attractions:
	    castles, palaces, monuments, archaeological ruins, old towns, churches, cathedrals, shrines, temples, statues
	Handicrafts (handmade products) which your friend can buy at a good price:
	    pottery, ceramics, leather goods, jewelry, copperware, brassware, silverware, clothes, textiles

II. Places to visit (itinerary)	Opening sentence of paragraph: mention the subject, *places to visit* (or *itinerary*)
	Use connectives such as first, second; after this; next; then
	Tell what your friend will enjoy in each place that is visited
	Grammar:
	that clause after *recommend, suggest:*
	    I recommend that you visit this market.
	    versus I recommend this market to you.
	    I suggest that you visit these interesting places.
	    versus I want to suggest some interesting places to you.
	Gerunds after verbs like *appreciate, enjoy, avoid*

III. Special advice about the trip
  A. What to bring
    1. Clothes: kind and quantity
 	
    2. Documents: passport, visa, etc.
  B. How and where to buy things
  C. Precautions
 	
Conclusion: repeat the invitation and welcome your friend
	Opening sentence of paragraph: mention the subject, *advice*
	For the weather
	For recreational, touring activities
	
	Need to bargain?
	What to avoid doing or saying
	
	Ask if and when your friend will come.
	Refer again to your friend's enjoyment of your country.
	Welcome him or her.

Outline (cont.)	Discussion (cont.)
Closing of the letter:	The closing begins about two-thirds over to the right.
Choices: Sincerely, Your friend, Yours, Affectionately, Love,	Use a comma after the closing. Use an initial capital only for the first word. These closings reveal degrees of friendship. *Sincerely* is used for someone who is not so well known, *Affectionately* and *Love* for a very good friend (more likely to be used by a woman).

2. COMPOSITION (to be done before or after the reinforcement practice)

A. ORGANIZING THE COMPOSITION

Before writing your composition, fill in the required information on this Organizational Worksheet. The Worksheet follows the preliminary outline used for the discussion. Guidance for writing each paragraph is given at the right side of this Worksheet. The pages of the discussion outline provide additional help for the composition.

You may use phrases on this Worksheet except where it calls for full sentences.

ORGANIZATIONAL WORKSHEET
(Preliminary notes for the composition)

Title of the composition _____
(Do not use quotation marks or a period for a title at the top of the page. Use initial capital letters for the first word of the title and for all other words except articles, short prepositions, and short conjunctions.)

(Address) _____	Single space (on the typewriter)
(City) _____	This information goes on the
(Date) _____	top right side of the paper
(Opening of the letter:)	Four spaces down from the date (on the typewriter)
Dear _____,	Opening begins on the left-hand margin
	A comma is used with the opening of a friendly letter

Introduction: greeting
Opening sentence of paragraph_____

Two spaces down (on the type-writer)

_____

_____

_____

_____

Transitional lead-in from the greeting in the introduction to the visit you are suggesting

Same paragraph as the introduction, or a new one
Include an invitation to be with you

_____

_____

_____

_____

_____

I. Tell why your friend would enjoy visiting your country
   Opening sentence of paragraph_____

New paragraph
Mention the subject, *enjoyment of your country*
Keep this paragraph general (the specific details will go with the next main point)

_____

_____

_____

_____

_____

Reasons for enjoyment_____

_____

_____

_____

_____

_____

II. Places to visit (itinerary)
    Opening sentence of paragraph_____

New paragraph
Mention the subject, *places to visit* (or *itinerary*)
Use some geographic order for the places

_____

_____

_____

_____

_____

Use connectives such as *first, second; after this; next; then*
(Point II may be more than one paragraph)

Places and the attractions of each _____

_____

_____

_____

_____

_____

_____

III. Special advice about the trip
    Opening sentence of paragraph_____

New paragraph
Mention the subject, *advice*
(Point III may be more than one paragraph)

_____

_____

_____

_____

_____

    A. What to bring _____

_____

_____

_____

_____

    B. How and where to buy things _____

_____

_____

_____

_____

C. Precautions _____

_____

_____

_____

_____

Conclusion: repeat the invitation and welcome your friend   New paragraph

_____

_____

_____

_____

_____

(Closing of the letter:)   Use a comma after the closing

_____   Use an initial capital letter only
for the first word

B. WRITING THE COMPOSITION

Write the composition based on your notes on the Organizational Worksheet. Be careful of your paragraphing. Use separate paragraphs for your introduction and your conclusion. (Long paragraphs may be broken in two at appropriate places, but single-sentence paragraphs should be avoided.)

Use 8½ - by 11-inch white paper, with lines for a handwritten composition and without lines for a typed composition. Double-space the body (contents) of a typewritten letter, and skip lines on a handwritten one.[1] Write on the front of the paper only, and leave wide margins on *both the left and the right sides* of the paper. Indent the beginning of each paragraph.

Look over your composition carefully before you hand it in.

Below is the form for a friendly letter that is typed. Follow this form whether your letter is typed or handwritten. However, leave space between the lines of the body (contents) of the letter to allow room for corrections.

---

[1] The double-spacing required for the body of this letter, which allows room for corrections, need not be used in an actual letter.

```
┌─────────────────────────────────────────────────────────────────┐
│                                                                   │
│  [Leave space for a top margin]                                   │
│                              [single-        (your street address)│
│                              space on the    ─────────────────────│
│                              typewriter]     (city)               │
│                                              ─────────────────────│
│                                              (date)               │
│                                              ─────────────────────│
│                                                                   │
│  [four spaces down on                                             │
│  the typewriter]                                                  │
│                                                                   │
│  Dear ─────────────────────,                                      │
│                                                                   │
│       (double-space before your first paragraph and between paragraphs) │
│                                                                   │
│                                              Your friend,         │
│                                           or Sincerely,           │
│                                           or Yours,               │
│                                           or Affectionately,      │
│                                           or Love,                │
│                                                                   │
└─────────────────────────────────────────────────────────────────┘
```

C. CORRECTING OR REWRITING THE COMPOSITION

When your teacher returns your composition, it will be marked with the symbols from the correction chart on page 257. Make the necessary corrections on the composition and hand it back to your teacher.

Place the corrections on the correction page, and note down the rule that is involved.

If you have made many mistakes, or if you wish to make some additions to your composition, you may need to write the composition again. In rewriting the composition, do not make extensive changes or additions without consulting your teacher.

(For more help with your problems in writing, consult the Index of Usage and Rhetoric in *Writer's Companion*. The items in this index are arranged in the same alphabetical order as in the correction chart.)

CORRECTION PAGE

Use this page to write down the correction of any mistakes you have made in your composition on "An Invitation to Visit (*name of your country*)." Include enough of the words surrounding the corrected part to make the meaning clear. (Do not copy down the mistake itself.) If possible, write down the rule that covers the correction you have made.

Review these corrections from time to time in order to avoid making the same mistakes again.

Corrections	*Rule* *(See the correction chart if necessary)*

REINFORCEMENT PRACTICE

EXERCISE 1: Participles in Main Verbs: -ing and -ed

As an auxiliary, a form of *be* (*is, are, was, were,* etc.) is used:
   (1) with an *-ing* participle to express action *in progress.*

They *are loading* the boat now.

   (2) with an *-ed* participle to express *passive* action.

The boat *was loaded* yesterday.
(active: They loaded the boat yesterday.)

With irregular verbs, the third principal part (find, found, *found*) corresponds to the *-ed* participle.

Many types of tropical plants are found in our forests.

If the verb expresses both progressive and passive action, the word *being* comes before the *-ed* participle.

The boat *is being loaded* now.
(active: They are loading the boat now.)

Use the correct form of the verb in parentheses. Remember that with the auxiliary *be:* (1) the *-ing* participle expresses action in progress; (2) the *-ed* participle expresses passive action.

1. Our tourist guide is (take) _____*taking*_____ care of everything.

2. You are (invite) _____*invited*_____ to stay at my home when you visit my city.

3. While you are (prepare) _____ for your trip, read the travel brochures I sent you.

4. Our country is now (be) __being__ (call) __Called__. the crossroads between the East and the West.

5. I am (look) _____ forward to your visit.

6. We will be (spend) __Spending__ several days at this beautiful beach.

7. Our beaches are (consider) _____ the most beautiful on the continent.

8. You will be (impress) _____ by the handiwork of these Indians.

9. In a few days we will be (stroll) _____ along the Pacific shore.

10. Many colorful birds can be (see) _____ in our jungles.

11. It is not (surprise) _____ that many people visit this beautiful temple.

12. You will be (interest) _____ in our ancient architecture.

13. Everything is (be) _____ (do) _____ to make your visit enjoyable.

14. Much money is (be) _____ (spend) _____ by my country to improve our roads.

15. The buildings were once (destroy) _____ by an earthquake and were (rebuild) _____ many years ago.

16. A sweater or coat must be (wear) _____ when you go up this mountain.

17. A subway was (be) _____ (construct) _____ but the work was (stopped) _____ for lack of money.

18. Our government has been (try) _____ for a long time to attract more tourists.

19. Our beautiful forests were (be) _____ (destroy) _____ by industry until they were (make) _____ into national parks by the government.

EXERCISE 2: Participles as Adjectives

The *-ing* and *-ed* participles may also be used as *adjectives*. Thus, from the sentence:

The dances *excited* the spectators.

We derive:

the *excitING* dances (active)	*-ing* is used with the *subject,* and tells what is *causing* the action
the *excitED* spectators (passive)	*-ed* is used with the *object,* and tells what is *receiving* the action

A. Use the correct *-ing* or *-ed* adjectives based on the verb in each sentence.

1. Our mountains have always *astonished* tourists.

   our _____*astonishing*_____ mountains _____*astonished.*_____ tourists

2. The customs of these Indians *interest* visitors.

   the _____ customs _____ visitors
   of these Indians

3. The cathedral *amazed* the sightseers.

   the _____ sight-   the _____ ca-
   seers   thedral

4. The walk usually *tires* the hikers.

   the ___*tiring*___ walk   the ___*tired*___ hikers

5. The experience *satisfied* the travelers.

   the _____ ex-   the _____
   perience   travelers

6. The poverty of the people *shocked* the tour group.

   the _____ tour   the _____ poverty
   group   of the people

7. The visit of the tourists *embarrassed* the villagers.

   the _____ villagers   the _____ visit of
                                 the tourists

B. Supply the *-ing* or *-ed* participle of the verb in parentheses.

1. The (frighten) _____*frightened*_____ deer ran away as we drove through the forest.

2. These people have very (charm) _____*charming*_____ customs.

3. The (puzzle) ___*puzzled*___ residents wondered what had brought the tourists to their small town.

4. The (delight) ___*delighted*___ audience applauded wildly at the end of the performance by the dancers.

5. Coming to my country will not be a (disappoint) ___*disappointing*___ experience. The trip will be very (reward) ___*rewarding*___

6. You may see all kinds of (interest) ___*interesting*___ sights in this village.

7. The (satisfy) _____ tourists tipped their guide very handsomely.

8. The (accommodate) _____ hotel clerk quickly assigned the (tire) _____ travelers to their rooms.

9. Many tourists are (interest) _____ in seeing the (reconstruct) _____ colonial village of Williamsburg.

10. You will be (excite) _____ by the pageantry of the bullfight.

11. It is not (surprise) _____ that many visitors find these dances very (excite) _____.

12. Because they were not allowed to enter the temple, the (frustrate) _____ tourists returned to their hotel.

EXERCISE 3: Participles in Reduced Adjective and Adverbial Clauses

A. Verbs in some clauses may be reduced to *-ing* or *-ed* forms. The subject and a form of *be* may be omitted with a progressive or passive verbs in an adjective or adverbial clause.

Adjective Clause:	*progressive:* The people (who are) living in this region are very friendly. *passive:* The pottery (which is) made in this town is of very fine quality.
Adverbial Clause:	*progressive:* While (they were) traveling in the East, they bought some antique jewelry. *passive:* Although (they were) warned about the dangers of the trip, they decided to go to the jungle anyhow.

Reduce the adjective clauses or adverbial clauses by omitting their subject and a form of *be*.

1. The sights which are waiting for you in Disneyland will astound you.

The sights waiting for you in Disneyland will astound you.

2. While they were wandering through the town, they were entertained by several mariachi bands.

   While wandering through the town, they were entertained by several mariachi bands.

3. This hotel offers gracious hospitality (which is) unmatched anywhere in the country.

4. Although they were advised to check most of their money with the hotel, they took a large sum of money with them when they went shopping.

5. Anyone (who is) looking for a chance to gamble will find lots of casinos in Las Vegas.

6. While you are eating dinner, you will enjoy a fantastic floor show.

7. The local people who are strolling along the beach will greet you pleasantly.

8. The cliffs which are located along the coast are very steep.

9. Although they were tired from their long tour, they decided to go dancing in the discotheque that had been recommended to them.

10. If you are given the opportunity, you should certainly make a side trip to see our famous rain forest.

11. The police have recovered the jewelry that was stolen from their hotel room.

B. The *-ing* reduction may also be made with active verbs that do not use the auxiliary *be.*

Adjective Clause:	Anyone visiting (from *who visits*) our country will want to return.
Adverbial Clause:	Before coming (from *you come*) to our country, you should look over the travel brochures.

Change the words in parentheses into a reduced adjective clause or a reduced adverbial clause.

1. Near San Francisco, you will visit a modern castle (it, contain, many works of art).

   Near San Francisco you will visit a modern castle containing many works of art.

2. While (you, visit, New York), you must be sure to go to a performance at the Lincoln Center for the Performing Arts.

   While visiting New York, you must be sure to go to a performance at the Lincoln Center for the Performing arts.

3. On a foreign flight, any passenger (the passenger, bring, more than 44 pounds, baggage) will have to pay extra for the excess baggage.

[handwritten: have seen / seeing] *[handwritten: had offer]*

4. After (you, see, amazing, sights, that, our town, offer), you will enjoy a fabulous dinner in your hotel.

[handwritten: has to be p-p]

5. Since (they, discover, wonderful, marketplace, outside the town), they have bought many handsome things from the local Indians.

6. Anyone (the person, not wish, take, the side trip, to the canyon) should inform the tour director.

7. Before (they, leave, for, their trip), they got as much information as possible about the countries they were traveling to.

8. Until (I, come, New York), I had never been to a circus.

9. While (I, watch, clowns, acrobats, aerialists, animals, perform), I realized how much enjoyment I had been missing in my life.

10. Although (they, not stay, that hotel), the visiting couple took advantage of all its facilities.

11. While (you, stay, Washington), you should take the short side trip to Mt. Vernon, George Washington's stately home in Virginia.

12. A trip (it, require, little more time, out of Washington) is the trip to Monticello, the classically beautiful home of Thomas Jefferson.

13. Some of the people (they, collect, tickets, in, this off-Broadway theater) are also the performers in the play.

C. In a reduced adjective or adverbial clause, the reduced verb may begin with *being* (for passive action) or *having* (for action that is past in relation to the action of the main verb).

---

being: *passive action*

Adjective clause: The members of the Alpine tour group *being* transferred (from *who were being transferred*) to the hotel annex were very angry.
(*being* for passive action in progress)

Adverbial clause: After *being* robbed (from *After they were robbed*), they were much more careful about their money.

having: *past action in relation to the main verb*

Adjective clause: The Alpine tour group, *having* been transferred (from *who had been transferred*) to the hotel annex, were very angry.

Adverbial clause: After *having* been robbed (from *After they had been robbed*), they were much more careful about their money.

The *having* participle is often chosen for the same reason that the past perfect tense is—merely to *emphasize* time that precedes the time of the rest of the sentence. If there is no desire for such emphasis, the *-ing* participle is used.

Change the words in parentheses into a reduced adjective clause or adverbial clause using a *being* or *having* participle.

1. (After they had walked along Fifth Avenue for a while), they decided to have dinner at Rockefeller Center.

    After having walked along Fifth Avenue for a while, they decided to have dinner at Rockefeller Center.

2. The sports stadium (which is being built now) will accommodate 50,000 people.

    The sports stadium being built now will accommodate 50,000 people.

3. (After it was delayed for two hours), the train finally pulled into the station.

4. Anyone (who has seen Bryce and Zion National Parks) will never forget their scenic beauty.

5. (Before they had discovered the marvelous restaurants in Little Italy), the visiting couple ate dinner in their midtown hotel.

6. The tour guide (who is being assigned to them) is a very pleasant and knowledgeable man.

7. All passengers must submit to a security search (before they are allowed to enter the plane).

8. Those tourists (who had paid for the theater tickets in advance) were the only ones who were able to see the play.

9. (Before they had gone into the desert), they never realized how unbelievably beautiful it could be.

10. The Impressionist paintings (which are now being exhibited at the Museum of Modern Art) are part of their permanent collection.

EXERCISE 4: Gerunds after Verbs

Some verbs may be followed by the *-ing* form of other verbs.

When you come to my country, you should avoid *discussing* politics.

The more common verbs of this type are:

anticipate	enjoy
appreciate	finish
avoid	look forward to
consider (meaning keep	mind
in mind, think	miss
favorably about)	postpone
delay	practice

put off	risk
recommend	stop
regret (for the past)[2]	suggest
remember (for the past)[3]	

These verbs also take simple noun objects.

When you come to my country, you should avoid any *discussion* about politics.

A. Change the italicized noun objects to -*ing* objects after the verbs.

1. You may risk *the loss of your money* if you do not keep it in a safe place.

   *You may risk **losing your money** if you do not keep it in a safe place.*

2. I am anticipating *your visit to our country* with great pleasure. (keep *your*)

3. I hope you will consider *a stay with me* in my home town for a while.

4. You will enjoy *a swim at our sandy beaches.*

5. You must not delay *your phone reservation.* (add *make*)

6. I recommend *traveler's checks.* (add *bring*)

7. After you practice *the use of the surfboard*, you will enjoy *the ride on the waves.*

8. The archaeological expedition stopped *the exploration of these ruins* for a while.

9. I suggest *an evening flight.* (add *take*)

10. Do you mind *a late arrival at our hotel?*

11. They finished *the construction of this highway* a short time ago.

12. I'll always remember *the sight of the sunset at Waikiki Beach.* (use *see* for the verb)

B. Complete the following sentences using -*ing* verbs after the italicized verbs. Use real sentences.

Many of the verbs in this exercise require a reference to some of the attractions in your country (*consider, suggest, appreciate, enjoy, not miss*). You may refer to any of the ideas given in the discussion outline about the people, the natural attractions, the recreational attractions, the historical and religious attractions, the handicrafts.

---

[2] *Regret* is followed by the infinitive when it does not refer to past time: We regret to inform you that the trip has been canceled.

[3] *Remember* is followed by the infinitive when it means "remind oneself about something in the future": We must remember to buy tickets for the ballet as soon as we arrive in town.

1. In my country a visitor should *avoid* _talking about politics_

    OR

    walking in the streets at night.

2. When you visit my country, you should *consider* (= think favorably about)

    _____

3. When you are preparing to come to my country, I *suggest* _____

    _____

4. When you get to my country, you will *appreciate* _____

    _____

5. To avoid getting sick while you are traveling in my country, I *suggest* _____

    _____

6. In my country, you will *enjoy* _____

    _____

7. You can relax in my home town. You can *stop* ___worrying___

    _____

8. While you are in my country, you must not *miss* _____

    _____

9. The weather in my country is very nice now. Don't *postpone* ___your coming___

    _____

EXERCISE 5: *would rather* versus *had better*

   Auxiliaries that are sometimes confused are *would rather* and *had better*. Keep in mind that *would rather* means *prefer*, and *had better* means *should* in the sense of advisability. The contraction for both *had* and *would* as auxiliaries is *'d*.

would rather (= prefer)	If you'd rather come by train than by plane, then leave a day earlier. (*choices* are involved; the second choice often begins with *than*)
had better (= should)	You'd better bring warm clothes with you if you want to be comfortable in the mountains. (*advice*, sometimes a warning)

Would rather has a past time, *would rather have.*

I would rather have gone to the mountains than to the beach.
(*My preference was for the mountains, but I went to the beach instead.*)

Had better has no past time.
Both auxiliaries are made negative by placing *not* right after them.

I'd rather not take a long trip at this time.
You'd better not take a long trip at this time.

A. Use *had better, would rather,* or *would rather have* with the words in parentheses.
Do not use *to* after these auxiliaries.

1. If you (take) ____*would rather take*____ a cruise than go swimming, I'll make a reservation on the boat for you.

2. You (telephone) ____*had better telephone*____ me when you arrive in my country.

3. I'm sure you (have) _____ someone reliable go with you to the
   marketplace than go alone.

4. You (take) _____ a little first aid kit with you.

5. I (relax-*past*) _____ more than rushed around seeing so
   many things.

6. If you (buy-*past*) _____ the Indian vase than the bowl, I can

   exchange the bowl for you. In that case you (send) _____ the
   bowl back to me as soon as possible.

7. We (take) _____ a taxi if we don't want to miss our plane.

8. I (take) _____ a taxi than a bus to get to the airport.

9. You (not bring) _____ much luggage if you plan to go camping.

10. If you (not go) _____ sightseeing in the city, then bring only
    sports clothes with you.

11. You (not go) _____ boating if the weather is bad.

12. I (stay) _____ at a hotel than inconvenience your family by
    staying at your house.

13. I (not have) _____ you come to my country this month
    because I will not be able to accompany you on your trip.

14. You (come) _____ next month when I can be with you.

15. Yesterday, I (visit) _____ Versailles than have stayed in
    Paris.

B. Use five sentences for each of the following.

1. Tell what a person *had better do* if he or she comes to your country as a visitor.

Anyone who visits my country had better get a visa.
(Note that *get* is the infinitive form without *to.*)

2. Tell what you *would rather do* if you visit another country.

If I visit another country, I would rather see the impressive architectural sights than the cities and towns.
(Note that *see* (after *would rather*) and *visit* (after *than*) are the infinitive forms without *to.*)

3. Tell what you *would rather have done* when you visited another place.

When I visited _____, I would rather have taken the train than the bus.
(Note that *taken* is the past participle after *have.*)

EXERCISE 6: Noun Structures after *suggest, recommend,* etc.

There are some common verbs that are followed by two objects. The first object has no preposition before it, the second is preceded by *to.*

I will $\begin{Bmatrix} \text{suggest} \\ \text{recommend} \\ \text{describe} \\ \text{explain} \end{Bmatrix}$ something to you.

The first object is often a thing, the second object a person.
If a verb is used after *suggest* or *recommend,* the verb is placed in a *that* clause.

I suggest $\Big\}$ that you visit the ruins of the castle.[4]
recommend

In such sentences, the verb in the *that* clause is in simple, unchanged form.

Make full sentences from the following. Some sentences will have two objects after the verb. Other sentences will require a *that* clause after the verb. Do not change the word order.

1. I, recommend, this city, you.

I recommend this city to you.

---

[4] In the previous exercise we saw that *suggest* or *recommend* can also be followed by *-ing* verbs: I suggest (or recommend) your visiting the ruins of the castle.

2. I, suggest, you, visit, our capital.

I suggest that you visit our capital.

3. I, will describe, my home town, you.

4. The travel brochure, explain, our currency regulations, tourists.

5. I, suggest, you, come, my country, spring.

6. I, strongly recommend, this beach, you.

7. I, will suggest, good airline, you.

8. The travel guide, will explain, significance of the archaeological ruins, us.

9. I, recommend, you, buy, some, silver jewelry made by the Indians.

10. The airline, suggest, all passengers, make reservations, as soon as possible.

11. It, difficult, describe, exquisite beauty of the palace, you.

12. The health authorities, recommend, tourists, not enter, this jungle. (do not use *do* with this negative)

13. It, recommended, tourists, not drink, water in the small villages.

14. I, suggest, you, not bring, too many things.

EXERCISE 7: Word Forms

Use the correct form of the word in parentheses, and complete the unfinished words.

(If you need help with the signals that tell whether a noun, verb, adjective, or adverbial form is needed, refer to *Writer's Companion,* Unit 2, in the Grammar Review and Practice section.)

1. My (suggest) _____*suggestion*_____ is that you come by plane.

2. Check the plane schedules (careful) _____ for the times of (depart) _____ and (arrive) _____ of your plane.

3. My (recommend) _____ is that you take as little lug-_____ as possible.

4. If you follow my advi-_____, you'll be able to see some very (beauty) _____ (nature) _____ (scene) _____.

5. Our people are very hospit- _____, (friend) _____, and (honesty) _____. They will help make your trip very (comfort) _____ and (enjoy) _____.

6. You'll find a good (describe) _____ of this splendid cathedral in the little travel folder I'm sending you. The brochure also gives an (explain) _____ of its (religion) _____ and (history) _____ significance.

7. In this region you'll see many (architecture) _____ remains of an ancient (civil) _____.

8. Water (ski) _____ and (surf) _____ are very popular sports at this beach.

9. You will be greatly impressed by the (tropic) _____ (vegetable) _____ in our country.

10. From the top of this mountain you will get a (panorama) _____ view that is breathtak-_____.

11. In that market, you can buy some very (color) _____ carpets and ceram-_____.

12. We will go dancing in a disco-_____ that accommo-_____ 1,000 people.

13. Some regions that are good for our (recreate) _____ activities are too (mountain) _____ for (farm) _____.

EXERCISE 8: Sentence Review

Make full sentences from the word groups below, and complete the unfinished words. Make whatever changes or additions are needed, but do not change the word order. Use commas, semicolons, or periods wherever necessary. Use the tense given at the beginning of each word group.

1. (present) Our beaches / consider / most beautiful / continent.

   Our beaches are considered the most beautiful on the continent.

2. (present) Many color- / birds / can see / our jungles.

3. (present) Much money / spend / now / improve / our roads.

4. (past) The frighten- / deer / run away / as / we / drive / through / forest.

5. (present) You / may see / all kinds / interest- / sights / this village.

6. (future) While / eat / dinner / you enjoy / fantastic / floor show.

7. (present) Cliffs / locate / along / coast / be / very steep.

8. (present) Before / come / our country / you / should look over / travel brochures.

9. (future) Near / San Francisco / you / visit / modern / castle / contain / many works of art.

10. (present) Anyone / not wish / take / side trip / should inform / tour director.

11. (past) After / delay / two hours / train / finally / pull / into / station.

12. (past) Before / go / into / desert / they / never / realize / how / beautiful / it / can be.

13. (future) After / practice / use / surfboard / you / enjoy / ride / waves.

14. (present) You / may risk / lose / your money / if / you / not keep / it / safe place.

15. (present) I / suggest / you / visit / ruins / castle. (give 2 possibilities)

16. (present) I / strongly recommend / this beach / you.

17. (present) It / recommended / tourists / not drink / water in the small villages.

18. (future) You / be / greatly / impress- / by / tropic- / vegeta- / our country.

EXTRA SPEAKING AND WRITING PRACTICE

EXERCISE 9: Spelling: Doubling Final Consonants before Added Vowels

A consonant is doubled if:

(1) a syllable beginning with a vowel is added, and
(2) the word originally ends in one consonant preceded by one vowel, and
(3) the stress is on the syllable where the doubling of the consonant might occur.

Examples: *plánned, rúnning, occúrred*

Do not double the consonant if:
(1) a syllable beginning with a consonant is added: *develop + ment = development,* or
(2) the original word ends in a vowel: *dine + ing = dining,* or
(3) the original word ends in two consonants or has two vowels: *bend + ing = bending, rain + ing = raining,* or
(4) the stress is not on the syllable where the doubling of the consonant might occur: *devélop + ed = devéloped*

Rewrite the words, adding the required endings.

pót + ery _____ *pottery* _____	bénefit + ed _____
begín + er _____	bíg + est _____
drúg + ist _____	múd + y[5] _____
súffer + ing _____	ráin + ing _____
shíp + ed _____	equíp + ed _____
préfer + ence _____	equíp + ment _____
shín + ing _____	márvel + ous[6] _____
límit + ed _____	cáncel + ed[6] _____
wráp + ed _____	díagram + ing[6] _____
sún + y[5] _____	wórship + er[6] _____

[5] For this spelling rule, *y* is regarded as a vowel.

[6] American usage follows the rule just given (*marvelous*). British usage doubles some *l*'s, *p*'s or *m*'s before added vowels (marvellous).

EXERCISE 10: Business Letter to a Tourist Office

You would like to travel to a particular foreign country for your vacation. Write a letter to their tourist office to get information for your trip. (In the United States most tourist offices are located in New York City.)

Some of the things you might ask about are:

interesting places to visit (tourist offices usually have brochures that describe such places)

the airlines that go to that country

the travel regulations (inoculations; what you may bring in or take out of the country, etc.)

the currency of the country

Thank the tourist office for the information you are asking for.

Since this is a business letter, it is best to type it. The form below is for a typewritten letter. If you do not have a typewriter, follow the form as closely as possible.

```
                                        Your street address
                          [all single   Your city
                          space]         Date


[skip 4 lines]


Name of Tourist Office
Street address [make one up]   [all single
New York, New York              space]
       [skip a line]
Gentlemen:
       [skip a line]

_____

_____

_____
              [skip a line between paragraphs]

                              Very truly yours,
                              [skip 4 lines—
                              sign your name in this space]
                              [type or print your name]
```

Leave 1 ¼ -inch margins on both the left and the right sides of the paper. Try to center the letter on the page so that there is as much space on the top as on the bottom.

EXERCISE 11: Composition with Descriptive Paragraphs

Write two separate paragraphs describing the same scene of nature. *Each paragraph should be only from your own particular viewpoint as you witness the scene.* The first paragraph should be an objective description, the second paragraph a subjective one that includes your feelings.

1. *Objective description*

In this paragraph tell only what you see as you walk or drive along. For example, for mountains, note whether they are high or low, whether they are covered with vegetation or are bare of vegetation. For lower land, note whether it is a valley, whether it is flat or rolling land, whether it is hilly or rocky land. Note the kind of vegetation (trees, flowers), farmland, buildings, and animals. For bodies of water (rivers, lakes, oceans), note the size (large or small, narrow or wide). You might mention the kind of movement of the water (waves, current), the color of the water. You might also describe what is on the water (boats, canoes), and what is on the shores.

2. *Subjective description*

In this paragraph describe the same scene of nature in a more colorful way. Your words should express your emotional reaction to the scene.

Here are some terms from travel brochures that can be helpful to you. However, do not use too many of them, since an overuse of such emotionally charged words will make your description sound exaggerated or insincere.

Adjectives

spectacular, breathtaking, unique, picturesque, splendid, exciting, enchanting, fantastic, thrilling, majestic, delightful

Adjectives plus Nouns

scenic view, colorful landscape, sun-drenched beaches, sparkling lakes, quaint villages, unspoiled natural beauty, panoramic view, indescribable beauty

LISTENING–WRITING PRACTICE

EXERCISE 12: Paragraphs for Dictation

Your teacher will dictate each paragraph three times. The first time is for listening only, the second time is for writing, and the third time is for checking what you have written.

Immediately after you give your teacher the dictation you have written, check the dictation in the book for any problems you had in writing it.

DICTATION 1

The visitor to New York City will greatly enjoy a trip to the New York Stock Exchange. Located in the Wall Street area, the Exchange is easily reached by bus and subway. The Exchange was established soon after the formation of the United States and kept growing to meet the increasing need for more investment capital and credit. Trading operations in the purchase and sale of securities are conducted orally on the floor of the Great Hall of the Exchange (one of the largest rooms in the world). The visitor may view these fascinating operations from a special gallery. At the same time a special recording device will explain to him how the Exchange works.

DICTATION 2

The tourist in Chinatown will find himself walking along narrow, winding streets. He will see importing houses and grocery stores selling a wide variety of special Chinese foods. He will also see many restaurants offering authentic Chinese dishes at moderate prices. He can enjoy looking at the gift shops that sell souvenir-type articles along with finer chinaware and art objects. At the end of January, when the Chinese celebrate their New Year, the visitor to Chinatown will see parades of dragons and lions (with someone at the head and at the tail of each animal) which stop at different stores to wish their owners happiness and prosperity. The loud noise of firecrackers as well as the many gongs that are sounded are supposed to frighten off the evil spirits.

EXERCISE 13: Dicto-comps

Take notes as your teacher reads each of these dicto-comps to you several times. Then reconstruct the dicto-comp from your notes. The dicto-comp does not need to be written exactly as you heard it, but it should be grammatically correct.

Before you write the dicto-comp, your teacher may ask the class to get together in groups to check with each other on what you heard.

Immediately after you give your teacher the dicto-comp you have written, check the dicto-comp in the book for any problems you had in writing it.

DICTO-COMP 1

On the west side of Manhattan are a number of tourist attractions. One that must be seen is Times Square. This "Great White Way" is lit with brilliant lights and neon signs. Every evening the streets are jammed with people, many of whom are going to the theaters on or near Times Square.

On New Year's Eve, huge crowds fill the streets at Times Square. Shortly before midnight a lighted globe is lowered slowly from the top of one of the buildings at Times Square. When the ball hits bottom exactly at midnight, shouts of "Happy New Year" go up from the crowd, and whistles and horns are blown wildly.

Another attraction on the west side is Madison Square Garden, America's chief indoor arena, which is built above Pennsylvania Station. In this arena visitors may see national political conventions and sports events such as boxing and hockey. They may also see the circus, ice shows, and, if they can afford it, the horse shows.

DICTO-COMP 2

Fifth Avenue is one of New York's biggest tourist attractions. Although some of the larger stores have moved away to the suburban areas, Fifth Avenue still retains much of its reputation for fashion. At Christmas time the stores on the Avenue create fabulous window displays. Admiring crowds come from everywhere to view them.

In the midst of these great stores on Fifth Avenue is Rockefeller Center. This architectural wonder consists of a vast skyscraper office center, a shopping center, an exhibition center, and the largest entertainment hall in the world, Radio City Music Hall. Mural paintings, sculpture, and metal work soften the effect of the straight, simple lines of these buildings. A skating rink and an open area for flowers also add interest and beauty to Rockefeller Center.

A few blocks south of Rockefeller Center, on Fifth Avenue and Forty-Second Street, is the New York Public Library, the second largest library in America. Its broad steps and sculptured lions are well known to New Yorkers. During the lunch hour on a warm day, many of them can be seen relaxing on the library steps.

UNIT 10

Courtship and Marriage

GRAMMAR AND USAGE

Infinitives versus gerunds after verbs
used to versus *be used to*
most, the most, almost, mostly
Passive voice
Structures that follow *after, before, while, since*
Spelling: final silent *e*

RHETORIC

Using an outline to guide the composition
Using an introduction and a conclusion
Using a transitional lead-in to the body of the composition
Using transitions between paragraphs

DISCUSSION AND COMPOSITION

1. DISCUSSION: Preliminary outline for the composition (prewriting stage)

Subject: *Traditional Courtship and Marriage Customs in* (name of your country)

Outline (To Be Placed on the Board)	Discussion (Ideas, Grammar and Usage, Vocabulary, Elements of Composition Building)
	Note: Students who are not familiar with traditional customs in their country may talk and write about modern customs of courtship and marriage.
Introduction: general statements	Possible comments:
	There is now a difference between past and present customs.
	Past customs often persist in the country rather than in the cities.
Transitional lead-in: to traditional customs	I will be concerned with (or, I would like to describe) traditional customs of courtship and marriage in my country.

I. Courtship
  A. Meeting of the boy and girl
  B. Further meetings
	Opening sentence of paragraph:
	mention the subject, *courtship*
	  in the neighborhood, school, church
	  by family arrangement
	  through a marriage broker (matchmaker)
	  U.S.: dating
	     going steady
	Consent of parents needed?
	A chaperone required?

II. Engagement
  A. Rings
  B. Celebration
	Opening sentence of paragraph:
	mention the subject, *engagement*
	  get (or become) engaged
	  fiancé (boy), fiancée (girl)
	  U.S.: an engagement ring for the girl (a diamond ring)
	  U.S.: parties:
	    shower for the girl (women only—to give her household gifts)
	    bachelor party for the boy (men only)

III. Marriage	Opening sentence of paragraph:
	  mention the subject, *marriage*
	  The girl marries the boy.
	  They get married.

Outline (cont.)	Discussion (cont.)
A. Financial arrangements, property agreements B. Wedding	dowry ~ dwelle of people trousseau civil, religious marriage bride, (bride)groom invitations payment for the wedding place of the wedding ceremony rings clothes worn reception honeymoon U.S.—maid (matron) of honor best man bridesmaids and ushers (attendants) wedding band, fourth finger of left hand bride wears white wedding gown, veil groom wears a formal suit U.S. superstition: the bride should wear "something old, something new, something borrowed, something blue"
Conclusion: general statements	Possible comments: the change to new customs OR hope for the future happiness of a newly married couple OR your comments about marriage for yourself OR If you are married, what customs did you follow? old or new? OR If you are not married, what customs will you follow?

2. COMPOSITION (to be done before or after the reinforcement practice)

A. ORGANIZING THE COMPOSITION

Before writing your composition, fill in the required information on this Organizational Worksheet. The Worksheet follows the preliminary outline used for the discussion. Guidance for writing each paragraph is given at the right side of this Worksheet. The pages of the discussion outline provide additional help for the composition.

You may use phrases on this Worksheet except where it calls for full sentences.

ORGANIZATIONAL WORKSHEET
(Preliminary notes for the composition)

Title of the composition _____

(Do not use quotation marks or a period for a title at the top of the page. Use initial capital letters for the first word of the title and for all other words except articles, short prepositions, and short conjunctions.)

Note: If you are not familiar with traditional customs in your country, you may write about modern courtship and marriage customs.

Introduction: general statements

Opening sentence of paragraph _____

_____

_____

_____

_____

Balance of paragraph _____

_____

_____

_____

Put in a separate paragraph

Use the present tense for the general statements in this paragraph and in the rest of the composition (except for past customs)

Transitional lead-in connecting the general statements of the introduction to the customs you will discuss

Full sentence _____

_____

_____

_____

New paragraph

I. Courtship

Opening sentence of paragraph _____

_____

_____

_____

_____

New paragraph (or may continue the paragraph beginning with the transitional lead-in

Mention the subject, *courtship*

A. Meeting of the boy and girl

_____

_____

_____

_____

B. Further meetings

_____

_____

_____

_____

II. Engagement
   Opening sentence of paragraph_____

_____

_____

_____

New paragraph
Mention the subject, _engagement_

A. Rings

_____

_____

_____

_____

B. Celebration

_____

_____

_____

_____

III. Marriage
   Opening sentence of paragraph_____

_____

_____

_____

New paragraph
Mention the subject, _marriage_
Point III may be more than one
paragraph

A. Financial arrangments, property agreements

_____

_____

_____

_____

B. Wedding

_____

_____

_____

_____

_____

_____

Conclusion: general statements   New paragraph

_____

_____

_____

_____

_____

_____

B. WRITING THE COMPOSITION

Write the composition based on your notes on the Organizational Worksheet. Be careful of your paragraphing. Use separate paragraphs for your introduction and your conclusion. (Long paragraphs may be broken in two at appropriate places, but single-sentence paragraphs should be avoided.)

Use 8½ - by 11-inch white paper, with lines for a handwritten composition and without lines for a typed composition. Double-space a typewritten composition, and skip lines on a handwritten one. Write on the front of the paper only, and leave wide margins on *both the left and the right sides* of the paper. Indent the beginning of each paragraph.

Look over your composition carefully before you hand it in.

C. CORRECTING OR REWRITING THE COMPOSITION

When your teacher returns your composition, it will be marked with the symbols from the correction chart on page 257. Make the necessary corrections on the composition and hand it back to your teacher.

Place the corrections on the correction page, and note down the rule that is involved.

If you have made any mistakes, or if you wish to make some additions to your composition, you may need to write the composition again. In rewriting the composition, do not make extensive changes or additions without consulting your teacher.

(For more help with your problems in writing, consult the Index of Usage and Rhetoric in *Writer's Companion*. The items in this index are arranged in the same alphabetical order as in the correction chart.)

CORRECTION PAGE

Use this page to write down the correction of any mistakes you have made in your composition on "Traditional Courtship and Marriage Customs in (*name of your country*)." Include enough of the words surrounding the corrected part to make the meaning clear. (Do not copy down the mistake itself.) If possible, write down the rule that covers the correction you have made.

Review these corrections from time to time in order to avoid making the same mistakes again.

Corrections	Rule *(See the correction chart if necessary)*

REINFORCEMENT PRACTICE

EXERCISE 1: Infinitives versus Gerunds after Verbs

A verb that follows another verb may be:
1. *an infinitive* (*to* plus the simple form of the verb)

Some parents won't permit their daughter *to go* with a boy unless the couple is chaperoned.

In some cases the infinitive is used without *to,* especially with *let, make.*

Some parents won't let their daughter *go* with a boy unless the couple is chaperoned.

Most parents don't make their daughter *marry* a man she doesn't like.

2. *a gerund* (*-ing* form of the verb)

Some couples postpone *buying* a house until they have some money saved up.

Common verbs that are followed by gerunds have already been given in Exercise 4 of the preceding unit. These verbs are: *anticipate, appreciate, avoid, consider, delay, enjoy, finish, look forward to, mind, miss, postpone, practice, put off, recommend, regret* (for the past), *remember* (for the past), *risk, stop, suggest.*
Some verbs can be followed by either the *to* or the *-ing* form.

Some couples prefer *to have* (or *having*) a June wedding.

Some common verbs that take either the *to* or *-ing* forms are: *begin, continue, hate, hesitate, intend, (dis)like, love, prefer, start.*

Use the *infinitive* form (with or without *to*) or the *gerund* (*ing*) form of the verbs in parentheses. Note where either form may be used. (If the verb is not on one of the above lists, use the infinitive after it.)

1. The bride and groom promise (love and honor)____*to love and honor*____ each other.

2. Many parents have stopped (choose) _____*choosing*_____ a mate for their children.

3. Young girls are now allowed (go out) _____ on a date without parental supervision.

4. Many parents now let their children (select) _____ their own mates.

to inherit

5. Children sometimes risk (lose) __losing__ their inheritance if

   they refuse (respect) __to__ their parents' choice of a mate.

6. Young couples often avoid (get) _____ married on the 13th of
   the month.

7. Couples sometimes put off (get) _____ married until June.

8. Young girls like (be) _____ June brides.

9. The girl's trousseau helps[1] the young newlyweds (meet) _____
   some of their housekeeping needs.

10. In the United States, young couples are required (take) _____
    a blood test in order to get a marriage license.

11. When the clergyman finished (perform)_____ the marriage
    ceremony, the bride and groom kiss each other.

12. Many parents hesitate (make) _____ their children (marry)

    _____ someone they don't like.

13. Today, most couples prefer (have) _____ their own home.

14. When a young man starts (go) _____ with a girl, he is very
    courteous and attentive. After they are married a while, he may begin (lose)

    _____ some of his courteous behavior.

15. She has often regretted (not marry) __marrying__ the boy she really
    loved.

EXERCISE 2: *used to* versus *be used to*

Used to and *be used to* both refer to custom. *Used to* is an auxiliary which refers to
a *past custom* that is no longer observed. It is followed by the simple form of a
verb.

   In very early days, a man *used to go out* and capture his bride.

Be used to is a synonym for *be accustomed to*. Most of the time it refers to *present custom*. It is followed by the *-ing* form of a verb.

   Today men *are used to courting* the women they want to marry.

Be used to may also be followed by a noun.

   Today men are used to the *idea* that their wives want equal rights in the marriage.

[1] *Help* is followed by an infinitive with or without *to*.

In speech, the auxiliary *used to* is generally pronounced together as one word (heard as [yustə]).

If progression toward acquiring a custom is intended, *get* or *become* replaces *be*.

> Parents are *getting* (or *becoming*) used to letting their children choose their own mates.

A. Supply *used to* or a form of *be used to*. Use the simple form of the verb after *used to* and the -*ing* form of the verb after *be used to*.

1. Young married couples often (live) _____*used to live*_____ with their parents, but now they (live) _____*are used to living*_____ in their own homes.

2. At one time, the bride always (wear) _____ a white gown in a religious service.

3. Today a young married couple[2] (be) _____ more independent of their parents.

4. Among the early Hebrews, the boy (give) _____ the girl a coin as a symbol of their engagement.

5. In earlier times, the engagement of a couple (call-*passive*)[3] _____ _____ the betrothal.

6. Today the girl (get) _____ a diamond ring, but even this custom is not as widespread as it (be) _____.

7. Nowadays young newlyweds (go) _____ on a honeymoon after the wedding.

8. In the Middle Ages, romantic love (flourish) _____ under a very elaborate chivalric code.

9. Marriages (arrange-*passive*)[3] _____ by their parents, but now young people (choose) _____ their own mates.

10. Much money (spend-*passive*)[3] _____ on wedding receptions, but now many young people (save) _____ this money for more practical purposes.

---

[2] *Couple* is often plural, but it may be singular. (In this sentence it must be plural because of *their* parents.)

[3] After *to*, use the word *be* + the -*ed* form of the verb.

B. The expressions *once* and *at one time* often refer to a custom that is no longer followed.

> In the wedding ceremony, the bride *once promised* to obey her husband.
> = In the wedding ceremony, the bride *used to promise* to obey her husband.

Change these sentences with *once* or *at one time* to sentences with *used to*.

1. Young couples once got married in solemn religious services, but now they often prefer simple civil services.

> *Young couples used to get married in solemn religious services, but now they often prefer simple civil services.*

2. A young girl once accumulated linens for her trousseau when she got married.

3. At one time some religious groups practiced polygamy.

4. People once believed that the groom had to carry his bride over the threshold of their new home.

5. At one time members of the wedding party tied old shoes to the bridal car.

6. At one time some young couples who didn't have their parents' consent eloped by going to another state to get married.

7. A dowry was once paid by the bride's family.

C. Give some courtship and marriage customs in your country that are not as widespread as they *used to be*. Then tell what people *are used to doing* in modern times. Use full sentences, following this example:

> A chaperon *used to accompany* the boy and girl when they went out.
> But now the couple are *used to going out* by themselves.

For this exercise, you may refer to customs about:

how the boy and girl meet
the use of a matchmaker
the role of the parents
the engagement party
the financial and property arrangements (including a dowry or a trousseau)
the wedding ceremony: when it takes place, who pays for the expenses, the
  exchange of rings, the clothes worn, the honeymoon

EXERCISE 3: *most, the most, almost, mostly*

Although *most, the most, almost, mostly* have some similarities in meaning, they are used differently according to the requirements of grammar.

	Meaning	**Use**
most	the greater part	before a noun: *Most* young people would prefer to marry for love.
		before *of* (usually + *the*): *Most of the* young people I know would prefer to marry for love.
the most	(superlative— this is the only time *the* precedes *most*)	before an adjective or an adverb: The young man bought his fiancée *the most* expensive diamond ring he could find.
almost	nearly	with a verb: The wedding ceremony was *almost* finished when some guests arrived.
		with a pronoun or an adjective: Almost all women want to get married.
mostly	in most cases	with a verb: Married couples now live mostly by themselves.

Use *most, the most, almost, mostly*.

1. _____*Most*_____ of the money for the wedding is contributed by the bride's family.

2. _____ of the guests who came to the wedding brought gifts.

3. In some countries, dowries are given _____ in small towns in the country.

4. _____ of the time the young man chooses the girl he wants to marry.

5. _____ wedding bands are made of gold.

6. The guests at the wedding reception were _____ friends and relatives of the bride.

7. _____ popular month for marriage is June.

8. Until quite recently, _____ all marriages were arranged by the parents of the young people.

9. In _____ countries, couples must get a license to get married.

231

10. For _____ young men and women, _____ important day of their lives is their wedding day.

11. The groom _____ forgot to bring the ring for his bride.

12. Her wedding gown is _____ beautiful I have ever seen.

13. _____ of her friends have had church weddings.

14. The bride's parents paid for _____ the whole wedding reception.

15. _____ everyone who was invited came to the wedding.

EXERCISE 4: Passive Voice

Change these sentences to the passive. Keep in mind that in a passive sentence the original object of the verb becomes its subject.

1. In some countries a young man's parents still choose his bride for him.

   In some countries a young man's bride is still chosen for him by his parents.

2. The family may employ a matchmaker to find a bride for their son.

3. Today many young couples marry whether or not their parents permit them to do so. (only *permit* becomes passive here)

4. Often female friends and relatives give a shower for an engaged girl.

5. In a civil wedding, a judge or justice of the peace performs the marriage ceremony.

6. In a church, a clergyman marries the young people.

7. At the end of the wedding ceremony, the young couple exchange rings.

8. The guests at a church wedding often throw rice at the newly married couple.

9. Each guest at a wedding reception eats a piece of the wedding cake.

10. The girl's family makes most of the wedding arrangements.

EXERCISE 5: Structures that Follow *after, before, while, since*

Time words like *after, before, while,* and *since* may be followed by:

a full subject and predicate	After *they decide to get married,* the young couple get a marriage license.
the *-ing* form of the verb	After *deciding to get married,* the young couple get a marriage license.
the noun form from a verb	After *their decision to get married,* the young couple get a marriage license.

Sometimes the *-ed* form for the passive follows these time words.

While *engaged,* the young man does whatever he can to please his fiancée.

Change the subject–predicates within parentheses so that: (1) the verb becomes an *-ing* form, and (2) the verb becomes a noun after the time word. Make whatever other changes are required.

1. Before (she definitely accepts the young man's proposal), the girl may want to get her parents' consent.

   Before definitely accepting the young man's proposal, the girl may want to get her parents' consent.

   Before her definite acceptance of the young man's proposal, the girl may want to get her parents' consent.

   (Note that the original adverb becomes an adjective, and the original object is preceded by *of.*)

2. After (they are introduced), the young couple start to go out with each other.

3. Before (they are officially engaged), the young couple must get the consent of the girl's father.

4. While (she is being courted), the girl often receives gifts of flowers or candy.[4]

5. While (he was performing the marriage ceremony), the clergyman once asked the young man whether he promised to love, honor, and protect the girl he was marrying.[4]

6. After (he acknowledged the young man's reply), the clergyman once asked the girl whether she promised to love, honor, and obey the man she was marrying.

[4] *While* is used if a subject and a predicate follow it. If only a noun follows the time word, *during* replaces *while.*

7. Since (they achieved their independence), young women have been choosing their own mates.

8. While (she is considering the young man's proposal of marriage), a girl may or may not ask for her parents' opinion.

9. After (he proposes to the girl), the young man gives her an engagement ring.

EXERCISE 6: Word Forms

Use the correct form of the word in parentheses, and complete the unfinished words.

(If you need help with the signals that tell whether a noun, verb, adjective, or adverbial form is needed, refer to *Writer's Companion,* Unit 2, in the Grammar Review and Practice section.)

1. After her (engage) _____*engagement*_____, the girl (usual) _____*usually*_____ gets a diamond ring.

2. In some countries, the parents (custom) _____ make some

(finance) _____ settlements before the young couple get

(marry) _____.

3. After a young man has (choice) _____ the girl he wants to

marry, he makes a (propose) _____ of (marry) _____

_____ to her.

4. Before they are (official) _____ (engage) _____,

the young couple sometimes must get their parents' (permit) _____.

5. If there is to be a (wed) _____ recept-_____,

(invite) _____ are sent out to relatives and friends.

6. Then the couple are (unite) _____ in holy matrim-

_____.

7. Most of the wedding (arrange) _____ are made by the girl's family.

8. The (perform) _____ of the marriage ceremony is either a

(religion) _____ one or a civ-_____ one.

9. Accord-_____ to some people, love is not (necessary)

_____ the best condition for marriage.

10. In some countries it has been (tradition) _____ for the parents to make the (select) _____ of a bride for their son.

11. Today, young couples are (use) _____ to (live) _____ alone.

EXERCISE 7: Sentence Review

Make full sentences from the word groups below. Unless a special auxiliary is given, use the present tense for the verbs. Make whatever changes or additions are needed, but do not change the word order. Use commas, semicolons, or periods wherever necessary.

1. Many / parents / have / stop / choose / mate / their children.

   Many parents have stopped choosing mates for their children.

2. Couples / sometimes / put off / get / marry / 13th / day / of / month.

3. When / clergyman / finish / perform / marriage ceremony / bride groom / kiss / each other.

4. Young couples / often / use / live / their parents / but / now / they / be / use / live / own homes.

5. In / wedding ceremony / bride / use / promise / obey / husband.

6. Marriages / use / arrange / by / parents / but / now / young people / be / use / choose / own mates.

7. Most / money / for / wedding / contribute / by / bride's / family.

8. Most / wedding bands / make / gold.

9. Most / her friends / have had / church weddings.

10. Her / wedding gown / be / most / beautiful / I / have / ever / see.

11. Matchmaker / may / employ / find / bride / for / young man.

12. Rice / often / throw / young couple / by / guests.

13. After / they / decide / get / marry / young couple / get / marriage license. (give 3 possibilities)

14. After / they / introduce / young couple / start / go out / each other. (give 3 possibilities)

15. Before / they / official / engage / young couple / must / get / consent / girl's / father. (give 3 possibilities)

EXTRA SPEAKING AND WRITING PRACTICE

EXERCISE 8: Spelling: Final Silent *e*

A. *Drop* final silent *e before a vowel* (or before *y*).

    admire + ation = admiration
    arrange + ing   = arranging

Keep final silent *e before a consonant.*

    arrange + ment = arrangement
    care + ful   = careful

Rewrite each word with the endings that are given. Remember to *drop* the final silent *e* before a vowel (or *y*) and *keep* the final silent *e* before a consonant.

please + ure _____*pleasure*_____	fortunate + ly _____
confuse + ion _____	continue + ing_____
engage + ment _____	practice + ing _____
advertise + ment _____	safe + ty_____
nine + ty_____	nature + al _____
arrive + al_____	complete + ly _____
excite + ment _____	nerve + ous_____
observe + ance _____	noise + y _____
immediate + ly _____	entire + ly_____
shine + ing _____	announce + ment _____
use + ful_____	judge + ment[5] _____
dine + ing_____	argue + ment[5] _____
accurate + ly_____	love + ly _____
shine + y _____	finance + ial _____
invite + ation_____	

B. There are some exceptions to the rule on final silent *e.*
   (1) To prevent *c* and *g* from becoming "hard" before *a, o,* or *u,* keep the *e:*
       serviceable, outrageous
   (2) Drop *e* before *-th: width, ninth*

[5] This word is an exception in American usage. British usage follows the rule.

Rewrite each word with the endings that are given.

wide + th _____*width*_____   change + able_____

notice + able_____   nine + th_____

advantage + ous _____   courage + ous_____

twelve + th (change the *v* to *f*) _____   five + th (change the *v* to *f*)_____

EXERCISE 9: Writing a News Story

Newspapers often print stories about weddings and engagements. Here is an example of a story about a wedding.

Diana Smith Is Married to Robert Kaiser

Diana Smith, daughter of Mr. and Mrs. John Smith, was married in Jacksonville yesterday to Robert Kaiser, son of Mr. and Mrs. David Kaiser. The Rev. Andrew Wilson performed the ceremony in the First Baptist Church.

The bride, a free-lance[6] photographer, is a graduate of Jacksonville College. Her father, who is also an alumnus of Jacksonville College, is an engineering consultant, and her mother is a high school teacher. The bridegroom is an intern at the Jacksonville Hospital. The bridegroom's father, now retired, was a senior partner in a law firm.

The bride's maid of honor was her sister, Alice Smith. James Robinson was best man.

Note the use of commas to enclose additional information after names or after words that apply to only one person, like *the bride, her father.*

Using the information given below, write a news story about the following wedding. Model your story on the one given above. Include the headline. Be careful of your use of commas.

headline (use *Wed* instead of *Married*)
bride: Madeleine McCormack
bride's parents: Harry J. McCormack and the late Caroline McCormack[7]
place and time of wedding: Tranquillity, yesterday
bridegroom: Jeffrey Harris
bridegroom's parents: Mr. and Mrs. Joseph Harris
ceremony: performed by the Rev. Jonathan Miller at Tranquillity Holy Church

[6] *Free-lance* is used for professionals who do their work independently and are not employees of any company.

[7] *The late* refers to a person who has died.

occupation of the bride: librarian
bride's education: alumna of Tranquillity College
occupation of her father: surgeon
occupation of the bridegroom: account executive in an advertising company
bridegroom's education: master's degree in business administration
occupation of the bridegroom's father: president of a real estate firm
occupation of the bridegroom's mother: lawyer
maid of honor: the bride's friend, Julia Stanton
best man: the bridegroom's brother, William Harris

LISTENING–WRITING PRACTICE

EXERCISE 10: Paragraphs for Dictation

Your teacher will dictate each paragraph three times. The first time is for listening only, the second time is for writing, and the third time is for checking what you have written.

Immediately after you give your teacher the dictation you have written, check the dictation in the book for any problems you had in writing it.

DICTATION 1

Marriage has developed through three stages. At first it was simply mating. As this stage progressed, the couple began to realize the obligation of having children. The second stage was legal, and the rights of each mate began to be defined. Customs and laws to regulate marriage were established. Property rights, the protection of children, rights of inheritance, interests of society, and the conditions of dissolving marriage were indicated. The third stage—the personal or moral stage of marriage—stresses ethical rights. The emphasis is on cooperation of husband and wife, the responsibilities and privileges of parenthood, and the relations of religion to marriage and family life.

Compton's Encyclopedia, 1980, Vol. 15, p. 117
("Marriage: The Most Important Contract")*

DICTATION 2

Most wedding customs are very old and come from many different lands. Throwing old shoes or tying them to the bridal car goes back to ancient Egypt. There the father handed the bride's sandal to the groom, symbolizing a transfer of authority. Throwing rice carries the wish that the couple will be blessed with children. Another widespread custom is for the bride to wear "something old, something new, something borrowed, and something blue." In ancient Israel the bride's robe had a blue border signifying purity, fidelity, and love. Centuries ago in France the bride threw her garter, and the girl who caught it was believed to be the next bride. Today the bride throws her bouquet.

Revised from Compton's Encyclopedia, 1980, Vol. 15, pp. 115–16
("Marriage: The Most Important Contract")*

EXERCISE 11: Dicto-comps

Take notes as your teacher reads each of these dicto-comps to you several times. Then reconstruct the dicto-comp from your notes. The dicto-comp does not need to be written exactly as you heard it, but it should be grammatically correct.

* F. E. Compton Company, a division of Encyclopedia Brittanica, Inc. Reprinted by permission.

Before you write the dicto-comp, your teacher may ask the class to get together in groups to check with each other on what you heard.

Immediately after you give your teacher the dicto-comp you have written, check the dicto-comp in the book for any problems you had in writing it.

DICTO-COMP 1

Throughout most of Western history, marriages have been arranged by parents, and young people have had little or nothing to say in the matter. Among the early Hebrews, the Greeks, and the Romans, it was customary for the parents to contract for a marriage. This contracting, or betrothal, was the forerunner of the modern engagement. A dowry was generally involved, and two witnesses were required at the betrothal ceremony.

It is probably wrong to think of parents as forcing their children into specific marriages. Indeed, in the case of both the Hebrews and the Romans, mutual consent of the participants was supposedly required. Since parents loved their children, it is unlikely that a father would force his son or daughter into unwelcome matrimony. On the other hand, it is just as unlikely that a well-bred boy or girl would object to a parentally arranged marriage. Young people did not marry for romantic love, for companionship, or for personality development. Marriages were based largely on economic considerations. Most men were farmers who needed a wife to manage the household and children to help on the farm.

"Courtship Customs," *Encyclopedia International,* 1980, Vol. 5, pp. 287–88 (abridged).*

DICTO-COMP 2

Throughout the United States, the legal age for marriage shows some variation. The most common age without parental consent is 18 for both females and males. However, persons who are underage in their home state can get married in another state with a more liberal law and then return to the home state legally married. The general rule in the United States is that a marriage which is valid in the state where it was performed is valid in all states.

Each state issues its own marriage license. Both residents and nonresidents are eligible for such a license. The fees, blood testing requirements, waiting period, and ceremonial aspects vary greatly from state to state. Most states, for instance, have a blood test requirement, but a few do not. Most states permit either a civil or religious ceremony, but a few require the ceremony to be religious. In most states a waiting period is required before the license is issued. This period is from one to five days, depending on the state. A three-day wait is the most common. In some states, however, there is no required waiting period.

"Marriage," *Encyclopedia International,* 1980, Vol. 11, p. 369*

* Reprinted by permission of Grolier Incorporated.

Partial Answers to Exercises

UNIT ONE—Traveling to Another Country

Exer. 1

4. very   6. so   8. so, very   10. so,   12. very

Exer. 2

A. 2. left, got, put   4. felt, felt   6. thought, had   8. came, come
10. said, hit, stolen

B. 2. It had been made for me by my girlfriend.   4. It was found by a customs inspector.   6. I was told by him to be very careful with money.   8. More money will be sent (to) me right away by my father (*or* by my father right away).

Exer. 3

4. change   6. preparing   8. make   10. pack (*or* to pack)   12. looking   14. beating   16. having   18. making

Exer. 4

A. 3. After I made, After making   5. After I was inoculated, After being inoculated   7. Before I boarded, Before boarding   9. After I arrived, After arriving

Exer. 5

A. 3. (in order) to learn   5. (in order) to pick up my plane ticket, for my plane ticket   7. in order not to be tired   9. (in order) to claim my suitcases, for my suitcases

B. 3. for   5. (in order) to   7. (in order) to   9. for

Exer. 6

3. There was   5. It was   7. There was   9. There was   11. It was

Exer. 7

2. objections, approval   4. anxiety, Embassy   6. departure, tearful
8. passengers   10. nervous, frightened

Exer. 8

2. a (doctor) medicine   4. a physicist   6. a psychiatrist   8. a chemist
10. a stenographer   12. an engineer   14. a (nurse), nursing

Exer. 9

2. Last month I flew to New York. (*or:* I had never flown on such a large airplane before.)   4. I had my tailor make some new clothes.   6. I applied for a visa after getting (*or* I got) my passport.   8. I went to the doctor to get a vaccination against (*or* for) smallpox.   10. There were many things that had to be done (*or* that I had to do) before I could leave.   12. There was a pretty girl sitting next to me. 14. When the day of departure arrived, I bid a tearful goodbye to my family and friends.

Exer. 10

A. carried, delaying, hurried, travel agencies, studying, enjoying, annoying, employed

B. loneliness, enjoyment, librarian, employment, beautiful, payment

Exer. 11

1. The airline passenger was Marcella Frank.   3. The travel agent (that issued the ticket) is Superior Travel Service.   5. The ticket cost $557.30. The tax was $3.00 (*or:* The passenger paid a tax of $3.00.)   7. After leaving Salt Lake City, the passenger went to Los Angeles, Miami, New York, and Casablanca.   9. The passenger took two flights in the morning and two flights in the evening.

UNIT TWO—Geography

Exer. 1

1. (b) To the east of Italy is the Adriatic Sea,   (c) To the south of Italy is the Mediterranean Sea,   (d) To the west of Italy is the Mediterranean Sea,   (e) to the northwest of Italy are France and Switzerland.   3. (b) Paris is located in the northern part of France,   (c) Lisbon is located in the western part of Portugal,   (d) Madrid is located in the central (or north central) part of Spain,   (e) Warsaw is located in the northeastern part of Poland,   (f) Rome is located in the western part of Italy,   (g) Bucharest is located in the southern part of Rumania,   (h) Athens is located in the eastern part of Greece,   (i) Berlin is located in the central (or north central) part of East Germany.

Exer. 2

2. ____, ____   4. The, the, ____   6. ____, ____   8. The, ____, ____
10. The, ____, the, the   12. The, ____, ____

Exer. 3

2. is surrounded, is attached   4. are found   6. are grown   8. are raised
10. are manufactured   12. are trapped

Exer. 4

vegetables, potatoes, coconuts, oats, feathers, pigs, oysters, textiles, handicrafts
meaning "kinds of": fruits, wools, wines

Exer. 6

3. Mexico City, (which is) the biggest city in my country, is located . . .   5. The Amazon, (which is) the largest river system in the world, drains . . .   7. Africa, (which is) a great plateau, is about . . .

Exer. 7

2. Saudi Arabia has two capitals, Riyadh and Mecca.   4. Rising from great depths of the sea, the islands of Japan are mostly mountainous. (or The islands of Japan, rising from great depths of the sea, are mostly mountainous.)   6. Once famous for its precious metals, Peru today produces . . . (or Peru, once famous . . .)

Exer. 8

A. 2. Scandinavia, which consists of (or consisting of) Norway, Sweden and Denmark), is in the northern part of Europe.   4. Holland, which lacks (or lacking) natural resources, has been a nation of sailors for centuries.   6. Chile, (which is) sometimes called the "Shoestring Republic," stretches along . . .

Exer. 9

2. (comma fault) We already have small industries, one of the largest of which is the textile industry.   4. There are many rivers in Venezuela, the most important of which . . .   6. Island groups off the Asian mainland are Japan, the Philippines, and Indonesia, all of which have become . . .   8. In Nepal are several of the world's highest mountains, one of which is Mt. Everest.

Exer. 10

(Note: There might be other acceptable combinations than the ones given below.)
2. The longest river in Japan is the Shinano River, (which is) located in . . .
4. The other famous city is Izmir, a port (which is) located on the west coast of Turkey.
6. The most famous mountain is Mt. Fuji, which is very beautiful and is one of the symbols of Japan.   8. Paraguay has two important rivers, the Parana and the Paraguay, both of which make . . .   10. My country is Malaysia, a small independent country situated in Southeast Asia.   12. We have two important cities: Caracas, the capital, and Valencia, where most of the factories are located.

Exer. 11

2. Among the many metals mined in this area of the continent are gold and silver.
4. Situated near the Persian Gulf are Iran's rich oil fields.   6. Located in the Elburz Mountains is Demavend, Iran's highest peak.   8. Lying in the western Pacific is Micronesia, or "little islands."

Exer. 12

2. mining   4. cultivation, mountainous (*or* mountain)   6. production
8. central   10. agricultural, manufactured, produced   12. commercial, industrial

Exer. 13

2. The United States is bounded on the north by Canada and the Great Lakes.
4. The Suez Canal separates Africa from Asia.   6. Dairy products are made from milk.   8. Manhattan is an island (which is) surrounded on all sides by water.
10. Mexico City, (which is) the biggest city in my country, is located in the central part of the Republic of Mexico.   12. The Sahara Desert extends from the Atlantic Ocean to the Nile River.

UNIT THREE—Biography

Exer. 1

2. in, (on) in   4. at   6. (on)   8. at   10. in, at   12. in
14. during

Exer. 2

2. My friend has been visiting (or has visited) me since January (or for three months). My friend came to visit me two months ago.   4. Anabel has been a lawyer since February (or for ten months). Anabel became a lawyer ten months ago.   6. I have been sick since October 20 (or for four days). I became sick four days ago.   8. Colette has been engaged since May (or for six months). Colette became engaged six months ago.

(In the above sentences the word *for* may be omitted.)

Exer. 3

A. 3. *it,* which gave me (the) most trouble   5. *she,* who was teaching this subject 7. *there,* where I was born   9. *he,* who helped me (to) learn the English language 11. *there,* where I studied (for) four years

B. *that* may be used instead of *who* or *which* in sentences 1, 3, 5, 6, 8, 9, 10.

C. 2. *it,* which I had (for) a long time   4. *them,* whom I met in elementary school 6. *it,* which I attended   8. *it,* which I liked the best

D. *Whom* or *which* may be omitted from all the sentences in C.

E. 2. *teacher,* of whom I was most fond   4. *teacher,* for whom I had the most respect 6. *thing,* about which I could think   8. *parties,* to which I was invited

F. 2. I was most fond of   4. I had the most respect for   6. I could think about 8. I was invited to

Exer. 4

3. The subject which gave me (the) most trouble was English.   5. Everyone on the block is helping the family whose house burned down yesterday.   7. I attended the same school where my brother went.   9. The education which (or that) I received in high school was excellent.   11. Everyone would enjoy visiting Paris, where I grew up.   13. A boy whose parents had money could afford to go abroad to study.   15. The children with whom I used to play (*or* whom, who, that I used to play with, *or* I used to play with) all lived on the same block where I lived.

Exer. 5

2. , considered the founder of modern psychoanalysis,   4. , the originator of the theory of evolution,   6. , a famous American poet,   8. , known as the founder of progressive education,

Exer. 6

2. infantile   4. was born, died   6. was engaged, engagement, died 8. engaged, married   10. neighborhood   12. married

Exer. 7

2. Albert Camus went to public schools in Algiers; (*or:* then he entered the University of Algiers.)   4. Leon Tolstoy, the great Russian novelist, attended the University

of Kazan but (he) never graduated from this school.   6. Abraham Lincoln was born in 1809 in Kentucky. He was assassinated in Washington (on) April 15, 1865. 8. Ford's Theatre, where Lincoln was shot, is (or was) located on Tenth Street in Washington, D.C.   10. Edgar Allan Poe married a young cousin of his in 1836. The marriage lasted until her death in 1847.   12. Everyone would enjoy visiting the town where I come from (*or* which, that I come from, *or* I come from).

Exer. 9

A. while,   at,   following or next,   soon or later

B. since,   ago,   at,   then or after this

C. At,   finally,   at,   while,   since

UNIT FOUR—Instructions (How to Make or Do Something)

Exer. 1

A. 3. The seeds are planted in even rows.   5. The tennis ball is thrown high in the air and (it is) served . . .   7. Plenty of fluids should be drunk if you have a cold. 9. The air in the tires should be checked before . . .   11. These exercises should be done regularly every morning.

Exer. 2

A. 2. You would get rid of your cold if you drank lots of fluids.   4. The piano would sound better if you had it tuned.   6. The car could last a long time if you took good care of it.   8. If you took some driving lessons, you would learn to park the car.   10. If you followed these instructions carefully, you would have no trouble.

B. 2. would have got(ten), had drunk   4. would have sounded better, had had 6. could have lasted, had taken   8. had taken, would have learned   10. had followed, would have had

C. 2. If you practiced a lot, you would be an excellent pianist.   4. If you shopped wisely, you would save money.   6. If you didn't look down at the typewriter keys, your typing speed would improve.

D. 2. had practiced, would have been   4. had shopped, would have saved 6. hadn't looked, would have improved

Exer. 3

3. Pin (*or* you must pin) the pieces of material together carefully; otherwise the dress won't come out right.   5. Hold (*or* you must hold) your fingers in the right position over the keys; otherwise you will make mistakes.   7. Turn on (*or* you must turn on) the ignition in the car with your key; otherwise the car won't start.

9. Learn (*or* you should, must learn) to skim in reading; otherwise you will never become a fast, efficient reader.

Exer. 4

3. don't have to put   5. mustn't leave   7. mustn't drive   9. don't have to do   11. don't have to be

Exer. 5

A. 2. the druggist fill my prescription, my prescription filled   4. the lawyer draw up my will, my will drawn up   6. the shoemaker repair my shoes, my shoes repaired   8. the painter paint the whole house, the whole house painted 10. the carpenter build some bookcases for me, some bookcases built for me   12. the handyman replace the light bulbs, the light bulbs replaced.

Exer. 6

2–6—All the replacements can be: then, next, after this

Exer. 7

2. Once the chicken is cooked, add the sautéed mushrooms.   4. After you hem the dress, the last step is ironing it.   6. When doing this dance step, place your arms on your partner's hips. (*or* When you do this dance step, your arms . . .) 8. Having cut each pattern piece of the dress, pin the pieces together. (*or* After you have cut . . . , the pieces . . .)   10. correct

Exer. 8

2. that we show respect . . .   4. that if we are wrong, we admit . . .   6. that we try . . .   8. that we dramatize our ideas.   10. that we talk . . .

Exer. 9

2. practical   4. attractive   6. enjoyable   8. sautéed   10. precaution   12. ingredient   14. accomplishment

Exer. 10

2. A screwdriver is used to loosen the screws.   4. The car would last a long time if you took care of it.   6. Your cold would have got(ten) better if you had stayed in bed.   8. You should (or must) learn to skim in reading; otherwise you will never become a fast, efficient reader.   10. You mustn't add much turpentine if you want the paint to cover the wood completely.   12. Dale Carnegie recommended that we (should) dramatize our ideas.

UNIT FIVE—Holidays

Exer. 1

A. 2. in   4. at   6. On, in   8. On, at, at   10. on, on

Exer. 2

3. the   5. the, ——   7. the   9. (the) twenty-fifth

Exer. 3

3. the enjoyment of holidays by children *or* children's enjoyment of holidays
5. the election of government officials   7. the exchange of gifts *or* exchanging gifts)

Exer. 4

2. commemorates   4. has, takes   6. enjoy   8. are, do   10. do, go
12. wishes   14. depends, has, cares   16. gets

Exer. 5

2. The dead servicemen are commemorated on Memorial Day.   4. Turkey is eaten on Thanksgiving Day.   6. Presents are given for Christmas.   8. Many holidays are observed on Mondays.   10. A lot of money is sometimes spent to . . .
12. Solemn music is heard in church . . .   14. Christmas carols are sung . . .
16. Santa Claus's "helpers" can be seen . . .

Exer. 6

2. few   4. much   6. much   8. a little   10. little   12. much, little

Exer. 7

2. customary   4. religious   6. appearance   8. pride, heritage or in-heritance   10. commemorates   12. symbolizes   14. basically,   gener-ally, especially, national

Exer. 8

2. Mother's Day is observed in May, Father's Day in June.   4. It is customary for families to eat Thanksgiving dinner together.   6. Memorial Day is observed (on) the last Monday in May.   8. Everybody likes to have a holiday from work.
10. Few people came to the parade because of the heat.   12. There is a lot of noise (on) New Year's Eve.   14. A lot of (*or* Lots of) money is (*or* was, will be) spent (in) preparing for the (*or* a) holiday.

Exer. 10

2. Boxes, sweethearts   4. leaves, trees   6. beliefs   8. parties, costumes, games   10. witches, symbols   12. cemeteries, wreaths, graves

UNIT SIX—Telling Stories

Exer. 1

A. 2. Cinderella told her stepsisters that she would help them get ready for the ball.
4. The Beast told Beauty that she had forgotten (*informal*—forgot) her promise, and so he decided to die, for he could not live without her.   6. The fairy told Beauty that she had chosen well, and that she would have her reward.   8. Sleeping Beauty told the prince that she had waited for him for a long time.

B. 2. They said, "Clothes made of this cloth are invisible to a stupid person."
4. The emperor said, "I have to have this cloth woven for me immediately."
6. A little child said, "The emperor has nothing on at all."

Exer. 2

A. 2. Cinderella asked her stepsisters whether (*or* if) they had enjoyed themselves at the ball.   4. Bluebeard asked his wife why there was blood on the key.   6. The emperor asked whether (*or* if) his suit didn't fit him marvelously.   8. At the ball, all the people asked who that beautiful girl was.

B. 2. The emperor asked himself, "Am I unfit to be the emperor because I cannot see the clothes?"   4. The Sultan asked his minister, "Have you ever seen (*or* "Did you ever see) such precious jewels?"   6. The princess asked the old lady, "What are you doing at the spinning wheel?"   8. The Sultan asked, "What has become (*or* "What became) of Aladdin's palace?"

Exer. 3

2. Her fairy godmother warned Cinderella not to stay . . .   4. The Moroccan magician urged Aladdin to put on his magic ring . . .   6. The bear told (*or* asked) Snow White and Rose Red to let him come with them and not to be afraid.

Exer. 4

1. c. What big legs you have.   2. a. What a clean cottage this is.   c. How good this food tastes.   e. How very far I have gone.   3. a. How lucky I am to see such a beautiful girl.   c. What a beautiful girl she is.   4. a. What a beautiful piece of cloth it is.   c. What a beautiful color the cloth is.   e. How magnificent your new clothes are.

Exer. 5

2. to the princess that she give him her old lamp for a new one (*or* that the princess give him . . .)   4. his wife that she would die at once because she had disobeyed him.
6. to Beauty that the spinning wheel made thread.   8. Aladdin to go into the cave (*or* that Aladdin go into the cave).   10. the magician to help him get out of the cave (*or* that the magician help him . . .).

Exer. 6

3. Aladdin's mother urged him to sell the enchanted lamp right away (*or* urged that he sell . . .).   5. Cinderella's fairy godmother implored her not to stay at the ball past midnight.   7. The prince told his messengers to find the girl who wore the glass slipper.   9. In "The Water of Life," each brother met a dwarf who asked where he was going.   11. Rumpelstiltskin told the princess that if she guessed his name in three days, she might keep her child.   13. Beauty begged her father to bring her back only one red rose (*or* that her father bring her back . . .).

Exer. 7

2. A fable is a fictitious narrative intended to teach some moral truth in which animals act like human beings.   4. A myth is a traditional story about gods and heroes, serving to explain some natural phenomenon, the origin of man, or the customs and institutions of a people.

Exer. 8

2. found, beginning   4. finally, heroine, strength, cleverness, assistance
6. caused, jealousy, wicked   8. purity, innocence   10. abandoned
12. Chinese, magician

Exer. 9

2. Cinderella said to her stepsisters, "I will help you (to) get ready for the ball."
4. The weavers said that they could weave the finest cloth in the world.   6. Bluebeard asked his wife, "Why is there blood on the key?"   8. The Sultan asked his minister whether (*or* if) he had ever seen such precious jewels.   10. Bluebeard said to his wife, "Don't open the door to (*or* of) one room."   12. When the prince saw Snow White (,) he exclaimed, "What a beautiful girl she is!"   14. The queen asked the magic mirror, "Who is the most beautiful woman?"

UNIT SEVEN—Superstitious Beliefs

Exer. 1

3. gets, will avoid   5. will not get, want   7. itches, will receive   9. wear, will wear
(*Note:* In Nos. 3, 4, 6, the verb in the main clause may be in the present tense.)

Exer. 2

2. If you walk under a ladder, you will have bad luck. Walking under a ladder will bring you bad luck.   4. If you spill salt on the table, . . . spilling salt . . .   6. If you find a penny, . . . Finding a penny . . .   8. If you open an umbrella in the house, . . . Opening an umbrella . . .

Exer. 3

A. 2. gave, would put   4. decided, would not have   6. gave, would give
B. 2. had given, would have put   4. had decided, would not have had
6. had given, would have given

Exer. 4

4. ; therefore,   6. ; however,   8. ; therefore,   10. ; therefore,

Exer. 5

A. 3. A–The, a, _____   5. a–the, _____, _____   7. the–a, _____, _____,
9. A, a
B. 2. a, _____, the, the _____   4. an, the, _____   6. a, a, the, a
C. 2. A, the–a, the   4. a, _____   6. _____, an, the   8. An–the, _____, _____
(*Note:* Sometimes *the* is used before the word *number,* as in sentences 5 and 9.)

Exer. 6

A. 4. most of the   6. most of the   8. most   10. the most   12. most of
the   14. most   16. most
B. 2. most, most of the   4. most, most of the

Exer. 7

2. superstition, unreasonable, belief, supernatural   4. _____, unknown, mysterious   6. Primitive, ignorant, superstitious, beliefs   8. Seeing, _____, death

Exer. 8

2. If a black cat crosses your path, you will be unlucky.   4. If a young girl took the
last piece of bread, she would be an old maid herself.   6. If someone sneezed, I
would say "God bless you."   8. He was worried because the–a mirror had fallen
(*informal*—fell) off the wall in the bedroom.   10. The house where he used to live
is–was haunted by ghosts.   12. There was once a belief that gold could be made by
man.   14. The most expensive gown was worn by the bride.

Exer. 10

1. orderly, cautious, self-disciplined, self-confidence, planner, organizer   3. imaginative, changeable, disorganized, subtlety, creativity, security, reality   5. determined, dependable, conservative, vitality, adaptability   7. possessive, changeable, jealous, intuition, security   9. modest, diligent, dependability, fanatic
11. patient, suspicious, determination, loyalty

UNIT EIGHT—Rules of Etiquette (Politeness)

Exer. 1

2. bring up, grow up   4. takes off, comes into   6. eat in, eat out   8. make up   10. picked up   12. puts out

Exer. 2

3. turned it down   5. have not raised him, didn't raise him, are not raising him, will not raise him   7. pick them out, does not try them on   9. put it out   11. call it off

Exer. 3

2. . . . Then we also thank . . .   4. . . . Finally we eat some dessert.   6. (use all *we*'s or all *you*'s)

Exer. 4

2. disobedient, misbehave   4. inconsiderate, indecent, disapproval   6. immodest   8. unable, inability   10. disapprove, disregards

Exer. 5

2. medieval, chivalrous   4. well-bred, ill-bred   6. courtesy, consideration, behaves, propriety, decency   8. permissive, politeness, courtesy   10. rises, seat, introduced, seated, introduction   12. lying   14. promptly, invitation

Exer. 6

A. 2. Parents should bring up their children to have good manners, so that when the children grow up, they will be well-bred.   4. They are worried about their son. They are afraid they have not brought him up (*or* didn't bring him up, *or* are not bringing him up, *or* will not bring him up) well.   6. She is wearing (*or* was wearing, *or* wore) a beautiful dress, but nothing else that she has (*or* had) on goes (*or* went) with it.

B. 1. It is impolite to be disrespectful to one's elders.   3. It is unpleasant to be with people who are discourteous.   5. Rules of etiquette tell us what kind of behavior is courteous and considerate.

UNIT NINE—Vacations

Exer. 1

3. preparing   5. looking   7. considered   9. strolling   11. surprising   13. being done   15. destroyed, rebuilt   17. being constructed, stopped   19. being destroyed, made.

Exer. 2

A. 2. interesting, interested   4. tiring, tired   6. shocked, shocking
B. 3. puzzled   5. disappointing, rewarding   7. satisfied   9. interested, reconstructed   11. surprising, exciting

Exer. 3

A. 3. unmatched anywhere . . .   5. looking for . . .   7. strolling along . . .
9. tired from . . . , recommended to them.   11. stolen from . . .
B. 3. bringing more than 44 pounds of baggage   5. discovering a–the wonderful marketplace outside the town   7. before leaving for their trip   9. watching the clowns, acrobats, aerialists and animals perform (*or* performing)   11. staying in Washington   13. collecting tickets in this off-Broadway theater.
C. 3. After being delayed . . .   5. Before having discovered . . .   7. before being allowed . . .   9. Before having gone . . .

Exer. 4

A. 2. your visiting our country   4. swimming at our sandy beaches
6. bringing traveler's checks   8. exploring these ruins   10. arriving late at our hotel   12. seeing the sunset at Waikiki Beach.

Exer. 5

A. 3. would rather have   5. would rather have relaxed   7. had better take
9. had better not bring   11. had better not go   13. would rather not have
15. would rather have visited

Exer. 6

3. I will describe my home town to you.   5. I suggest that you come to my country in (the) spring.   7. I will suggest a good airline to you.   9. I recommend that you buy some (of the) silver jewelry made by the Indians.   11. It is difficult to describe the exquisite beauty of the palace to you.   13. It is recommended that tourists not drink the water in the small villages.   15. I suggest that you not bring too many things. (*Note*—sometimes the word *that* is omitted.)

Exer. 7

2. carefully, departure, arrival   4. advice, beautiful natural scenery   6. description, explanation, religious, historic(al)   8. skiing, surfing   10. panoramic, breathtaking   12. discotheque *or* discothèque, accommodates

Exer. 8

2. Many colorful birds can be seen in our jungles.   4. The frightened deer ran away as we drove through the forest.   6. While eating (*or* you eat) dinner, you will enjoy a fantastic floor show.   8. Before coming (*or* you come) to our country, you

should look over the travel brochures.   10. Anyone not wishing (*or* who does not wish) to take the side trip should inform the tour director.   12. Before having gone (*or* going) *or* Before they had gone (*or* went) into the desert, they never realized (*or* had realized) how beautiful it could be.   14. You may risk losing your money if you do not (*or* don't) keep it in a safe place.   16. I strongly recommend this beach to you. 18. You will be greatly impressed by the tropical vegetation in (*or* of) our country.

Exer. 9

druggist, shipped, shining, wrapped, benefited, raining, equipment, canceled (British—cancelled), worshiper (British—worshipper)

UNIT TEN—Courtship and Marriage

Exer. 1

2. choosing   4. select   6. getting   8. to be or being   10. to take 12. to make *or* making,   14. to go *or* going, to lose *or* losing

Exer. 2

A. 2. used to wear   4. used to give   6. is used to getting, used to be 8. used to flourish   10. used to be spent, used to saving

B. 2. A young girl used to accumulate . . .   4. People used to believe . . . 6. Some young couples who didn't have their parents' consent used to elope . . .

Exer. 3

2. most   4. most   6. mostly   8. almost   10. most, the most 12. the most   14. almost

Exer. 4

2. A matchmaker may be employed by the family to . . .   4. A shower is often given for an engaged girl by female friends and relatives. *or* . . . given by female friends and relatives for an engaged girl.   6. In a church, the young people are married by a clergyman.   8. Rice is often thrown at the newly married couple by the guests at a church wedding.   10. Most of the wedding arrangements are made by the girl's family.

Exer. 5

2. being introduced, their introduction   4. being courted, during her courtship 6. acknowledging the young man's reply, his acknowledgment of the young man's reply   8. considering the young man's proposal of marriage, during her consideration of . . .

Exer. 6

2. customarily, financial, married   4. officially engaged, permission
6. united, matrimony   8. performance, religious, civil   10. traditional, selection

Exer. 7

2. Couples sometimes put off getting married on the 13th day of the month.
4. Young couples often used to live with their parents, but now they are used to living in their own homes.   6. Marriages used to be arranged by parents, but now young people are used to choosing their own mates.   8. Most wedding bands are made of gold.   10. Her wedding gown is (*or* was) the most beautiful I have ever seen.
12. Rice is often thrown at the young couple by (the) guests.   14. After they are introduced (*or* After being introduced, *or* After their introduction), a–the young couple start to go out (*or* going out) with each other.

Exer. 8

A. confusion, advertisement, arrival, observance, shining, dining, shiny, fortunately, practicing, natural, nervous, entirely, judgment (British—judgement), lovely

B. noticeable, twelfth, ninth, fifth.

Symbol Chart
for Correction
of Compositions

Note: starred symbols indicate more elementary types of faults.

* agree   *agreement.*   Make the verb singular or plural according to the main word in the subject.

> The architecture of these buildings *is* very interesting.

If *each* or *every* is part of the subject, the verb must be singular.

> Everybody *is coming* to the party.

* ap   *apostrophe.*   An apostrophe has been incorrectly added or omitted. Apostrophes are used for contractions with auxiliaries (*who's* = *who is*) or for possessives of nouns (*the girl's hat*) but not for the possessive of pronouns (*its function, whose book*).

* art   *article.*   The article (*a, an, the*) is incorrect or omitted. Use an article with a singular countable noun. Do not use an article with a noncountable noun that stands alone (*I am studying history*). Use *the* if the noncountable noun is followed by a modifier (*the* history *of the United States*).

* C   *capital letter.*   Correct for capitalization. Use an initial capital letter for a word referring to nationality or religion (*an Italian custom; the Catholic religion*), a day of the week, a month, a holiday, a geographic name.

257

*⌒   *close up.*   Join together as one word—them⌒selves.

***comp**   *comparison.*   Use the correct word-form, preposition, pronoun or auxiliary required in a comparison.

concl   *conclusion.*   Add a conclusion, or rewrite a weak conclusion.

con   *connection.*   Use an appropriate connection within a paragraph.

coor   *coordination.*   Too many short sentences have been written separately or joined by *and.* Subordinate some of the sentences.

dangl   *dangling.*   Correct the *-ing* or *-ed* phrase that has no subject to be attached to.

DANGLING: While *watching* TV, *her dinner* was burning on the stove.

CORRECTION: While watching TV, she didn't notice that her dinner was burning on the stove.

OR: While she was watching TV, her dinner was burning on the stove.

***frag**   *fragment.*   Do not cut off a part of a sentence from the rest.

FRAGMENT: She has many hobbies. *For example, tennis and dancing.*

CORRECTION: She has many hobbies, for example, tennis and dancing.

OR: She has many hobbies. Among them are tennis and dancing.

***H**   *hyphen.*   Correct or add a hyphen within a word or at the end of a line. Do not use a hyphen at the beginning of a line.

inform   *informal.*   Change the informal expression to one that is more appropriate for formal English.

intro   *introduction.*   Add an introduction, or rewrite a weak introduction.

***neg**   *negative.*   Avoid the use of a double negative.

DOUBLE NEGATIVE: There isn't nobody here.

CORRECTION: There isn't anybody here.

OR: There's nobody here.

***N**   *number (of nouns and adjectives).*   Use the correct singular or plural form for a noun.
Adjectives do not have any plural form except for *this* (plural *these*), *that* (plural *those*), *much* (plural *many*), *little* (plural *few*).

par   *paragraph development.*   The paragraph does not develop one main point, or it includes more than one point, or its main point is not sufficiently developed.

¶   *new paragraph.*   The paragraph is too long, or the wording suggests that you are turning to another aspect of the point you are developing, or a new point is being made.

no ¶   *no new paragraph.*   This paragraph is very closely related to the one that precedes it.

Avoid single sentence paragraphs.

//   *parallelism.*   Use the same grammatical form for word groups connected by words like *and, or, than.*

> FAULT IN PARALLELISM: The girl promised to stay home that week and that she would study for her tests.

> CORRECTION: The girl promised to stay home that week and to study for her tests.

prep   *preposition.*   Correct the preposition fault.

*pro   *pronoun.*   Correct the pronoun fault. The fault may be:
1. an incorrect form of the pronoun
2. a confusion between *it* and *there*
3. a vague or unclear reference of a pronoun
4. a change in pronoun number (singular or plural)
5. a shift in person (*we, you, one*) in a general statement
6. an unnecessary pronoun

*P   *punctuation.*   Correct the punctuation. Watch especially for a comma or a semicolon that has been added or omitted. Correct a run-on sentence (two sentences incorrectly joined into one by a comma or no punctuation) by using a period or a semicolon.

> RUN-ON: I will have to read more in college, consequently I will improve my reading skill.

> CORRECTION: I will have to read more in college; consequently I will improve my reading skill.

repet   *repetitious.*   Cut out the unnecessary expressions or ideas that repeat what has already been said.

*SS   *sentence structure.*   Supply the missing subject, verb, or object. Or correct the form of a phrase used as a subject or an object.

*sp   *spelling.*   Use the correct spelling. Observe the rules for doubling final consonants, keeping or dropping final *e*, changing *y* to *i*, combining the letters *i* and *e*.

*trans   *transition.*   Rewrite the opening sentence of a paragraph so that it connects with the preceding paragraph, or so that it makes the point of the paragraph clear.

lead-in transition.   Add a connection, or rewrite a weak connection between the general statements of the introduction and the beginning of the specific topic of the composition.

vague   *vague.*   Make the expression or the statement more specific in relation to the point being made.

* V   *verb.*   Use the correct verb tense, verb form, or auxiliary.

FORM: **be** + ____-*ing* (progressive)

be + ____-*ed* (passive)

have + ____-*ed* (perfect tenses)

will

do

may

must

can

should

+ ____-(no ending)

Use the -*ing* form of a verb after a preposition.

* WF   *word form.*   Use the correct ending for the word (determined by the word's part-of-speech function in the sentence).

* WO   *word order.*   Use the correct word order for: questions and indirect questions; adverbials; adjectives.
Do not separate a verb and its object.

∿ Reverse the word order.

wordy   *wordy.*   Remove the excessive wording that has been used for the idea being expressed.

* WW   *wrong word.*   Choose the exact word for the intended meaning.

Index of Exercises

General Index